Lawns
1-2-3®

Meredith® BOOKS

Lawns 1-2-3®
Editor: Marilyn Rogers
Contributing Writer: Jeff Day
Copy Chief: Terri Fredrickson
Publishing Operations Manager: Karen Schirm
Senior Editor, Asset and Information Manager: Phillip Morgan
Edit and Design Coordinator: Mary Lee Gavin
Editorial and Design Assistant: Renee E. McAtee
Book Production Managers: Pam Kvitne, Marjorie J. Schenkelberg,
     Rick von Holdt, Mark Weaver
Contributing Photo Researcher: Susan K. Ferguson
Contributing Copy Editor: Carolyn Garrick Stern
Contributing Proofreaders: Tom Blackett, Sara Henderson, Elise Marton,
     Carolyn Petersen
Contributing Indexer: Kathleen Poole

**Additional Editorial and Design contributions from
     Abramowitz Creative Studios**
Publishing Director/Designer: Tim Abramowitz
Graphic Designer: Joel Wires
Illustrator: Kelly Bailey
Photography: Image Studios
     Account Executive: Lisa Egan
     Photographer: Bill Rein, John von Dorn
     Assistants: Dave Claussen, Bill Kapinski
     Technical Advisor: Rick Nadke

Meredith® Books
Executive Director, Editorial: Gregory H. Kayko
Executive Director, Design: Matt Strelecki
Managing Editor: Amy Tincher-Durik
Executive Editor/Group Manager: Benjamin W. Allen
Senior Associate Design Director: Tom Wegner
Marketing Product Manager: Brent Wiersma
National Marketing Manager—Home Depot: Suzy Emmack

Publisher and Editor in Chief: James D. Blume
Editorial Director: Linda Raglan Cunningham
Executive Director, New Business Development: Todd M. Davis
Director, Sales—Home Depot: Robb Morris
Executive Director, Sales: Ken Zagor
Director, Operations: George A. Susral
Director, Production: Douglas M. Johnston
Director, Marketing: Amy Nichols
Business Director: Jim Leonard
Vice President and General Manager: Douglas J. Guendel

Meredith Publishing Group
President: Jack Griffin
Executive Vice President: Karla Jeffries

Meredith Corporation
Chairman of the Board: William T. Kerr
President and Chief Executive Officer: Stephen M. Lacy
In Memoriam: E.T. Meredith III (1933–2003)

Contributing Photographers: William D. Adams, Adam Albright,
     Jim Baron, Patricia Bruno, Lyle Buss, David Cavagnaro,
     Dr. Nick E. Christians, Dale Clark, Karl Danneberger, Ed Degginger,
     Alan & Linda Detrick Photography LLC, Wally Eberhart, Derek Fell,
     John Himmelman, Jerry Howard, Bill Johnson, Jim Kalisch,
     John Kaminski, Tom Koske, David Liebman, Nicholas Mitchell,
     Positive Images, Ann Reilly, Forest & Kim Starr, Joseph G. Strauch,
     Jr., Michael Thompson

The Home Depot®
Marketing Manager: Tom Sattler

Note to the Reader: Due to differing conditions, tools, and individual
skills, Meredith Corporation and The Home Depot® assume no
responsibility for any damages, injuries suffered, or losses incurred as
a result of following the information published in this book. Before
beginning any project, review the instructions carefully, and if any doubts
or questions remain, consult local experts or authorities. Because codes
and regulations vary greatly, you always should check with authorities
to ensure that your project complies with all applicable local codes
and regulations. Always read and observe all of the safety precautions
provided by any tool or equipment manufacturer, and follow all accepted
safety procedures.

We are dedicated to providing accurate and helpful do-it-yourself
information. We welcome your comments about improving this book and
ideas for other books we might offer to home improvement enthusiasts.
Contact us by any of these methods:

Leave a voice message at: 800/678-2093

Write to: Meredith Books, Home Depot Books
     1716 Locust St.
     Des Moines, IA 50309-3023

Send e-mail to: hi123@mdp.com.

How to use this book

Did you know that there are more than 32 million acres of tended lawns in North America? That's a lot of grass framing homes, providing a soft playing surface at the park, helping to cool the environment, and holding soil in place. Obviously, lawns fill an important role in society and probably in your yard too. With *Lawns 1-2-3* you'll find ways to get the most out of your lawn as well as to save time and money while caring for it.

Whether you've just moved into a brand-new home or live in one that was built at the turn of the century, you probably already have a lawn. For that reason Lawns 1-2-3 opens with the tasks you'll use the most: mowing, watering, fertilizing, and, of course, troubleshooting. If you mow, water, and fertilize properly, you can avoid many of the most common lawn problems and may never need to refer to the troubleshooting section. In fact, mowing, watering, and fertilizing properly can often help improve your lawn without having to resort to using pesticides.

There are instances where you may need to install a lawn—you worked with a builder who did not provide one, your lawn has deteriorated so far that no amount of pesticides or better care can bring it back, or your lawn consists of an old variety that is prone to problems no matter what you do. In the last third of the book you'll learn how to prepare the soil as well as to lay sod or start a new lawn from seed.

Here's a rundown of the various chapters:

Chapter 1: Lawn Fundamentals
Before reading anything else, read this chapter. It explains terms that will help you understand the rest of the book. It tells you how a grass plant grows, which will help you understand how and why you mow, water, and fertilize a lawn. Exactly how and when you tackle some chores, like mowing, watering, and fertilizing, depends on the type of grass. Profiles in this chapter will help you identify the grass in your lawn, as well as help you decide on a new grass if you're starting a new lawn.

Chapter 2: Mowing and Trimming
Mowing's not hard, but a few steps help make the job easier and your lawn healthier. In this chapter you'll learn about those steps as well as find information on servicing your mower and sharpening the blades. The next time you're in the market for a new mower or a string trimmer, edger, or leaf blower, check the buying guide at the end of the chapter.

Chapter 3: Watering
Chapter 3 tells you how to know whether your grass is getting enough water and helps you prepare to deal with drought and watering restrictions. In addition, you'll find a buying guide for sprinklers and learn how to install a rudimentary irrigation system.

Chapter 4: Fertilizing
Lawns can survive without fertilizer, but they'll be thicker, healthier, greener, and have a stronger root system if you fertilize at least once a year. Twice is even better. Learn what to apply, how to apply it, and when to do the job.

Chapters 5 and 6: Solving Problems and Weeds
A healthy lawn rarely has problems. A dense turf provides no openings for weed seeds to fall in, germinate, and take over. Healthy grass can outgrow or quickly recover from insect or disease problems. Even so, it doesn't hurt to be vigilant in watching for problems and treating them quickly if you find them. In Chapters 5 and 6, you'll gain advice for diagnosing and treating lawn diseases and insects, identifying and eliminating weeds, and for solving problems with thatch and shade.

Chapter 7: Soil Basics
You can't grow grass without getting your hands dirty. The soil in your yard will make or break your lawn. Find out what it's made of, and what it needs.

Chapter 8: Planting a Lawn
Chapter 8 walks you through the steps of preparing your yard for a new lawn and shows you how to start it with seed, sod, and other planting methods. You'll also find the steps for repairing the holes in your lawn after eliminating pests and weeds.

Lawns 1-2-3®
Table of contents

Chapter 1
LAWN FUNDAMENTALS 6

Chapter 2
MOWING AND TRIMMING 36

Chapter 3
WATERING 60

Chapter 4
FERTILIZING 76

Chapter 5
SOLVING PROBLEMS 86

Chapter 6
WEEDS 118

Chapter 7
SOIL BASICS 140

Chapter 8
PLANTING A LAWN 162

Lawn fundamentals

You know that a healthy, well-kept lawn is beautiful and peaceful looking and a good place to play and relax. What you may not know is that your lawn keeps your house cooler and quieter, helps purify the air while fighting pollution, knits the soil together to prevent erosion, and adds substantially to the value of your home.

Fortunately, a good lawn is less hard to create and maintain than you might think. All it takes is a little know-how and a commitment to regular watering, mowing, and basic care to grow a lush, thick lawn that naturally resists insects, diseases, and drought. But first, you need to understand how grass grows and you need to know what kind of grass you're growing so that you can give it the right care at the right time. That's where this chapter comes in. Depending on where you live, your lawn will consist of either a bunch or a creeping grass and either a warm-season or a cool-season grass. Check out the following pages for help in identifying your grass, as well as for help in choosing a new grass if you are starting from scratch.

Chapter 1 highlights

In the pages that follow this chapter, you'll learn about mowing, watering, and fertilizing. You'll get a chance to analyze your lawn, become familiar with insects, weeds and diseases, and see how to evaluate your soil and how to solve problems. This chapter helps you begin to think about your commitment to your lawn as you learn about it. Decide if you're a high-, medium-, or low-input lawn person. Then you can analyze your lawn's problems, mix the solutions into the package, and end up with a healthy lawn that makes you proud.

How grass grows

Grasses have a unique way of growing, and it's this uniqueness that allows them to be used as lawns.

Think of the trees, shrubs, and other plants in your yard and how they grow from the tips of their stems. If grasses grew in the same way, mowing would kill the plants and you'd never get that lovely carpet of green to frame your home.

Instead, the growing point of a grass—called a crown—is at its base, and all new leaves come up through the older leaves. With the growing point buried at the base of the plant, you can repeatedly cut the leaves to keep them at a uniform height. And the more you cut them, the thicker the grass becomes.

If you let your grass go for long periods without mowing, however, the grass plant may start to send up seed stalks. As these develop, the growing point starts to rise with them so that when you do mow, you cut it off. Do this too often and your lawn will start to thin out. Also, since seed stalks are thicker and less flexible, the lawn loses its inviting texture.

▲ **If you were small enough to crawl through the grass, you'd be crawling over what's called the crown, where all the growth takes place. Towering above you would be the green leaves, which like the leaves of a tree, can be trimmed without damaging the plant.**

Growth patterns

Grasses can be characterized by the different ways they spread across open ground. These growth patterns influence whether you can plant a new lawn from seed or sod, how quickly the lawn fills in after it is seeded, and the lawn's ability to recover from damage such as the kids might inflict on it with their football games.

Bunchgrasses grow tall and narrow, almost straight up from their roots. They spread via "tillers" that sprout immediately next to the existing plant. (One variety of tall fescue spreads via underground stems called rhizomes.) Growth radiates out from the original plant, so bunchgrasses form clusters grouped around the parent plant. They spread slowly, and if part of the lawn is damaged, bunchgrasses can't be counted on to fill bare spots before weeds do. However, the tillers of tall fescue

and other bunchgrasses form such dense turfs that they aren't easily damaged.

Creeping grasses appear to sprawl. They spread more quickly via horizontal stems that grow out from the original plant to form new plants. The new plants in turn send out stems. If the horizontal stems are aboveground, they are called stolons; those that travel underground are rhizomes. Grasses that spread via rhizomes, such as Kentucky bluegrass, form dense, uniform lawns. Grasses with both stolons and rhizomes, such as bermudagrass and zoysiagrass, also form dense, uniform lawns and spread aggressively.

Most warm-season grasses are creeping grasses. Cool-season grasses are more varied and may be either bunchgrasses or creeping grasses.

▶ ▶ **Bunchgrasses such as tall fescue don't have stolons and rhizomes. Because they spread by forming new plants next to the crown, they grow in clumps.**

▶ **Creeping grasses such as Kentucky bluegrass spread by underground stems called rhizomes and aboveground stems called stolons.**

Most likely you inherited your lawn when you moved into your home; either the previous owners or the builder put it in. If you're lucky, they may be able to tell you what the lawn is. Otherwise, you'll need to do a little exploring.

From a distance, all grasses may look pretty much alike. Up close, however, each has unique characteristics that will help you identify it.

Start the process of figuring out your grass with your location: You're not going to find a warm-season grass in Chicago, for example. Then look at the lawn's general appearance. For example, if it's coarse textured, it could be tall fescue or centipedegrass, depending on whether you're in the North or the South.

Turf experts then look at the plant itself for clues to its identity. Once you learn to recognize different parts of a grass plant, identification is simple. The descriptions of the grasses, which run from pages 18 to 35, explain what to look for with each one.

The first part of the plant to check is the easiest: the leaf. A grass leaf is broad at the top and wraps around a stem at the bottom. The broad part is the blade; the bottom is the sheath. Look first at the tip of the blade (one that hasn't been cut off by your mower). It will be either blunt, pointed, or shaped like the bow of a ship. Next examine the sheath. It will be either hairy or smooth, flat or round.

Then look for newly forming leaves. Unlike other plants whose leaves develop all along a stem, you'll find new grass leaves growing up through the base of the previous leaf. Cut one of these new leaves in half and check whether it is rolled or folded.

Pull the blade away from the grass stem. The point where the leaf blade and sheath meet is called the collar. The collar sometimes appears as a light-colored band that is visible in the front or back of the leaf. Collars are often hard to see; their width is the distinguishing feature.

Some collars have an extension called a ligule. Ligules will be either hairy or membranous (thin and transparent).

At the outside edge of the collar where it clasps the grass stem, you may find auricles. These look like little ears extending from the collar. Their size, shape, and presence are the identifying clues to check.

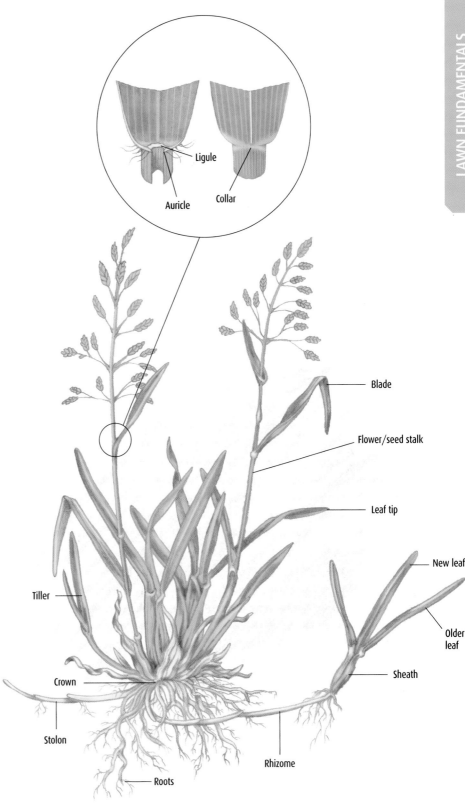

Ligule

Auricle

Collar

Blade

Flower/seed stalk

Leaf tip

New leaf

Older leaf

Sheath

Tiller

Crown

Stolon

Rhizome

Roots

Texture and color

Two traits—leaf texture and color—have less to do with identification than they do with the quality of the lawn.

Texture

Grasses with blades ¼-inch wide or less are considered fine-textured grasses. Those whose leaves are wider than ¼ inch are coarse textured. The texture of the grass has nothing to do with the way it spreads, with its hardiness, or with its color. Either type of grass will form an attractive lawn. Dense, fine-textured lawns, however, appear more uniform and are preferred by experts, who are constantly trying to breed finer grasses.

Color

Everyone wants a green lawn. While all grasses are green, the shade varies from grass to grass. You can make your lawn greener by following a good fertilizing program, but you cannot alter the grass's underlying genetic makeup. Some grass varieties will always be greener than others. If you really want a deep green lawn, you'll find it easier to replant with one of the new varieties bred for dark color than to fertilize often to keep the lawn at the color you desire.

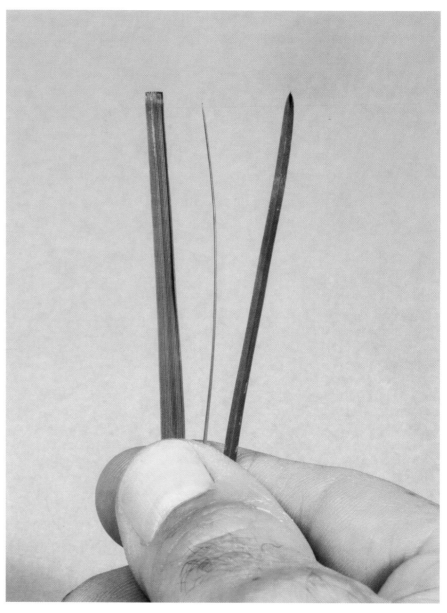

▲ The texture of grass leaves varies from very broad (St. Augustinegrass, tall fescue, bahiagrass and others) to slender (fine fescues).

Fine-textured grasses

Bentgrass
Bermudagrass, improved varieties
Bluegrass
Buffalograss
Fine fescue
Perennial ryegrass, improved varieties
Some turf-type tall fescues
Zoysiagrass

Coarse-textured grasses

Bahiagrass
Centipedegrass
Common bermudagrass
Common zoysiagrass
St. Augustinegrass
Some turf-type tall fescues

Most suburbanites can't imagine having a lawn-free yard, and yet there are people who suggest that lawns waste resources and should be outlawed. Don't listen to them. As these facts show, lawns are great for the environment and great for your yard.

- Real estate agents estimate that a beautiful lawn can add as much as 15 percent to a home's value. A beautiful lawn signals that the rest of the home is well kept and worth top dollar.

- A healthy lawn keeps your home cooler and quieter. When hot, sunny weather turns streets, sidewalks, and driveways into sizzling strips of pavement, the grass next to them remains pleasant. In fact, when the concrete is 100°F (38°C), lawn temperatures will be around 75°F (24°C). This cool surface keeps the air around your home cooler, thus reducing air-conditioning costs.

- Lawns absorb and deflect sound, especially when they are part of a landscape with trees and shrubs.

- Like other plants, grasses help purify air and produce oxygen. Only 25 square feet of healthy lawn supplies all the oxygen that one adult requires for a day. An average 5,000-square-foot home lawn produces as much oxygen as two 100-foot-tall trees, more than enough for a large family.

- Lawns fight pollution. Over a year, the leaf blades and grass roots in an acre of healthy lawn absorb hundreds of pounds of pollutants from air and rainwater, including nitrates, sulfur dioxide, nitrogen oxide, and hydrogen fluoride.

- Grass roots knit soil particles together. This prevents slopes from washing away and keeps your property cleaner and mud-free.

- A healthy lawn prevents runoff during rainstorms. Thick, dense turf absorbs 7½ inches of rainfall in an hour, while a thin turf soaks up only 2½ inches of rain.

- Grass also serves as a dust trap, rather like a vacuum cleaner filter. As air flows across the surface of a lawn, dust particles filter out and settle on the grass blades, where they are washed back into the soil by rain. Every year, grass traps millions of tons of dust that would otherwise be airborne, making for difficult breathing, irritated eyes, and dirty air.

- In regions prone to wildfires, a mowed lawn can help slow the spread of the flames around your house.

Warm season or cool-season grass?

The types of grasses that will grow in your yard are determined by a number of factors, the most important of which is where you live. Most of the grasses that grow in Florida can't stand the cold of a Maine winter, while those that thrive in Michigan will fry in Texas sun. Turfgrasses fall into two broad groups: warm season and cool season—depending first on *when* they grow and second on *where* they will grow.

Which type you have determines what you do to your lawn and when you do it. Warm season grasses, for example grow during the summer and should be fertilized in the summer as a result. Cool-season grasses put on the most growth in spring and fall, and the best time to fertilize them is in fall.

Warm-season grasses

Warm-season grasses grow during the summer. They are able to withstand heat and thrive in the intense sun of southern states. Most readily withstand drought; some can cope with high humidity.

Most warm-season grasses will survive a –10°F (–23°C) winter, but St. Augustinegrass and a few others are limited to areas that get no colder than 20°F (–7°C). One—zoysiagrass—survives very cold temperatures. However, it is not a good choice for northern areas because, at most, it will be green for only three months of the year.

The grasses in this group show no sign of life until temperatures rise to 75°F (24°C)

▲ **Warm season grasses do best in warm climates. They grow most actively during the summer, and go dormant in the winter.**

or so in spring and quickly stop growing—go dormant—when temperatures start to drop in fall. Leaf growth is most rapid when air temperatures are between 80°F (27°C) and 95°F (35°C), which means you'll mow a warm-season lawn several times a week all summer but have a nice reprieve in fall, winter, and spring.

Warm-season grass roots grow the most when the soil is 75°F (24°C) to 85°F (29°C), so plan to

do any maintenance that disrupts roots, such as aerating, in mid- to late spring. This will give your lawn a maximum amount of time to grow and recover. The best time for planting warm-season grasses is from spring, after all danger of frost is past, through early summer.

Fertilize a warm-season lawn as often as once a month during the summer.

Warm-season grasses

Bermudagrass is the most widely used warm-season grass; it grows well in both dry and humid climates. As you near the humid coast, bahiagrass and St. Augustinegrass grow well. Because warm-season grasses go into decline during the winter, cool-season grasses are often seeded over the existing grass to create a lawn that is green year-round.

Warm-season grasses include:

Bahiagrass	Buffalograss	St. Augustinegrass
Bermudagrass	Centipedegrass	Zoysiagrass

WARM-SEASON GRASS GROWING CYCLE

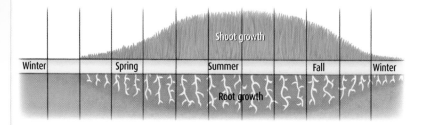

▲ Cool season grasses thrive in cool climates. They grow rapidly in the spring and fall, slow down during the heat of summer, and go dormant with winter temperatures.

Cool-season grasses

Not surprisingly, given their name, cool-season grasses thrive in cool temperatures, when the air is 60°F (15°C) to 80°F (27°C). For northerners, they're often the first sign of life in the spring landscape, greening up as temperatures start to rise. In some climates, they stay green all year.

Cool-season grasses grow rapidly in spring and fall, but slow down or go dormant as temperatures hit the mid- to high 80s. Some will remain green in hot weather if they receive plenty of water. Even so, cool-season grasses never look their best during the dog days of summer.

The leaves of cool-season grasses grow the most when the air is between 65°F (18°C) and 75°F (24°C), and most root growth occurs when the soil temperature is between 50°F (10°C) and 65°F (18°C).

The best time to fertilize cool-season grasses is in the fall when they are growing rapidly in the cool weather. Plant cool-season grasses when temperatures have reached 60°F (15°C) and are rising in spring, or when they have hit 75°F (24°C) and are falling in late summer or fall.

COOL-SEASON GRASS GROWING CYCLE

Shoot growth

Shoot growth

| Winter | Spring | Summer | Fall | Winter |

Root growth

Root growth

Cool-season grasses

Cool-season grasses grow best in the northern part of the continent and are usually the grass of choice in the Transition Zone (see page 16). Kentucky bluegrass is widely grown, because of both its appearance and its ability to grow in a variety of climates. Perennial ryegrass is popular and often mixed with other grasses because it sprouts quickly. Tall fescue is perhaps the most versatile: It wears well, is drought resistant, withstands hot and cold weather, and is shade tolerant.

Cool-season grasses include:

Colonial bentgrass
Fine fescue
Kentucky bluegrass

Perennial ryegrass
Tall fescue

Levels of lawn care

How much time should you spend on your lawn? To some people, lawns are nothing but hard work; to others they are pure joy. The majority of people fall somewhere in between. An important part of lawn care is deciding which group you belong to and how much effort and expense you want to devote to your lawn. Very few people will do everything in this book. Everyone will find a level of lawn care with which they are comfortable.

Lawn care, after all, is something you do in your spare time. You want the best lawn you can get in the time you have. If you're balancing lawn care with other activities—and we all balance our activities with other activities—you need to decide how high lawn care is on the list. As you look at what you want to do, there are three basic approaches to lawn care: low input, medium input, and high input. The following describes each approach and shows you how to get better results from your efforts.

Low input

Low-input regimes are for people who really don't want or have time to think about their lawns. Of the three main tasks associated with lawn care—mowing, fertilizing and watering—low input care is limited to the first two. You should water the lawn when it's under stress, but for the most part, you can leave the watering to Mother Nature. In the face of a drought, the lawn will go brown and dormant, but if the drought doesn't linger, it will come back to life when regular rainfall resumes.

You can make a big difference in the quality of your lawn by concentrating on mowing and fertilizing. In fact, proper mowing lays the foundation for grass care. It ensures adequate roots that help grass survive drought; it provides fertilizer as the clippings decay and return to the soil; it prevents the build-up of undecayed organic matter, called thatch, which keeps air and water from reaching the roots.

The rules of proper mowing are simple, and may even save you work. Let the grass grow to its optimum height. Each grass is healthiest at a particular height, though the height varies from variety to variety. (The plant profiles beginning on page 18 list the optimum height for each grass.) The optimum height is the level at which the roots are longest, and the blades are healthiest and long enough to produce food. Let the grass grow one-fourth to one-third taller than its optimum height, then mow.

Fertilize at least once a year; twice a year is even better. Exactly when to fertilize depends on whether your lawn is a cool-season grass or a warm-season grass. Fertilize cool-season grasses once in early fall and once in late fall, if you plan on two feedings. Fertilize warm-season grasses after the second mowing and again two months later. (For more on cool- and warm-season grasses, see Warm-Season or Cool-Season Grass? page 12.)

Barring a drought, proper cutting and minimal fertilization alone will encourage a thicker lawn. In so doing, you will reduce the need for weed control: The thicker the lawn, the less the weeds are able to get a foothold. However, you will not get rid of all the weeds, and your lawn will be paler and not quite as healthy as it would be if it received optimal amounts of fertilizer.

Lawn care calendar

SEASON	COOL-SEASON GRASS	WARM-SEASON GRASS
Early to Midspring	Fertilize after initial growth spurt if using medium- or high-intensity feeding programs.	Fertilize after the second mowing in low-, medium-, and high-intensity feeding programs.
Midspring		Fertilize one month after first application if using medium- or high-intensity feeding programs.
Spring	Dethatch, lime	Sow warm-season grass.
Summer		Aerate
Midsummer	Fertilize if using a high-intensity feeding program.	Dethatch. Fertilize two months after first spring application if using low- or high-intensity feeding programs.
Late Summer	Sow cool-season grass.	Fertilize three months after first spring application if using medium- or high-intensity feeding programs.
Early Fall	Fertilize whether using a low-, medium-, or high-intensity feeding program.	
Fall	Dethatch, aerate, topdress, lime. Apply fertilizer after last mowing if using medium- or high-intensity feeding programs.	Topdress, lime
Winter		Overseed lawn with annual ryegrass.

Medium input

This regime results in a healthier, greener, thicker lawn with few weeds. The main difference between medium-input care and low-input care is fertilizer. Feed your cool-season lawn in early fall, in late fall, and again in spring. Fertilize a warm-season lawn after the second mowing, again a month later, and end with an application three months after the first. Also begin to treat at least some of the problems that affect the lawn: insects, disease, compaction, poor soil, shade, thatch, and all the rest.

In the face of a drought, water your lawn to keep it alive and green, but once the drought ends, let the lawn rely on the rain for irrigation.

All of this attention will make your lawn grow faster. Faster growth does means more frequent mowing. Even so, the mowing rules remain the same—grow grass to its optimum height and never cut off more than one-fourth to one-third of the total height.

High input

A high-input lawn is the crowning jewel of the neighborhood. Give it still more fertilizer than a medium-input lawn, up to four applications for both warm- and cool-season grasses. For cool-season grasses, you fertilize in early fall, late fall, spring and midsummer. For warm-season grasses, fertilize after the second mowing, and then one, two, and three months later.

Water infrequently, but heavily—not to save work, but to encourage roots to reach down deeply for the water they need. Longer roots can pull more water and more nutrients from the soil.

Identify and treat problems such as insects and disease. Apply lime to address soil acidity or sulfur to address alkalinity. Remove thatch from the lawn as needed; in some cases you may need to do so every year.

You might consider applying seed over your existing lawn to invigorate it with a stronger variety of grass. Down south you may even overseed with a cool-season grass once it turns brown and goes dormant in the winter. The cool-season grass will pop up quickly, keep the yard green all winter long, and die back as your summer lawn starts to regrow.

Stay safe

Whether you're mowing, running a power edger, or clipping grass with your string trimmer, do what it takes to prevent serious injury.

■ **Never disable safety shutoffs.** As annoying as you might find them, putting up with the inconvenience is much less costly than losing toes or fingers.

■ **Wear sturdy shoes while mowing** to avoid slipping and falling and to protect your feet in case the safety shutoff fails.

■ **Use earplugs.** Mowing once or twice every week for years can take its toll on your hearing. The high-pitched whine from string trimmers can damage hearing even faster. Earplugs are inexpensive and disposable, so wear them.

■ **Wear thick gloves.** They'll help absorb the vibrations of the machine so that your wrists, elbows, and shoulders don't suffer.

■ **Put on safety glasses, especially when running a string trimmer.** Trimmers readily kick up pebbles and rocks that have an uncanny knack for hitting an eye.

■ **Clean up the lawn** before mowing and trimming to avoid turning rocks and debris into missiles.

■ **Travel so that the mower chute points away from areas where pedestrians could be hit** by clippings and flying debris. At the very least, stop the blade as people pass by.

■ **Keep children and visitors away from the area** as you work to ensure you don't hit them with debris or accidentally run over them.

■ **Never let children ride along** with you on a rider or tractor mower.

Growing zones

If you're getting ready to plant a new lawn, you'll need to think in broader terms than merely cool-season and warm-season when deciding which grass to grow. As you can see on the map below, North America can be divided into five growing areas, depending on rainfall. Certain grasses grow better than others in each of these areas.

Cool, humid climate

This region is highly diverse and includes areas with mild, wet winters and warm, dry summers, as well as ones with frigid winters and hot summers. Rainfall totals 30 inches or more per year. This area is best suited to cool-season grasses such as bluegrass, fescue, ryegrass, and bentgrass. However, these grasses may go dormant for short periods in summer unless you water them. Buffalograss—a native North American grass—grows in the dry, warm parts of this climate. Zoysiagrass also grows in the southern portion of this region and along the Atlantic Coast. Both grasses have a short growing period in these climates and are brown much of the year.

Cool, arid climate

This region has cold-to-mild, snowy-to-dry winters and warm-to-hot, dry summers. Rainfall totals less than 20 inches per year. All cool-season grasses grow here but will need watering. Buffalograss does well on rainfall alone and is often used on nonirrigated sites in the warmer areas of Kansas, Nebraska, and Colorado.

Warm, humid climate

In this region, winters are mild, rainfall is high, and summers are hot and humid. The area along the Gulf Coast is almost tropical, with rainfall totaling 60 inches or more per year. Warm-season grasses dominate in this region.

Bermudagrass is the most widely used, but it is subject to cold damage in the northern sections. Zoysiagrass works well in those areas. Bahiagrass and St. Augustinegrass grow well along the southern coast. Cool-season grasses are good choices for mountainous sections. They are also often seeded over an existing lawn to create a grass that is green year-round; perennial ryegrass, especially, is used in this way.

Warm, dry climate

This region has hot summers, mild winters, and little to no rain at any time of year. Bermudagrass is most commonly grown in this climate, but any warm-season grass will grow here if you keep it watered. Buffalograss works in the driest parts of the region. Cool-season grasses are used to overseed here in the winter too. Because the soil is alkaline and often saline, check with your local Home Depot garden associate for specialized grasses that are appropriate for some parts of this region.

Transition Zone

The Transition Zone has characteristics of all four other regions. It has hot summers, cold winters, and wet and dry periods throughout the year. Both cool- and warm-season grasses will grow here, but no one type does well. The cool-season grasses suffer in summer, while warm-season grasses suffer in winter. However, a handful of grasses do better than most. These include tall fescue, a cool-season grass that is better suited to hot summers than most others and that can survive the winter in most of the region. Of the warm-season grasses, cold-tolerant varieties of bermudagrass do well in the southern part of the zone and zoysiagrass grows farther north, although it is brown for much of the year.

NORTH AMERICAN GROWING ZONES

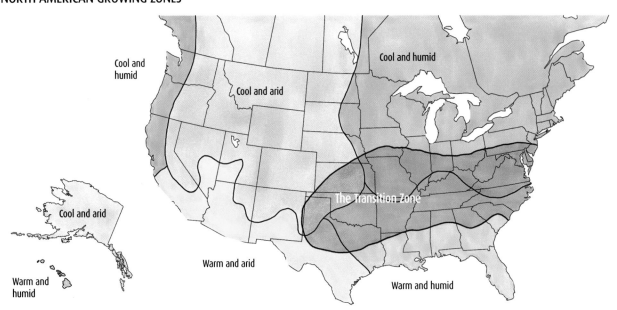

Cool and humid

Cool and humid

Cool and arid

Cool and arid

The Transition Zone

Warm and arid

Warm and humid

Warm and humid

About the grasses

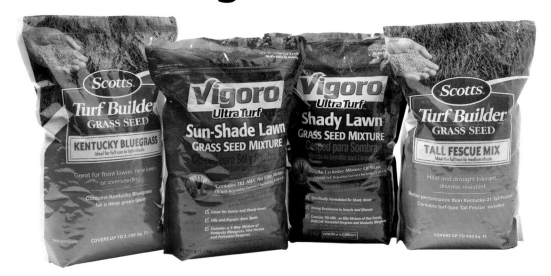

The pages that follow give you an in-depth look at the major grasses used in lawns, cool season first, followed by warm season. You'll find discussions of each grass's color, texture, heat resistance, cold tolerance, and where it grows best. Use the descriptions to identify the grasses growing in your lawn or to help you select a grass if you are planting a new lawn.

But don't stop there. Get some on-the-ground advice too. Ask at the garden center about what works best in your area. Check with the extension service run by your state university. They'll have both an office in your county and a website on-line. Check with neighbors. Get all the local information you can get. The more you know, the better your choice of grasses will be.

One of the things you'll discover, as you look at your yard and talk with locals, is that most lawns are a combination of grasses. And when you buy seed, you'll discover that most grass seed is sold as either a mix or a blend. A popular *mixture* for shaded lawns in the North, for example, is a combination of Kentucky bluegrass, fine fescue, and ryegrass. *Blends,* on the other hand, combine several varieties of the same grass, such as America, Award, Eclipse, Glade, Jefferson, Midnight, NuGlade, Odyssey, Quantum Leap, Rugby II, Total Eclipse, or Unique Kentucky bluegrass, in the package.

No matter where you live, there are probably only two or three grasses that do well in your area and only four or five—at most—that are grown. Some grasses grow best in shade; most require full sun. Some turfgrasses prefer dry climates; still others thrive on humidity. This chapter will help you determine what you've got growing in your yard, so that you can give it the best care. If you need to patch part of your lawn—or want to replace it entirely at some point—take a close look at the grass types listed here to find one that meets your needs.

PURE SEED	VARIETY KIND	GERMINATION	ORIGIN
47.23%	EVENING SHADE PERENNIAL RYEGRASS	90%	OR
28.95%	BOREAL CREEPING RED FESCUE	85%	CAN
19.34%	KENBLUE KENTUCKY BLUEGRASS	85%	WA

OTHER INGREDIENTS
2.11% OTHER CROP SEED
2.28% INERT MATTER
0.09% WEED SEED
NOXIOUS WEEDS: NONE FOUND

NET WGT. 3 POUNDS

PURE SEED	VARIETY KIND	GERMINATION	ORIGIN
97.75%	KENBLUE KENTUCKY BLUEGRASS	85%	WA

OTHER INGREDIENTS
0.05% OTHER CROP SEED
2.11% INERT MATTER
0.09% WEED SEED
NOXIOUS WEEDS: NONE FOUND.

NET WGT. 3 POUNDS

PURE SEED	VARIETY KIND	GERMINATION	ORIGIN
34.67%	ADOBE TALL FESCUE	87%	OR
24.59%	LS 1000 TALL FESCUE	87%	OR
19.82%	CODY TALL FESCUE	87%	OR
18.64%	GREENKEEPER-WAF TALL FESCUE	87%	OR

OTHER INGREDIENTS
0.35% OTHER CROP SEED
1.64% INERT MATTER
0.09% WEED SEED
NOXIOUS WEEDS: NONE FOUND

NET WGT. 3 POUNDS

▲ **A seed mixture is a combination of several grass species.** The resulting lawn can thrive in a variety of conditions. For example, one species may do well in full sun, another in shade. When mixed, each takes hold where it does best.

▲ **Packages of straight seed contain only one species of grass.**

▲ **A blend contains several varieties of the same grass species.** The seeds in a given blend would all be tall fescue, for example, but each would be a different variety of tall fescue.

Cool-season grasses

Kentucky bluegrass *(Poa pratensis)*

Kentucky bluegrass sets the standard by which all other cool-season grasses are judged. It forms a high-quality turf that is dense, dark green, and fine to medium textured. The roots are extensive and deep. It originated not in Kentucky but in Europe and Asia and was brought here very early in the country's history.

When raised by seed, Kentucky bluegrass is a slow starter. For that reason, you'll often find it mixed with grasses that germinate more quickly—fine fescues and ryegrasses in particular. Bluegrass spreads aggressively via underground stems called rhizomes that knit the turf together, making it a favorite for sod. More important for homeowners, the rhizomes also spread to crowd out weeds and fill in thin spots.

Kentucky bluegrass forms minimal thatch buildup unless you overfertilize.

Varieties of bluegrass have improved greatly during the last few years. New varieties are more resistant to drought, disease, heat, and insects. Older bluegrass may be a candidate for overseeding or replacement.

▲ **Kentucky bluegrass forms a dense, deep-green lawn with medium-to fine-textured leaves. It is a popular grass for sod because its dense roots hold together during installation.**

Kentucky bluegrass at a glance

Planting method: Seed or sod

Type of grass: Creeping. Spreads via underground stems called rhizomes which help it fill in thin areas and crowd out weeds.

Drought resistance: Goes dormant during a drought but recovers.

Shade tolerance: Fair

Heat resistance: Good. Cut at upper end of height range during drought.

Cold resistance: Excellent

Wear resistance: Can stand occasional abuse, from which it quickly recovers.

Best mowing height: 2 inches. Mow when lawn height reaches 3 inches.

Comments: Kentucky bluegrass is plagued by pests in Southern California, where it is better in the shade than fescue. It dies in the southern heat, making it an annual in states like Georgia. A heat-tolerant variety is being tested at Tifton, Georgia.

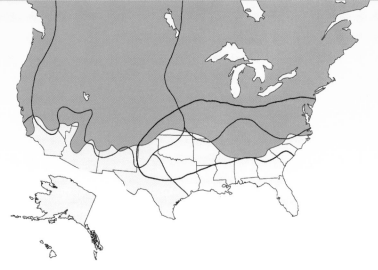

OPTIMAL GROWING CONDITIONS

Kentucky bluegrass grows well in cool-humid and cool-arid climates. Although it is often touted as a shade-tolerant grass, it actually needs full sun for three to four hours a day; some varieties will take more shade. Kentucky bluegrass requires moderate amounts of moisture.

Keys to identification

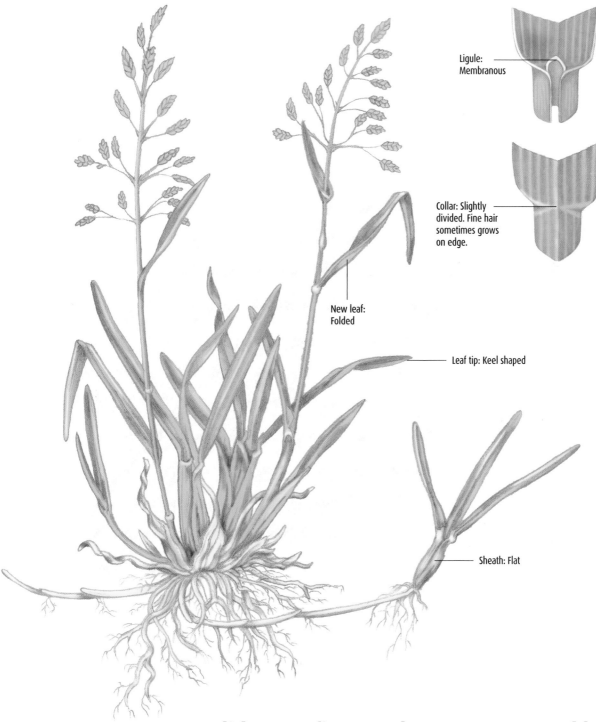

Ligule:
Membranous

Collar: Slightly
divided. Fine hair
sometimes grows
on edge.

New leaf:
Folded

Leaf tip: Keel shaped

Sheath: Flat

Slide your fingers along an unmowed leaf
blade. If the tip splits into a V, the lawn is
most likely Kentucky bluegrass.

Perennial ryegrass *(Lolium perenne)*

Perennial ryegrass forms a moderately dark green, dense, fine-textured lawn. Because its seeds sprout rapidly, with germination in as little as four days, it's possible to plant perennial ryegrass and get a good lawn in only a few weeks. Although generally easy to maintain, perennial ryegrass is susceptible to brown patch, Pythium blight, and gray leaf spot, which can mean using lots of fungicide on your lawn. Thatch is not a problem.

In seed packages, you often find perennial ryegrass blended with Kentucky bluegrass. Because it germinates so quickly, it can act as a sort of nurse crop while the bluegrass takes its time to germinate. Southern homeowners and turf managers use perennial ryegrass to overseed their lawns so they have green grass all year. Golf fairways are often 100 percent perennial ryegrass.

Although perennial ryegrass will grow in partial shade, it's not the best choice if your yard is very shady. However, seed companies include it in mixes for shade because it helps bridge the areas of sun and shade.

▲ **Perennial ryegrass seeds sprout quickly to form a dark green, dense lawn with fine-textured leaves. Because it sprouts as soon as four days after planting, it's often included in grass mixes to provide some color while the other grasses germinate.**

Annual ryegrass

Annual ryegrass is related to perennial ryegrass—the difference of course being that annual ryegrass dies every year while perennial ryegrass doesn't. Because it dies off, annual ryegrass isn't used as a permanent turf. It does germinate and grow quickly however, so it is often mixed with longer-lived seeds in starter mixes and mixes designed for patching. The quick-growing annual ryegrass comes in, providing color and controlling erosion during the time that the slower growing permanent grass is germinating. In the South, it's often spread over dormant perennial grasses to give them color during the winter.

Annual ryegrass is a bunch grass with fair to good shade tolerance, fair drought tolerance, good cold tolerance, and is very wear resistant. Beyond its use as a temporary turf that greens up an area quickly, it's used for erosion control and a pasture grass.

Perennial ryegrass at a glance

Planting method: Seed. In some areas, it is also found in bluegrass sod.

Type of grass: Bunchgrass. Germinates quickly, creating a thick lawn when seeded properly. Spreads slowly, with growth radiating outward from the parent plant.

Drought resistance: Fair

Shade tolerance: Poor

Heat resistance: Fair

Cold resistance: Good

Wear resistance: Fair

Best mowing height: 1 inch. Mow lawn when it reaches 3 inches. Because of its rapid growth rate, perennial ryegrass may require twice-weekly mowing in spring.

Comments: Perennial ryegrass is an annual when planted in the South.

OPTIMAL GROWING CONDITIONS
Perennial ryegrass likes mild winters and cool, moist summers. It grows in full sun to partial shade and requires moderate amounts of water.

Keys to identification

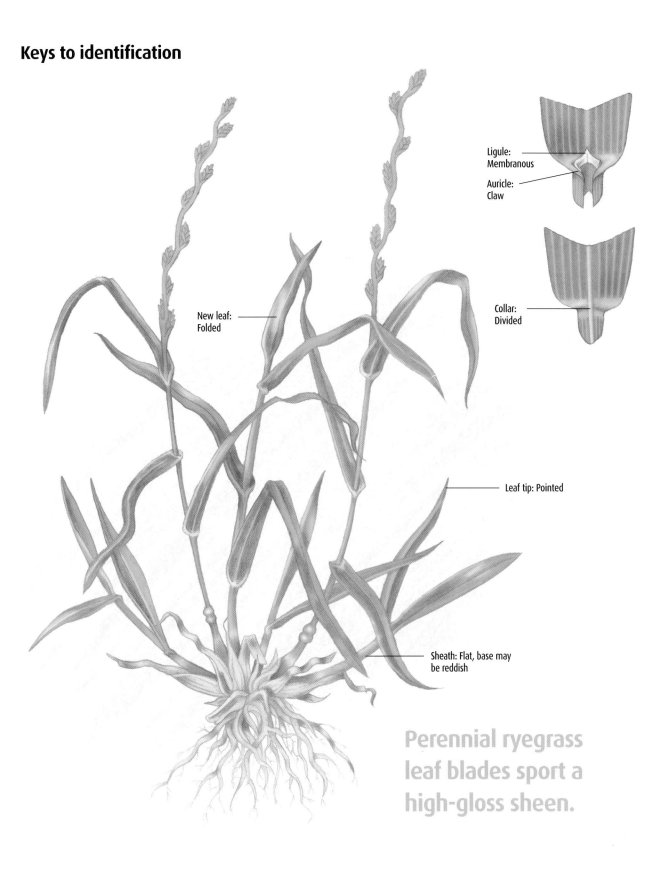

Ligule:
Membranous

Auricle:
Claw

Collar:
Divided

New leaf:
Folded

Leaf tip: Pointed

Sheath: Flat, base may
be reddish

Perennial ryegrass
leaf blades sport a
high-gloss sheen.

Tall fescue *(Festuca arundinacea)*

Tall fescue forms a medium- to dark-green turf with a medium to coarse texture. This grass has the deepest roots and the most extensive root system of any cool-weather grass. As a result, tall fescue has the best heat and drought resistance in this group, so it tolerates warmer weather. And with proper care, it uses 25 percent less water than Kentucky bluegrass. It is especially well suited to the Transition Zone.

Older varieties of tall fescue have coarse-textured leaf blades, which are not to everyone's liking. Newer varieties, called turf-type tall fescues, have thinner leaves than older types and they form a denser lawn. Some even newer varieties, known as dwarf and double dwarf type tall fescues, are also available. These are short, fine-textured grasses that grow more slowly. While these require less mowing, they are also less drought resistant and disease tolerant than turf-type tall fescues.

Another new type of tall fescue, rhizomatous tall fescue (RTF) spreads via rhizomes, underground runners that grow from the roots. As a result, RTF fescues spread more evenly than their non-rhizomatous cousins.

All types of tall fescue grow well in shade. They form very little thatch.

▲ Of all the grasses, tall fescue has the longest roots, making it a good candidate for dry areas. It's medium to dark green with a medium to coarse texture.

Tall fescue at a glance

Planting method: Seed or sod

Type of grass: Bunchgrass. Radiates slowly outward from the parent plant. Damaged areas will not fill in quickly and should be reseeded.

Drought resistance: Excellent

Shade tolerance: Good. Tall fescue thins out in full shade, but does well if it gets about five hours of sun.

Heat resistance: Very good

Cold resistance: Very good

Wear resistance: Good

Best mowing height: Mow when the grass reaches 3 inches. Dwarf tall fescue is best mowed to a height of 2 inches; mow when it is 2½ inches tall. Double dwarf tall fescue is best mowed to 1½ inches. Mow when it reaches 2 inches tall.

Comments: This is the most common grass in both Atlanta and Southern California. At the southern end of its range, it needs partial or afternoon shade. It's fine in full sun in the Midwest. Brown patch is a significant problem in the South and Midwest. In the South, it is routinely overseeded with ryegrass in the fall.

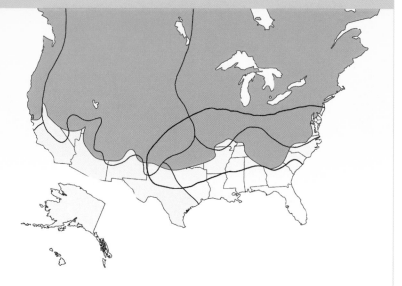

OPTIMAL GROWING CONDITIONS

Tall fescue is a good choice for the Transition Zone. It likes warm summers and winters that are moderately cold. Tall fescue grows in sun and in partial shade and in all types of soil. It tolerates relatively dry conditions.

Keys to identification

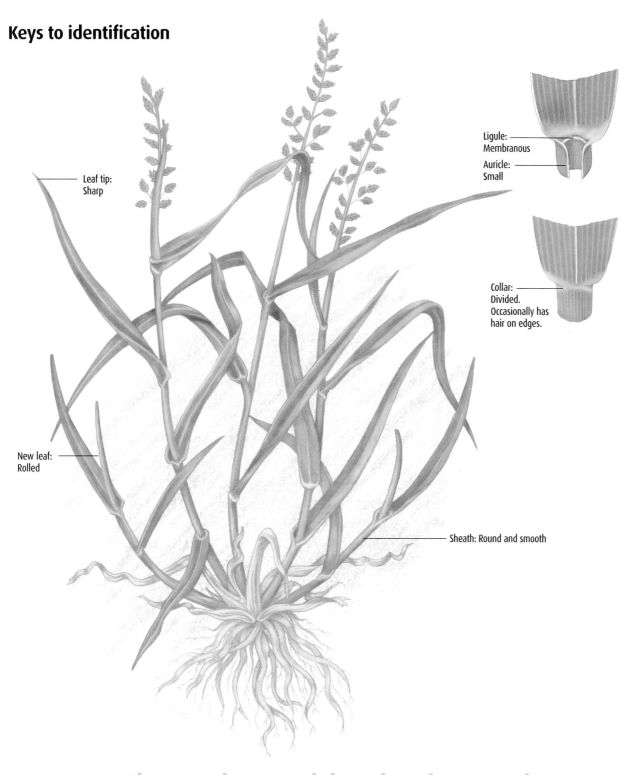

Leaf tip:
Sharp

New leaf:
Rolled

Ligule:
Membranous

Auricle:
Small

Collar:
Divided.
Occasionally has
hair on edges.

Sheath: Round and smooth

The most heat- and drought-tolerant cool-season grass, tall fescue is tough enough to be used on sports fields.

Fine fescue *(Festuca* spp.)

Fine fescues form a deep green lawn with the narrowest leaves of all cold-weather grasses. Of all the grasses, it is the most shade tolerant. It does well in cold, dry climates and is used both for lawns and as a low-maintenance grass in dry or unmowed areas. It requires little fertilizer.

Fine fescue actually refers to several species of grass—creeping red fescue, chewings fescue, hard fescue, and sheep fescue. Creeping red fescue is a creeping grass, unlike other fescues. It has a very fine texture, good drought resistance, and does well in shade. Chewings fescue is a fine-leafed bunchgrass that is often the best choice for a shady lawn. Hard fescue is a high-maintenance grass that has better tolerance to heat, drought, and disease than other fine fescues. Sheep's fescue is a low-maintenance grass that is also tolerant of heat, drought, and disease.

Fine fescue seed is often combined with Kentucky bluegrass seed to create a lawn that adjusts to whatever conditions may be found in a yard. When conditions favor fine fescues, they'll dominate the lawn; when conditions favor bluegrass, it is the predominant species in the lawn.

Most fine fescues are bunchgrasses, which form daughter plants next to the crown and radiate slowly outward. Creeping red fescue is the exception, spreading along underground stems called rhizomes. Fine fescues sprout and establish themselves quickly.

▲ **Fine fescue is actually a group of grasses that includes creeping red fescue, chewings fescue, hard fescue and sheep fescue. It has the finest texture and is the most shade-resistant of the cool-season grasses.**

Fine fescue at a glance

Planting method: Seed
Type of grass: Bunchgrass. Growth radiates slowly outward from the parent plant.
Drought resistance: Very good
Shade tolerance: Excellent
Heat resistance: Fair
Cold resistance: Excellent
Wear resistance: Moderate. Durable but won't recover quickly from severe injury.
Best mowing height: 2 inches. Mow when grass reaches 3 inches.

OPTIMAL GROWING CONDITIONS
Fine fescue prefers cool summers at high altitudes but tolerates cold weather and arid climates.

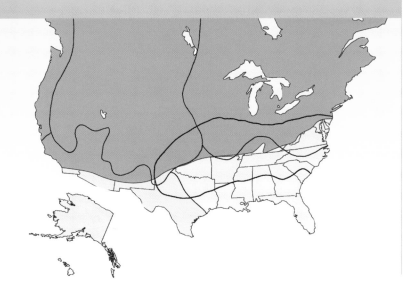

Keys to identification

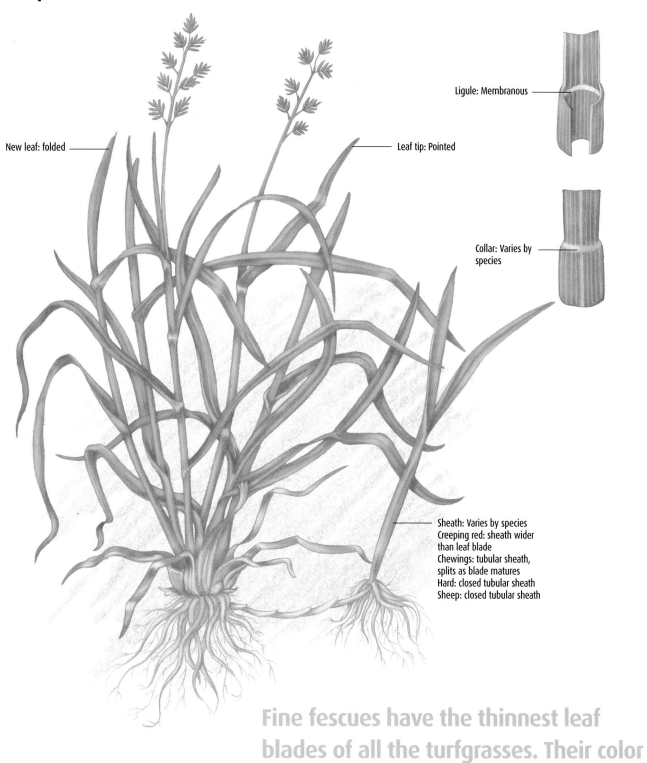

New leaf: folded

Leaf tip: Pointed

Ligule: Membranous

Collar: Varies by species

Sheath: Varies by species
Creeping red: sheath wider than leaf blade
Chewings: tubular sheath, splits as blade matures
Hard: closed tubular sheath
Sheep: closed tubular sheath

Fine fescues have the thinnest leaf blades of all the turfgrasses. Their color varies from pale green to gray green.

Warm-season grasses

Bermudagrass *(Cynodon* spp.*)*

Bermudagrass forms a dense dark green lawn with fine- to medium-textured leaves. Despite its name, bermudagrass originated in a hot, dry African climate, and it is both heat and drought tolerant. It is the predominant grass in the South and Southwest and is also popular for use on sports fields. It prefers full sun and has very little tolerance to shade.

Bermudagrass requires less water than any other turfgrass except buffalograss. If properly mowed and fertilized, it has no significant disease or insect problems. It does, however, go dormant when temperatures drop below 60°F (15°C) and stays brown most of the winter before reviving again in spring.

There are two types of bermudagrass— common and hybrid. Hybrid bermudagrass is considered the better of the two. It is dense and dark green, with fine- to medium-textured leaves. It is popular on golf courses, although it does turn brown with the first cold weather. Common bermudagrass, with its medium-textured leaves is better suited for sports fields. It turns white when it goes dormant in the winter.

Bermudagrass can be planted by sod, sprigs, or plugs. Common bermudagrass can also be planted

▲ **Bermudagrass, the most common grass in the South, requires less water than any other warm-season grass. It's also a durable grass, making it popular for use in sports fields.**

from seeds, which take 30 days to germinate. If you do buy seed, make sure you buy a named variety, which will be an improvement over common bermudagrass, although not as much of an improvement as the hybrid bermudagrasses are. (For more information on planting grass, see the chapter beginning on page 162.)

If you have a flagging hybrid lawn, don't attempt to revive it by overseeding with common bermudagrass. Common bermudagrass is quite

invasive, and will quickly overtake the lawn as well as move into your flower beds.

Older varieties were known for spreading into areas such as gardens where they weren't wanted. Newer varieties are less invasive, have finer leaves, and wear well. They require more sun and more fertilizer, however, and need to be mowed twice a week during the summer when growth peaks.

Bermudagrass at a glance

Planting method: Seed, sod, plugs or sprigs. (Hybrid bermudagrass cannot be started from seed.)
Type of grass: Creeping. Spreads aggressively by rhizomes and stolons.
Drought resistance: Excellent to average, depending on variety
Shade tolerance: Poor
Heat resistance: Good
Cold resistance: Fair
Wear resistance: Good
Best mowing height: 1 to 2 inches.

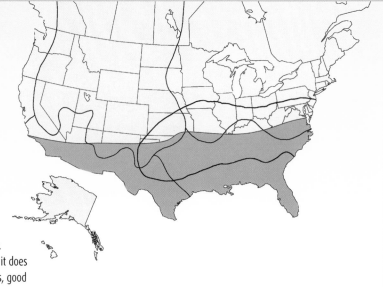

OPTIMAL GROWING CONDITIONS

Bermudagrass likes hot, dry climates as well as more humid tropical climates. It needs full sun and tolerates shade poorly. Bermudagrass grows in a wide range of soil types. Although it does best in moist soil, it tolerates drought well. It is a tough grass, good for yards that get a lot of use—or abuse—from children and pets.

Keys to identification

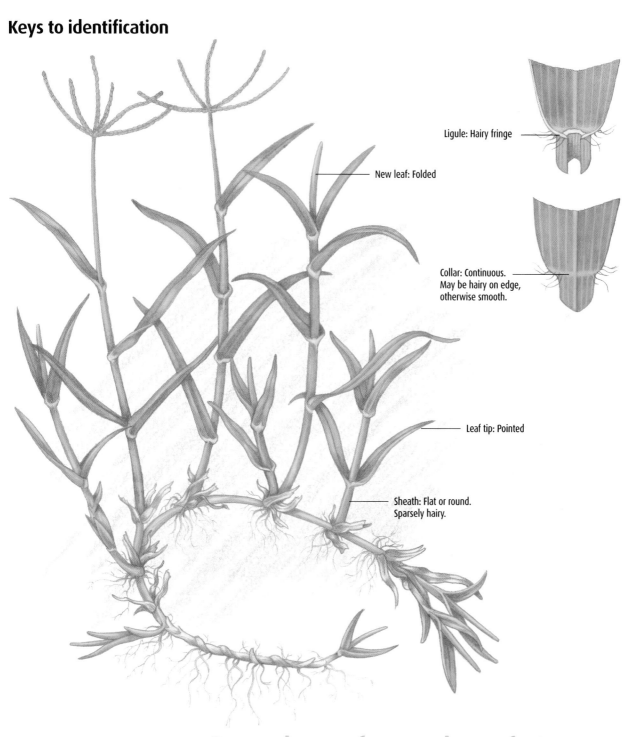

Ligule: Hairy fringe

Collar: Continuous. May be hairy on edge, otherwise smooth.

New leaf: Folded

Leaf tip: Pointed

Sheath: Flat or round. Sparsely hairy.

Bermudagrass forms a dense, fast-spreading, fast-growing, healthy green turf. Newer or improved varieties are especially handsome.

St. Augustinegrass (Stenotaphrum secundatum)

St. Augustinegrass grows best in humid coastal areas from Florida to Southern California. Its wide leaves form a coarse, medium- to dark-green turf. The resulting lawn is dense and nearly weedproof. St. Augustinegrass thrives in the sun, but it also has the greatest shade tolerance of the warm-season grasses. It grows rapidly and recovers quickly from damage.

St. Augustinegrass creates a low- to moderate-maintenance lawn, but it does have a tendency toward forming thatch. It suffers from a disease called St. Augustinegrass decline (SAD), so make sure you buy a grass seed that is labeled "SAD resistant." You can improve an existing lawn by planting plugs of a disease-resistant variety around your yard.

In spring and fall St. Augustinegrass may only need to be mowed every other week. During the summer, however, you will need to mow it weekly, if not more often. Because it requires fertile soil, you should fertilize regularly. If you use a weed-and-feed fertilizer, make sure you use one that is labeled safe for St. Augustinegrass. Dicamba and 2-4,D will kill St. Augustinegrass.

Different varieties have differing resistance to cold. Make sure the variety you buy matches your climate.

▲ **St. Augustinegrass thrives in warm, humid coastal regions. It grows best in full sun, but is also the most shade-resistant warm-season grass.**

St. Augustinegrass at a glance

Type of grass: Creeping
Planting method: Sod, sprigs, or plugs, which you cut yourself from sod grown in flats.
Drought resistance: Good
Shade tolerance: Excellent
Heat resistance: Excellent
Cold resistance: Poor
Wear resistance: Moderate
Best mowing height: 2 inches. Mow when grass reaches 3 inches tall.

OPTIMAL GROWING CONDITIONS
St. Augustinegrass prefers hot, tropical climates in coastal regions. It grows well in both sun and shade but prefers well-drained, sandy but fertile soil.

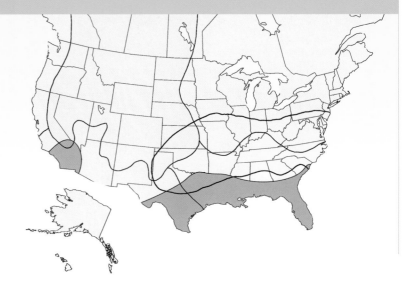

Keys to identification

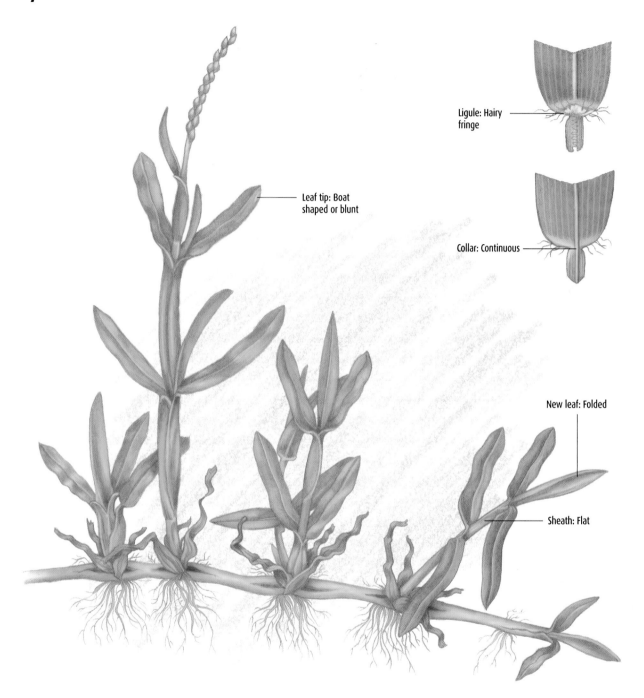

Ligule: Hairy fringe

Collar: Continuous

Leaf tip: Boat shaped or blunt

New leaf: Folded

Sheath: Flat

St. Augustinegrass has a distinctive coarse texture that stands out from other warm-season grasses in the way that it spreads across the ground.

Buffalograss *(Buchloe dactyloides)*

Buffalograss has fine blue-green blades but is not as dense as other warm-season grasses. Once a part of the natural landscape in the plains from Montana to New Mexico, buffalograss is the only native grass used for lawns. As you might expect from what was originally a prairie grass, buffalograss tolerates drought and dry weather, requires little fertilizer, and is low maintenance. Left alone with lots of sun and a little water, it grows to a maximum of 4 to 5 inches tall, so it can be left unmowed. In cooler climates with a short growing season, buffalograss can be clumpy. In areas of higher rainfall, bermudagrass and weeds do better than buffalograss and will take over a buffalograss lawn.

Buffalograss can be planted from either seeds or sod. If started from seed, it will have both male and female plants. The male seed stalks can be tall and unsightly. Sod, which can be propagated strictly from female plants, does not have the seed stalks. (Ask your source to be sure it sells female-only sod.)

No matter how you start your lawn, thatch is not a problem with buffalograss. Although buffalograss doesn't need fertilization, an application of nitrogen will green it up.

▲ **Buffalograss is a native prairie grass that has adapted well to lawns. Because it grows only about 5 inches tall, it can be left unmowed.**

Buffalograss at a glance

Planting method: Seed or sod
Type of grass: Creeping. Spreads through aboveground stolons.
Drought resistance: Excellent. It requires dry soil and low humidity, and it won't do well in humid areas or areas where there is a lot of rain.
Shade tolerance: Poor
Heat resistance: Excellent
Cold resistance: Very good
Wear resistance: Poor
Best mowing height: 2 inches. Mow when the grass reaches 3 inches tall.

OPTIMAL GROWING CONDITIONS
Buffalograss grows best in areas that receive as little as 15 inches and no more than 30 inches of rainfall per year. It does not do well in shade, in areas that undergo heavy wear, or where it rains a lot. It prefers sunny locations and medium- to fine-textured alkaline soil, and tolerates dry conditions. Although it is a warm-season grass, it is hardy in cold areas.

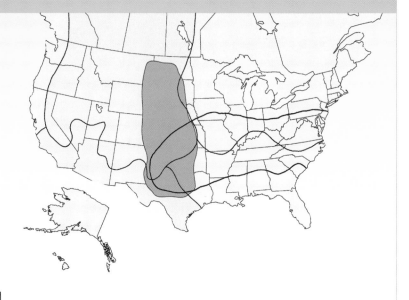

Keys to identification

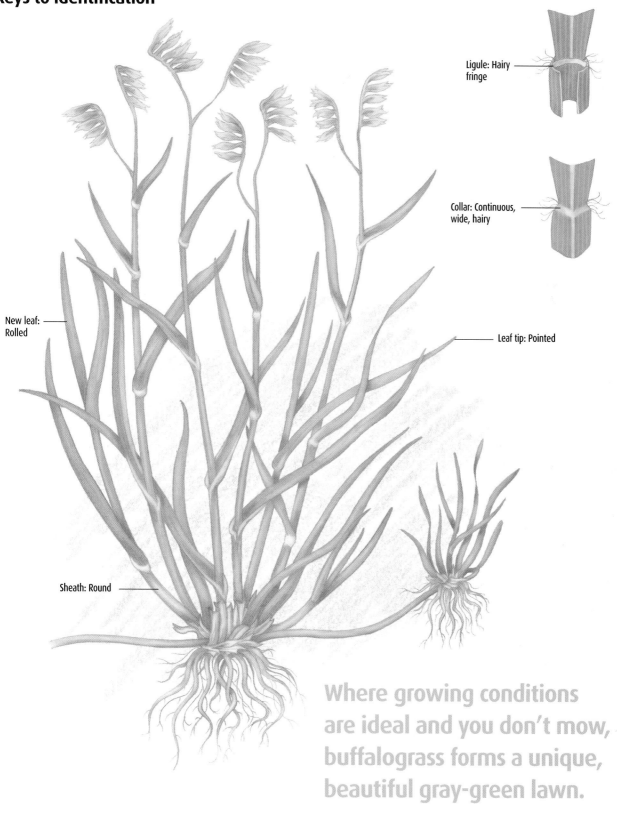

Ligule: Hairy fringe

Collar: Continuous, wide, hairy

New leaf: Rolled

Leaf tip: Pointed

Sheath: Round

Where growing conditions are ideal and you don't mow, buffalograss forms a unique, beautiful gray-green lawn.

Centipedegrass *(Eremochloa ophiuroides)*

Centipedegrass is one of the newer turfgrasses in the United States, having been brought in from China around the time of the First World War. It grows well on the Gulf Coast but not as well in arid regions. Its leaves are yellow green with a medium to coarse texture.

Centipedegrass likes acid soil, and tolerates shade well. Because it is an easy grass to care for requiring little fertilizer and no lime, it's often called "poor man's grass." Since it grows slowly, it needs mowing less often than other grasses. Under some conditions, you can get by with mowing a centipedegrass lawn every 10 to 14 days. Although centipedegrass grows slowly, it also grows aggressively, crowding out weeds and reducing the need for herbicides.

Because centipedegrass grows slowly, lawns made of it are slow to recover from damage. It has a poor tolerance to traffic. Bermudagrass and St. Augustinegrass produce a nicer lawn but are harder to care for. Overfertilizing can lead to thatch in a centipedegrass lawn.

▲ **Centipedegrass grows well in acidic soil, and requires very little fertilizer. Because it's a slow-growing grass, it requires less mowing than other turfgrasses.**

Centipedegrass at a glance

Type of grass: Creeping, with upright stolons that resemble a centipede and account for the grass's name.
Planting method: Seed, sprigs, or sod
Drought resistance: Good
Shade tolerance: Good
Heat resistance: Excellent
Cold resistance: Poor
Wear resistance: Poor
Best mowing height: 1½ inches. Mow grass when it reaches 2¼ inches.

OPTIMAL GROWING CONDITIONS
Centipedegrass prefers hot, humid climates and areas of high rainfall. It likes sunny locations and does well in the sandy, infertile acid soil of the Southeast. It spreads only above ground, making it easy to keep out of flower beds.

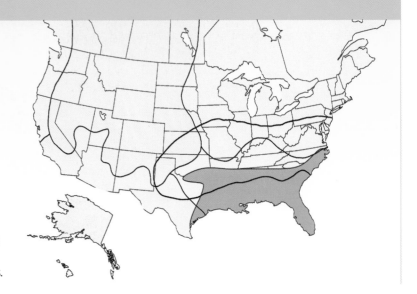

Keys to identification

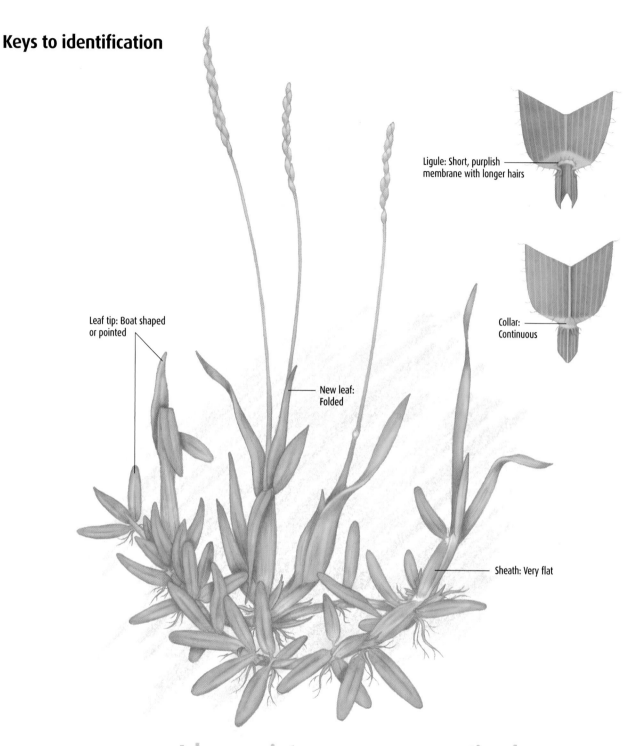

Ligule: Short, purplish membrane with longer hairs

Collar: Continuous

Leaf tip: Boat shaped or pointed

New leaf: Folded

Sheath: Very flat

A low-maintenance grass, centipedegrass grows slowly so it needs less mowing, and it resists insects and diseases such as chinch bugs and brown patch.

Zoysiagrass *(Zoysia* spp.)

Zoysiagrass is a dense turf that is light to medium green with fine to medium leaf texture. It is a tough, aggressive grass that is low maintenance. The leaves are high in silica, making zoysiagrass the best wearing of any grass. On the downside, the leaves are also wiry and can be sharp underfoot; the tough, stiff blades can also be hard to mow. Because old rhizomes and stems break down slowly, zoysiagrass tends to have problems with thatch.

Zoysiagrass is the most cold tolerant of the warm-season grasses, so it does better in the northern part of the warm-season area and in the Transition Zone. The leaves go dormant and turn brown below 55°F (13°C). In the northern end of its range, zoysiagrass turns brown well before other grasses, and it is slow to green up in spring. It's at its best in the summer, when it forms a dense turf that crowds out weeds.

Zoysiagrass requires relatively little fertilizer and few pesticides because it has no significant insect or disease problems if properly maintained. When properly managed, it requires only half the water that a Kentucky bluegrass lawn needs.

It takes a long time to establish a zoysiagrass lawn, and it recuperates slowly from damage. Zoysiagrass is usually planted as either sod or plugs, and the plugs can take up to two years to cover an area completely. Take care when reading Sunday supplement ads for a miracle grass in the

▲ **Zoysiagrass has tough, wiry leaves that wear well but can be hard to mow. It's a low-maintenance grass, though thatch can be a problem.**

newspaper. Usually the grass being sold is zoysia, and you won't get enough to grow a lawn as fast as the ads claim.

There are several varieties of zoysiagrass. Emerald has a fine texture, spreads quickly, and is considered by some to be the most attractive of the zoysias. It is somewhat prickly to the touch, however. El Toro, Zenith, and Meyer all have a nicer feel. El Toro is durable but slower growing. Zenith has good texture and turf quality and can be grown from seed. Meyer has good color, disease resistance, and excellent cold tolerance.

Zoysiagrass at a glance

Type of grass: Creeping. Spreads aggressively through rhizomes and stolons.
Planting method: Seed, sprigs, or sod
Drought resistance: Very good
Shade tolerance: Fair to good
Heat resistance: Excellent
Cold resistance: Poor but recovers
Wear resistance: Excellent
Best mowing height: 1½ inches. Mow when the grass reaches 2¼ inches tall.

OPTIMAL GROWING CONDITIONS
Even though it grows in the North, zoysiagrass prefers hot, humid tropical climates. It does well in both sun and shade and in a wide variety of well-drained soils. It needs little if any watering, having excellent drought tolerance. It is a good play and sports lawn that survives heavy use.

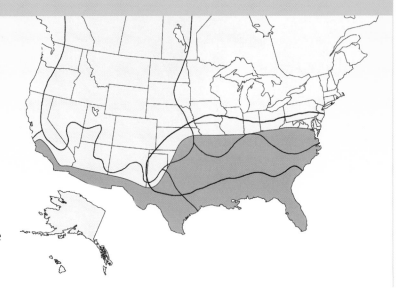

Keys to identification

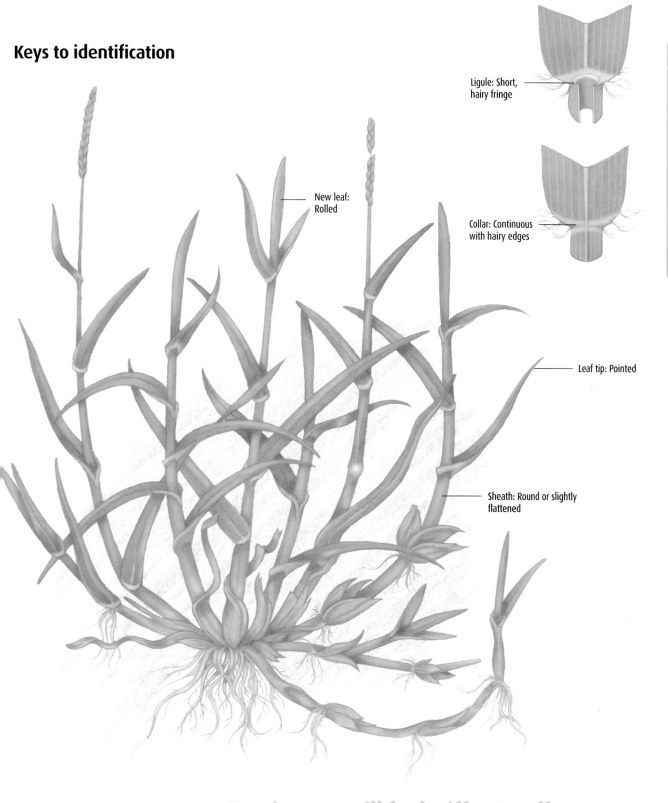

Ligule: Short, hairy fringe

New leaf: Rolled

Collar: Continuous with hairy edges

Leaf tip: Pointed

Sheath: Round or slightly flattened

Zoysiagrass will feel stiff yet puffy when you walk across it. It makes a tough, fine-textured, light green lawn.

Mowing and trimming

The ability to tolerate mowing is the one characteristic that separates grasses from all other plants. Whether you love or hate the job, without this ability there would be no lush carpet of green to set off your house or provide a smooth surface on which to practice your golf swing. So while mowing may be a dreaded lawn task for you, it is also a very important one.

When you mow correctly, your lawn is thicker, healthier, and weed-free. It has deeper roots and is better able to withstand all the hard knocks the weather, kids, or dogs may dish out. Mowing correctly even helps the grass get by with less water and suffer from fewer insects and diseases.

What is mowing correctly? It's cutting the grass to the right height—usually at the top of the recommended range for the grass—and mowing often enough that you never take off too much at one time. It's also making sure that your mower blade is good and sharp and well-tuned so that it doesn't damage your grass.

On the following pages you'll find help in learning to mow correctly as well as hints for making the job easier.

Chapter 2 highlights

Mowing for success

► Set your lawn mower to cut off one-quarter to one-third of the overall height of the grass. Wait until your grass is at optimum height—2 or 3 inches in most cases—before mowing it again. This encourages root growth that helps the plant get water during droughts.

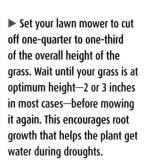owing a lawn is simple, but getting it wrong is simple to do too. A bad job is worse than no job.

If you're like most people, you run the lawn mower or tractor across the lawn once a week. You may enjoy it—at least a little bit—or you wouldn't bother learning more about lawn care. During the long, dry days of summer, when a regular mowing leaves the lawn a bit ragged, you may cut the grass a bit shorter. If vacation takes you away for a week or two, you may even cut the grass as short as you can, hoping that it won't get too long while you're gone.

Start looking at your lawn differently. Mow it because the grass is too long, not because it's the weekend. When you do mow, never cut off more than one-third of the length of the leaves.

Low-cut grasses don't have enough leaf mass to thrive. When you cut off more than a third of the blade length, you remove the tissues that grass uses to produce the food that fuels its root growth. When root growth suffers, the grass is left without enough water and nutrients, and it becomes vulnerable to disease and drought.

High-cut grasses, on the other hand, have both more leaves and more and deeper roots. With better roots, grass can draw in more water and nutrients from the soil—nutrients that make the plant vigorous and help it outcompete weeds sneaking into the lawn. During dry spells, the deeper roots, which can be as much as 8 inches deep, are vital to getting the nutrients and water that grass needs. During more moderate weather, deep roots result in a stronger grass that is resistant to disease.

Taller grass also creates its own shade. Although excessive shade is enough to stunt or even kill grass, the shade that grass produces can be important to its survival. Cutting the grass long keeps the sun from overheating the grass crown and roots; it protects the roots and helps conserve water. Short cut grass has nothing to protect it, and the crown will sunburn, killing the grass, especially in hot weather.

Mowing heights for different grasses

GRASS	OPTIMUM HEIGHT	MOW WHEN THE GRASS REACHES
Bluegrass	2 inches	3 inches
Perennial ryegrass	2 inches	3 inches
Tall fescue	2 inches	3 inches
Fine fescue	2 inches	3 inches
St. Augustinegrass	2 inches	3 inches
Buffalograss	2 inches	3 inches
Bermudagrass	1¼ inches	2¼ inches
Zoysiagrass	1¼ inches	2¼ inches

Lawn mower safety

■ Leave the safety features intact. Guards and dead men switches are there to protect you from danger. Don't disable them.

■ Never reach into the mower while the blade is running. If grass clogs the discharge chute, shut off the engine before trying to remove the clog. Mow the grass only when it's dry to help prevent clogs and to keep from slipping on wet grass.

■ Don't let children run the mower. They are neither mature enough nor large enough to operate it safely

■ Remove sticks, stones, and trash from the mowing area before you mow.

■ Keep your feet clear of the deck and blade at all times.

■ Wear long pants to protect your legs, and heavy shoes to protect your feet.

■ Wear safety glasses and hearing protection.

■ Refill the gas tank carefully. Don't smoke while refueling and don't do the job indoors. Let the engine cool before refilling, and never refill while the engine is still running.

■ If you're using a bagger, make sure there aren't any holes in it. Stones grabbed by the blade can fly through the holes. Don't operate a rear bagger without the bag unless the discharge door is closed.

■ Pay attention. Don't operate a mower after drinking, taking medication, or any other drugs.

▲ Cut off no more than one-third of the height at a time. Cutting shorter exposes plant crowns, reduces root growth, and stresses the lawn.

▲ Repeatedly scalping a lawn—cutting it too short—eventually results in a thin weedy patch.

Grass height: How high is too high?

In theory, each variety of grass grows best when cut to a certain height, so the setting on your lawn mower should be based on the grass in your lawn. In practice, however, the grass in most lawns was planted ages ago, and few people have any idea what they're cutting. Check the grass profiles beginning on page 18 for help identifying exactly which grass you have and for the proper mowing height.

One mower manufacturer recommends a general guideline, which while not perfect, comes close to what you should do: Cut warm-season grasses—the ones suited to the South—2 to 2½ inches tall, the height at which they grow best. Cool-season grasses—those suited to the North—grow best when cut a little longer. Keep them at 3 to 3½ inches tall.

Once you know the proper height for your grass, remember that you don't want to cut off more than one-quarter to one-third of its height. Cutting off more than that stresses the grass and dumps a layer of clippings on the lawn that can smother it. Follow the one-quarter to one-third guideline, however, and the clippings generally decompose and act as a natural fertilizer. (If you're in an area such as California, where the grass is prone to disease, bagging the clippings can help prevent problems.)

Mowing simplified

Most people find mowing to be somewhat of a chore. But even if it appeals to your inner sodbuster, it doesn't have to be as much of a chore as it seems.

Start with the right mower—a lawn mower that is too big for your yard will slow you down as much as one that is too small. Try maneuvering a 60-inch tractor across a tight, tree-filled yard, for example. You'll spend as much time backing up and turning as you will mowing. On the other hand, it will take 2½ hours to mow a half-acre lot with an 18-inch, gas-powered rotary mower, while you could do the job in ½ hour with a 36-inch riding mower.

Cut in long, straight patterns. The fewer turns you make, the sooner you'll finish. If your front yard is 30 feet by 40 feet, for example, cut it in 40-foot-long swaths.

In almost all cases, you won't need a grass catcher or bag as long as you are cutting off only a fourth to a third of the lawn's height. The exception—areas like Southern California where leaving clippings on the lawn encourages disease. Otherwise, let the clippings fall on the ground where they'll decompose and feed the grass. Use a mulching blade if you're concerned about the clippings. One isn't necessary if you're taking off only the top one-quarter to one-third of the grass, but it will cut the clippings into smaller pieces so they are less visible and decompose more quickly.

Don't mow a wet lawn unless it's impossibly tall and more rain is in the forecast. Wet grass is more likely

to tear as it is cut, especially if the mower blade is a bit dull. Wet clippings blow out and fall in thick chunks rather than a fine haze. And the wheels of your mower can compact wet soil, especially if you're driving a tractor or riding mower.

Remember the standard rules. Mow at the recommended height for your lawn. Never cut off more than one-third of the height. Keep mower blades sharp. Dull blades introduce disease, leading to less leaf growth and a sparser lawn. They also use about 20 percent more gas.

▲ **To do the job right—and quickly—choose a mower to match the size of your yard and mow in long straight patterns.**

Keep mower blades sharp

A whitish cast to the lawn is a sure sign that you're cutting with a dull blade. But don't wait for a sure sign before you sharpen your blade. A dull blade—particularly on a rotary mower—tears the grass and weakens it long before the whitish cast appears. (Ryegrass is especially prone to tearing.) At the very least, sharpen the blade—or have it sharpened—at the beginning of the season.

Once the blade is sharp, keep an eye out for two things. First, look at the blade after every mowing. If it's uneven or dinged like the one on the right (above right), it needs to be resharpened. Second, take a look at the ends of the grass and the clippings (above left). The first time you cut the grass after a sharpening, the ends will be straight and clean. When the ends of the grass blades start to look ragged or fuzzy, it's time to resharpen.

1

MOW AROUND THE PERIMETER

Start by mowing around the perimeter of the yard—along the sidewalk, against the house, and along the fence, if there is one. Travel so that you're blowing the clippings back onto the lawn. This will let the cutting blade get as close as possible to the fence and house so you don't have to follow up with a lot of trimming. Along the sidewalk, send the grass toward the lawn so you won't have to sweep the walk clean.

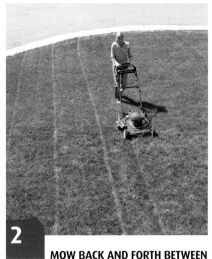

2

MOW BACK AND FORTH BETWEEN THE EDGES

Once you've cut around the edges, mow back and forth between the perimeters. Travel between the farthest edges of the yard in a direction that sends the clippings onto the grass you've already cut. Blowing it onto uncut grass only creates piles you'll have to plow through, giving you more work to do and slowing you down.

Change the pattern every few mowings, working diagonally or traveling along the short dimension of the yard. Grass tends to lay flat after it's mowed, and changing directions will pull it back up and give you a more even cut. It also helps avoid soil compaction under the wheels, and in uneven terrain, spots that are scalped will get a bit of relief when you change directions.

3

IF THE GRASS IS TOO LONG, MAKE TWO PASSES

If you've waited out a rain and ended up with overly long grass, cut it in two passes. Remove half of what you have to cut on the first pass; then change directions, lower the blades, and cut the rest on a second pass. You'll get a more even cut and a finer layer of clippings.

Patterns in the grass

No doubt you've seen the patterns in the grass at baseball games, the light and dark strips between the yard lines at football games, or the stripes on the PGA Tour.

If you've looked closely at your yard after you mow it, it's not quite the PGA Tour, but you've probably noticed some subtle stripes. Mowing the grass forces the lawn to lay down in the direction the lawn mower travels. Light playing across strips of grass laying in opposite directions creates subtle differences in color. With some extra mowing, you can create the patterns you've seen on sports fields.

To make a checkerboard pattern on your lawn, cut normally, going back and forth in adjacent rows. Overlap the rows slightly to make sure you don't leave any uncut blades between rows.

When you finish the lawn, cut it again, traveling back and forth at 90 degrees to the original cut. When you finish the second pass, emphasize the pattern with a third pass, cutting every other row in the direction of the original cut.

Mowing slopes

Slopes greater than 5 degrees look almost flat, but are dangerous to mow. Never mow a slope steeper than 15 degrees.

If you're using a walk-behind mower, mow across the face of the slope. The mower is less likely to hit you if you fall and less likely to run out of control downhill.

If you're mowing with a tractor, mow up and down the hill so that the tractor is less likely to turn over on top of you. If the wheels slip, the slope is too steep for the tractor. Disengage the blade, and back straight downhill.

Sharpening a mower blade

PROJECT DETAILS

SKILLS: Ability to use a wrench and file
PROJECT: Removing, sharpening, and reinstalling a rotary lawn mower blade

TIME TO COMPLETE

EXPERIENCED: 30 min.
HANDY: 45 min.
NOVICE: 1 hr.

STUFF YOU'LL NEED

TOOLS: Socket wrench, clamp, blade sharpener and balancing kit, vice, torque wrench (optional)
MATERIALS: Block of wood

SAFETY ALERT

DISCONNECT THE SPARK PLUG

When working on a lawn mower—whether you're sharpening the blade or scraping grass buildup from underneath the deck—always disconnect the spark plug. Turning the blade, even by accident, is the equivalent of turning the crank on a Model T. It causes the motor to turn, and if the spark plug is connected, it can cause the motor to start when you can least afford it. Once the plug is disconnected, the motor will not start.

A dull lawn mower blade will tear the grass instead of cutting it cleanly, stressing the grass and leaving it vulnerable to disease. The best way to tell if your blade needs sharpening isn't by looking at the blade—it's by looking at the grass. No matter what kind of mower you have, clean-cut edges indicate a sharp blade. Ragged edges mean it's time for a sharpening.

Sharpening reel mowers is a very precise operation, and setting the space between the bed knife and the blades is crucial. Have your reel mower sharpened professionally. With a rotary mower, you have a choice: You can have it sharpened at the shop, or you can remove the blade and sharpen it yourself.

If you plan on having the blade sharpened at the shop, you can take in the entire mower, or just the blade. If you're removing the blade, either for the shop or to sharpen it yourself, it's pretty straightforward. You just loosen a bolt or two. Make sure you do a couple of other things, however. First, disconnect the spark plug so you won't accidentally start the engine while turning the blade. Second, mark the bottom of the blade and make sure you put it back on the way you took it off. It's possible to put the blade on upside down—and then it's *really* dull.

▲ You can sharpen a lawn mower blade with a file or with a grinding wheel. A file gives you more control; a grinding wheel makes quicker work of the job.

Removing the blade

1 **DISCONNECT THE SPARK PLUG AND TURN OFF THE FUEL VALVE**
Turning the blade as you work turns over the motor. Unless you disconnect the spark plug, it's often enough to make the mower start up—even if the mower has a safety shut-off. Pull the spark plug wire off the plug to keep this from happening. Most lawn mowers also have a valve that shuts off the flow of fuel to the carburetor. Turn the valve to the off position.

2

TURN THE LAWN MOWER ON ITS SIDE

Position the mower so that the carburetor side faces up. If you put the carburetor side down, it can fill with oil, making it hard to start and blowing a black cloud of smoke into the air in the process. Spray some penetrating oil onto the bolts that hold the blade in place. This will make loosening the bolts easier.

3

CLAMP A WOODEN BLOCK TO THE DECK

The engine shaft and mower blade will turn when you try to loosen the bolts holding the blade. Clamp a wooden block to the inside of the mower to keep the blade from turning as you try to loosen it.

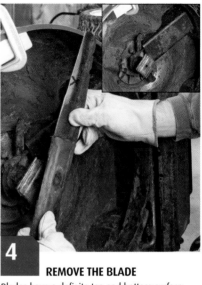

4

REMOVE THE BLADE

Blades have a definite top and bottom surface. Mark the bottom so that you'll be able to get the blade back on in the correct position. Rest the blade against the wooden block and loosen the bolts that hold the blade in place with a socket wrench. Remove the bolts and lift off the blade.

Sharpening the blade

1

INSPECT THE BLADE

Take a good look at it. Replace the blade if it's bent, cracked, or if part of the blade is missing. If you'd rather not sharpen it yourself, or if it's badly nicked like this one, take it to a dealer for sharpening.

2

SHARPEN THE BEVEL

Put the blade in a vise, protecting it with a couple of pieces of scrap wood. Grind nicks and burrs off the bottom of the bevel with the sharpening kit grinding wheel. Turn the blade over and guide the wheel along the outer 3 to 4 inches of the blade. Take care near the end of the blade where the wheel may catch.

3

BALANCE THE BLADE

If the blade's center of gravity isn't in the middle, the blade will wobble and wear out the motor's bearings. Put the blade on the sharpening kit's wheel balancer. If one side is lower than the other, grind the bevel on the low side a bit more and check the balance again. Repeat until the blade balances perfectly.

Remounting the blade

CLEAN THE HOUSING AND BLADE HOLDER

Use a scraper or putty knife to clean off any debris or grass from the blade holder or undercarriage.

2 **PUT THE BLADE ON WITH THE MARK FACING YOU**

If there were any plates that helped fasten the blade, put them in place. Thread the bolts through the blade and start tightening by hand. Tighten firmly with a wrench. Stand the mower upright, reconnect the spark plug, and put the fuel control valve in the open position.

TIMESAVER

GET AN EXTRA BLADE

It doesn't take long to sharpen a blade. If you have it professionally sharpened, however, you have to leave the blade at the shop and wait for it to be sharpened. Depending on the shop and season, it can take the shop quite a while, and until they get around to it, your mower is useless. Buy an extra blade that you can use while the dull one is in the shop. When you get the sharpened blade back, hang it on the wall until the blade you're using gets dull.

TOOL SAVVY

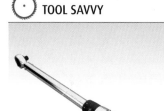

TORQUE WRENCH

Some manufacturers specify that you tighten the bolts on the blades with a torque wrench. A torque wrench measures the amount of pressure you apply when you tighten the bolt against the blade or holder. It's a good tool to use to make sure the blade is properly tightened. Check the owner's manual for your lawn mower to see if a torque wrench is recommended and how tight the nuts should be. If a torque wrench is recommended, get one and tighten as directed.

Setting the cutting height on a rotary mower

utting the grass to the right height is one of the most important—and easiest—things you can do to keep your lawn green and healthy. Cut the grass too short, and the roots suffer. Cut off too much grass at any one mowing, and the clippings will smother the lawn. How high is right? Grasses suited to the South, known as warm-season grasses, grow best when they are cut to 2 or 2½ inches. Cool-season grasses, suited to the North, grow best when cut a little longer—3 to 3½ inches.

The best way to set the cutting height on your mower is to do a little measuring. Measure the distance from the bottom of the mower housing to the bottom of the blade and mark the distance on the outside of the mower. Measure from the ground to the mark to see what your setting is; then do a bit of cutting to see how the mower and the terrain interact. Adjust the setting as necessary.

1　**DISCONNECT THE SPARK PLUG**
Always disconnect the spark plug before working on the lawn mower. Even a small accidental push of the blade may be enough to start the motor and cause serious injury.

2　**TURN THE MOWER ON ITS SIDE**
Turn the lawn mower on its side so that you can get to the blade. Make sure the carburetor is uppermost. If the carburetor faces down, it will fill with oil and produce a cloud of black smoke when you start the mower.

3　**MEASURE THE DISTANCE FROM THE BOTTOM OF THE HOUSING TO THE BLADE**
Measure from the bottom of the mower housing, or deck, to the blade using a ruler, a square, or a tape measure.

▼ On most mowers you adjust the cutting height by setting a lever that moves the wheels up and down. On other models, you unbolt the wheel to move it. Whichever you do, make sure you've got all four wheels at the same height.

4　**MARK THIS DISTANCE ON THE OUTSIDE OF THE DECK**
Measuring from the bottom of the housing, mark the blade height on the outside of the deck.

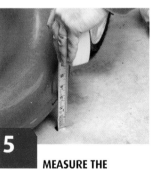

5　**MEASURE THE DISTANCE FROM THE MARK TO THE GROUND**
Put the lawn mower on a flat, solid surface like the driveway or garage floor. The distance between the surface and the mark is the height to which the mower will cut. Adjust as necessary.

6　**MAKE A TEST CUT**
Start the lawn mower and cut a swath across a flat section of your yard. Measure, using the same rule, tape, or square that you used before to get the actual cutting height. Measure in several places to account for any irregularities in the surface. The reading you get most often is the actual height of the cut.

Buying a new mower

Since cutting your lawn is one of the best things you do for it, buying a lawn mower deserves more than passing attention. When you get to the store, you'll come face to face with a broad range of lawn mowers: push mowers, electric mowers, battery-powered mowers, gas mowers, riding mowers, and tractors. Despite the variety, all fall into two broad categories: rotary and reel.

■ Reel mowers, invented in 1830, have four to six blades joined to form a spinning cage powered by the motion of the wheels. Old reel mowers seemed to work best when you flipped the handle to the front so you could walk them to the garage; they seemed to work worst when cutting the lawn. New reel mowers, however, are easy to use and do a great job.

■ Rotary mowers have a blade that spins parallel to the ground. Most mowers on the market are rotary. They include gas-, battery-, and electric-powered mowers, as well as tractors and riding mowers.

▲ A large lawn requires a large mower, and a small yard calls for a small mower, but there are other factors too. A small yard with a steep incline may call for a self-propelled mower. A small, flat yard may be the perfect candidate for a quiet electric mower.

▼ Reel mowers are ideal for small yards and for some types of grass—hybrid bermudagrass and bentgrass among them.

Reel mowers

Pros: Turf managers consider them to be the best type of mower. Cuts are clean and heal quickly. Grass is cut to a uniform height. Mowers are simple to operate.
Cons: May cut grass too short, even at highest setting. Push models cut a narrow swath. Must be professionally sharpened.

The cutting action of a reel mower has always been better than that of rotary mowers. A bar at the base of the reel, called a bed knife, forces the grass to stand up, and the turning blades pinch the grass against the bar, shearing it off. Unlike rotary mowers, which leave a ragged edge, the cut is always clean and heals quickly.

Reel mowers cut grass to a uniform height. The clippings are very fine—finer than those left by a rotary mulching blade—and decompose quickly. A reel mower is simple to operate, and does such a good job of

cutting that gas-powered ones are used by grounds managers for mowing golf greens. In fact, hybrid bermudagrass and bentgrass are best cut with a reel mower. They'll cut zoysiagrass well, too, but it can be too puffy and dense for a manual reel mower if not managed properly.

Reel mowers are not perfect. They have problems cutting extra-long grass and thick-stemmed weeds. Some cut the grass too short, even at their highest setting.

If you're considering a reel mower, shop around—some models offer more height adjustment options and can cut considerably higher than others. Most reel mowers are manual push mowers, and manufacturers recommend them for lawns no larger than a quarter-acre. Gas-powered models are good for larger expanses. Commercial models are expensive, but ask about the availability of more reasonably priced residential models.

Gas-powered rotary mowers

Pros: Cuts a wider swath than either reel or electric mowers. Powerful. Handles long grass and weeds easily. Most start easily.

Cons: High maintenance when compared with electric and reel mowers. Leaves a ragged edge on the grass it cuts. Noisy. Creates exhaust fumes. Not good for low-cutting heights.

If your lawn is larger than one-quarter acre, you've pretty much moved into ground that requires a gas-powered mower. Gas-powered rotary mowers cut a wider swath than reel or electric mowers—20 to 22 inches—are powerful, and have an unlimited range. On the downside, they're noisy and require regular maintenance. (For more on maintenance, see page 52.)

The blade on a rotary mower rotates with tremendous speed and (dangerous) force. The spinning blade works in combination with the mower deck to vacuum the grass into an upright position, and then the blade lops off the top of the grass. The cut edge is a bit more ragged because the grass is unsupported during the cut and the top tends to tear. Because they're powered by gas engines, these mowers make a lot of noise. What the rotary mower lacks in subtlety, however, it makes up for in power. It can cut longer grass (not that you should) and is well suited for cutting weeds (not that you'll have that many once you start cutting, watering, and fertilizing properly).

Rotaries come in a variety of sizes, with a variety of motors. Obviously, the wider the cut, the sooner you are done. Horsepower doesn't necessarily play a major role, however. A 5½ hp motor is plenty for a push rotary mower. You're cutting grass, not trees.

You'll want a bigger motor for a self-propelled mower, however. Self-propelled models are good for hilly properties—the drive mechanism not only pulls the lawn mower up the hill, it keeps it from racing downhill. And of course, a self-propelled model is easier to push.

Self-propelled mowers have a variety of drive mechanisms from which to choose. Front-wheel drive is the least expensive. Rear-wheel drive mowers are easier to turn, however. You push down on the handle, and pivot the lawn mower with an assist from the wheels.

The drive mechanism may be either single speed, three-speed or variable speed. Single speed is the most affordable, but it may cause the mower to run faster or slower than you like. Three speeds may come closer to setting the right pace. Variable speed mowers pretty much assure that you and the lawn mower travel at the same speed. Some models are designed so that the harder you push, the faster the mower travels.

▲ Gas powered rotary mowers are a good fit for medium-sized lawns. Self-propelled models ease pushing and are especially helpful on inclines.

◀ Electric starters effortlessly turn over the engine.

Self-propelled or owner-propelled, rotary mowers have a wide variety of available options. An electric starter may come in handy, especially as you get older, though mowers are much easier to start by hand than they once were. An oversized rear wheel makes for a smoother trip across rough lawn. If you're cutting the proper amount off the top of the grass, you won't need a bagger unless you're in an area like California, where grass build-up contributes to disease. Mulching blades aren't necessary, though they chop the clippings more thoroughly so that they will decompose on the lawn more quickly.

⊘ **SAFETY ALERT**

DON'T OVERRIDE SAFETY FEATURES

A rotary mower has a handle-shaped lever called a "dead man's switch." You have to hold it against the actual handle in order for the mower to run. Don't override it. It's there so that if you slip or step away from the mower, the blade stops turning, making if far less likely that you'll get hurt.

Riding mowers and tractors

🚫 **SAFETY ALERT**

TRACTOR SAFETY

- Tractors require you to follow all the safety recommendations for a push mower, plus some others.
- Ride solo. A passenger could slip off and be badly injured.
- Look behind you when backing up. Make sure there's no one behind you. Turn off the blade to eliminate the danger of running over something unintentionally while the blade is turning.
- Don't pop the clutch. Ease the mower into gear.
- Be extremely careful on hills. Anything over 5 degrees is dangerous; anything over 15 degrees is off limits. Mow up and down the hill, rather than across it.

Pros: Cut large areas quickly with little effort. Snow blowers, carts, garden tools, and other accessories are often available.

Cons: Expensive; difficult to operate on small lawns; mechanically complex drives and transmission can require maintenance and are expensive to repair.

If your lawn is a half-acre or more, you have entered the market for a riding mower or tractor—and the larger it is, the more you're in the market.

The most important variable among riding mowers and tractors is the least obvious. Riding mowers have a single blade inside the deck; tractors have three blades. Single blades can usually be driven by a smaller motor, and tractors with single blades are less expensive as a result. The blade is usually on a rigid carriage, and if your lawn is uneven, the blade can leave the grass long on one side while scalping the other. Multiple-blade mowers are on a floating deck that follows the contour of your lawn and are less likely to scalp.

Choosing between the two types of mowers depends in part on your budget—single-blade mowers can be dramatically cheaper. The contour of your yard plays a role too. The more uneven the yard, the more likely a single-blade machine is to scalp parts of it.

Take the size of your yard into consideration as well. Practically speaking, motor size and scalping problems limit the blade size of single-blade mowers to between 28 and 32 inches long. Multiple-blade tractors may have blades that are 20 inches long but combine for a cutting width of up to 60 inches. A multiple-blade tractor with its wider swath can cut the yard in nearly half the time of a single-blade riding mower.

▲ Smaller tractors, like this one, often have a single blade that stays parallel to the plane of the wheels. They do a good job, but if high spots in the lawn cause the tractor to tilt, the blade will tilt too, causing it to scalp the lawn.

▲ Larger tractors have three blades side by side and a "floating" mower deck that follows the contour of the yard. Because the blades follow the terrain, they are less likely to scalp the lawn.

Electric-powered rotary mowers

Pros: Easy to operate, quiet, start easily, require little maintenance, no exhaust emissions.

Cons: Corded models require an outdoor outlet and will go only as far as the longest extension cord. Battery-operated models are free to roam but considerably heavier. Both types cut a narrower swath than gas-powered mowers.

If your lawn is the right size for a reel mower but you'd rather not push quite so hard, consider an electric mower. Electric mowers are rotary mowers—a bit harder on the grass than a reel mower, but somewhat easier to push. They require little maintenance, operate quietly, and start easily. They typically cut an 18- to 19-inch swath. If you use a model with a cord, you can cut as far as the longest extension cord will let you—usually 100 feet. Cordless models give you all the advantages of an electric mower but free you of the extension cord. You can go as far as you'd like, and you can mow between one-quarter and one-third acre before recharging. A disadvantage: Battery-powered models weigh up to 30 pounds more than their corded counterparts.

▲ Electric mowers are quiet, need little maintenance, and are exhaust free. Models that plug in are limited by the length of the extension cord they use. Battery-operated models go anywhere, but are as much as 30 pounds heavier.

💲 BUYER'S GUIDE

ELECTRIC MOWERS NEED A THICK CORD

When you buy an extension cord for your electric lawn mower, make sure it's rated for outdoor use, and that the wire is thick enough. Voltage drops as it travels through a wire, and the thinner the wire the more it drops. You'll need at least a 14-gauge wire in a 50-foot cord to power a 12-amp mower. The motor will run on thinner cords, but you're likely to damage it. If you get a 100-foot cord, you'll need a 10 gauge cord—10 gauge is thicker than 14 gauge.

Zero-turning-radius mowers

Most tractors are like cars: Turn the wheel and you move in a circle—a circle around a 3-foot-wide center of uncut grass. Zero-turning-radius mowers, on the other hand, can mow a tight circle around a pencil stuck in the ground, easily moving around the pencil while cutting the grass up to it.

They do this in one of two ways. Some have a steering wheel that controls a single rear wheel. Others have a lever on each side of the mower. These control drive wheels on opposite sides of the mower that operate on separate hydraulic motors. When the wheel on one side turns faster than the other wheel, the mower turns in the direction of the slower wheel. Pulling back on the lever slows the wheel; pushing forward speeds it up. Both steering-wheel and steering-lever tractors do the job equally well, although those with lever-type steering tend to be more compact, which may be important if you have a small garage or tight spaces to mow.

Zero-turning-radius mowers reduce cutting time on large lots with lots of trees and bushes. The more obstructions, the more time they save. In open spaces, however, zero-turn steering has no particular advantage. These mowers are more expensive than others.

■ Zero-turning-radius mowers make quick, sharp turns and are far more maneuverable than traditional riding mowers and tractors.

Mower comparisons

TYPE OF MOWER	PROS	CONS	TERRAIN	PRICE
Push Reel Mower	Quiet. No exhaust. Cuts cleanly. Best for St. Augustinegrass, hybrid bermudagrass, zoysia, and bentgrass.	Does a poor job in tall grass.	Best in small, flat yards.	$100–$200
Gas-powered Reel Mower	Cuts cleanly. Smaller models are affordable.	Does a poor job in tall grass.	Can handle medium-sized lawns.	$500–$2,000
Electric Mower	Quiet. No exhaust.	Lacks power to mow tall grass. Extension cord can be awkward.	Best in small, flat yards.	$200–$400
Battery-powered Electric	Quiet. No exhaust.	Heavy; lacks the power to mow tall grass.	Best in small, flat yards.	$400–$500
Gas-powered Rotary Mower	Powerful; handles high grass well. Cuts a wider swath than electric and reel mowers.	Noisy, produces exhaust. Higher maintenance than manual and electric mowers.	Best in flat yards up to ¼ acre.	$150–$500
Self-propelled Gas Rotary Mower	Powerful; handles high grass well. Cuts a wider swath than electric and reel mowers. Good on slopes.	Noisy, produces exhaust. Higher maintenance than manual and electric mowers.	Good for hilly areas, ½ acre or larger lawns, and ones where you routinely bag clippings. Front-wheel drive is least expensive; real-wheel drive is more maneuverable.	$400–$900
Riding Mower	Very powerful; handles high grass well. Cuts a swath up to two times wider than rotary mower. Less expensive than a tractor.	Has a single long blade, which may scalp uneven terrain. Shares other disadvantages with gas-powered rotary mowers.	Good for ½ acre lawns or larger. Handles hills well.	$1,300–$4,000
Tractor	Has three blades mounted in a deck that follows the terrain. Very little scalping. Very powerful; it and the zero-turning radius mower cut the widest swath of all mowers. Handles high grass well. Attachments such as snow plows, tillers and trailers make tractors very versatile.	May be difficult to maneuver in tight spaces. Noisy, produces exhaust. Higher maintenance than push mowers.	Good for ½ acre lawns or larger. Handles hills well.	$800–$12,000
Zero-turning Radius Tractor	Has same advantages as other tractors, but is more maneuverable.	Noisy, produces exhaust. Higher maintenance than push mowers.	Good for ½ acre lawns or larger. Handles hills well.	$3,000–$9,000

 TOOL SAVVY

MUFFLE IT

A muffler is important not only to your peace and quiet, it's important to your safety and to your mower. Mufflers act as spark arrestors, especially in mowers where the exhaust exits under the deck. If the muffler is working poorly, backfires and sparks can ignite dry grass that collects on the mower. The motors of two-cycle engines won't operate correctly without a muffler.

An extremely noisy engine is a sure sign that the muffler has failed. If your muffler is worn out, replace it. Consider looking into an aftermarket model that is extra quiet.

Keep your mower in shape

Take care of your mower to keep it running right. Keep the blade sharp, and double check to make sure the wheels are all at the same height setting. If one or more of the wheels is lower than the others, the cutting deck tilts and one side cuts shorter than the other. At best you'll get a scalloped surface; more likely the low side will scalp the grass.

The number one problem with lawn mowers is that the motor burns out when people forget to refill the oil—a problem not covered by warranty. Check the oil before each use with the mower on a level surface. Add the type, weight, and amount of oil called for in the owner's manual; do not overfill. Overfilling can lead to harder starts, dirty spark plugs, and engine damage.

Check the air filter before starting, and clean or replace it if necessary. (Some filters need to be removed with a wrench.) When you finish mowing, clean grass from underneath and on top of the deck, as well as from around the engine and air filter.

Clean off your lawn mower after each use. Built-up grass clippings rust the mower deck, help to spread turf diseases, and interfere with mulching blades. Before cleaning, disconnect the spark plug so that moving the blade won't start the mower by accident. Turn the mower on its side with the carburetor facing up. Hose off the debris or scrape it off with a putty knife.

Winterizing your lawn mower

2

MOWING AND TRIMMING

Before you put your gas-powered lawn mower away for the winter, do something nice for it and for you: Winterize it. Winterizing prepares the mower for the ravages of time, namely rust and gas that turns gummy. Either problem can make it very difficult to start the mower in the spring—in fact, a good case of rust can make it impossible to ever start the mower again.

Pouring a little oil in the cylinder will stave off rust. Adding fuel stabilizer keeps good gas from going gummy. Neither is hard to do, and as long as you're working on your mower, it makes sense to do some routine maintenance. Change the oil once you've got the motor warm so that the oil flows readily. Replace the spark plug after you pour oil in the cylinder. Change the filters, clean off grass buildup, sharpen the blade, and you're ready for spring.

1

ADD A FUEL STABILIZER

Gasoline left in your power mower will turn gummy over the winter, making it hard to start the mower come spring. Buy fuel stabilizer from your home and garden center, mix it into a gas can as directed. Use the stabilized gas the last couple of times you fill the tank so any gas that remains in the tank over the winter doesn't gum up.

2

START THE MOWER

Run the mower for a minute or two to draw stabilized gas into the cylinder.

3

CHANGE THE OIL

Though not strictly winter maintenance, you should change the oil once a year, and this is a good time to do it. Loosen the oil drain plug while the motor is still warm and while oil, which is usually thick when cold, will flow out easily. Collect it in a pan and take it to your service station for recycling. Remove the oil filter if your mower has one.

4

REFILL WITH OIL

Replace the drain plug and pour in fresh oil until it's at the proper level.

5

REMOVE THE SPARK PLUG

Let the engine cool until it is cool enough to work with. Put a spark plug wrench over the spark plug and remove the plug.

🔍 CLOSER LOOK

SHELF LIFE OF GASOLINE

Gas kept at a moderate temperature in an airtight container that is 95 percent full will last for up to a year, according to the companies that make it. (Never fill a container completely. Gas expands as it gets warm.) If gas is stored at temperatures consistently above 80°F (27°C) or in direct sunlight, it will go bad more quickly, gumming up the fuel line and carburetor, and making it hard to start the engine. In the right conditions, gas can go bad in as little as a month. As a result, most small engine manufacturers recommend that you use gas no more than 30 days old or that you add a fuel stabilizer to it when it's fresh.

If you have some gas that's gone bad, pour it in the gas tank of your car. The bad gas will be diluted by the gas in the tank and won't affect the more powerful engine.

6

PUT OIL IN THE CYLINDER

Pour a tablespoon of motor oil in the spark plug hole to prevent rust. Pull the cord a few times to distribute the oil around the cylinder. Put in a new spark plug. Reattach the wire when you're ready to use the mower again.

7

PERFORM OTHER ROUTINE MAINTENANCE

Change the air filter and brush any grass buildup off the mower. Scrape any encrusted grass from inside the mower and sharpen the blade or have it sharpened.

Buying a string trimmer

String trimmers go boldly where no lawn mower has gone before—along fences, houses, trees, and countless other objects. Without string trimmers, the grass would grow impossibly long next to all of the above, and you'd have to do what they did in days not so long ago—cut the grass by hand.

With all the string trimmers on the market, how do you choose one? The first, and easiest, choice is between electric and gas models.

Electric models are inexpensive, lightweight, low maintenance, and start without the bother of pulling a rope. When you buy an extension cord for an electric string trimmer, make sure it's rated for outdoor use and that the wire is thick enough. Because voltage drops as it travels through a wire, a 50-foot cord needs to be at least 16-gauge wire to carry enough power for most trimmers. A 100-foot cord would require a 14-gauge wire (14 gauge is thicker than 16 gauge). You can avoid cord problems altogether with a cordless model, though they tend to be heavier and not as powerful.

Gas models, on the other hand, are quite powerful and will go anywhere in the yard. They usually handle a thicker line that doesn't break easily and often have two lines coming out of the head, as opposed to one. As a result, they are better at trimming high weeds, dense weeds, and weeds with thicker stalks. While more expensive, they are also more versatile, and several have accessories that you can buy separately—including edgers, pruners, brush cutters, tillers, and leaf blowers.

Other considerations: Some trimmers have curved shafts, others have straight shafts. A curved shaft is easier to maneuver; a straight shaft lets you reach under bushes more easily, is better when you're working on a slope, and is more comfortable for tall people to use. Straight shafts are more expensive, but the drive shaft lasts longer.

The balance and weight of the machine are important. Slide the handle to a point on the shaft that is comfortable for you. Hold the trimmer with both hands as if you were trimming the yard. The weight should be evenly distributed or slightly top-heavy. Some trimmers are heavier than others, usually because of the motor size. If a trimmer feels heavy—or feels as though a half-hour's work with it might tire you out—compare it with a model that has a slightly smaller motor.

Check the controls while you're checking the balance. Make sure the important controls—trigger, choke, and on/off switch—are easy to reach without having to change your grip.

Gas trimmers have become much easier to start than they once were. Look for trimmers with a choke and a bulb that you pump to prime the engine. Check the package for references to quick or easy starting and talk with friends about their experience.

 BUYER'S GUIDE

HOW TO CHOOSE A GAS TRIMMER

Trimmers come in two grades—commercial grade and home grade. The commercial grade, while it may be more expensive, is a better deal. It's lighter. It's stronger. It starts easier. It can run eight hours straight with no problem. It has a full cam shaft, and best of all it can be entirely rebuilt if something goes wrong.

Don't be fooled by engine size when you're comparing commercial and home grades. A home model with a 30 cc engine isn't as strong as a commercial model with a 21.2 cc engine.

The best way to tell a home model from a commercial model is by looking at the starter rope. If the starter is on the back, it's commercial. If it's on the side, it's home grade.

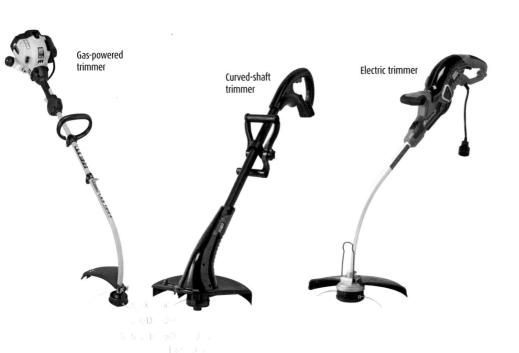

Gas-powered trimmer

Curved-shaft trimmer

Electric trimmer

Straight-shaft trimmer

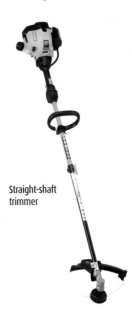

How to use a string trimmer

Mow first, trim last. Mowing first lets you match the height of the trimmed grass with the height of the mown grass. For a controlled cut, hold the trimmer at the desired height and sweep it back and forth parallel to the ground as you walk slowly along the area to be trimmed. If you come to a patch of tall weeds, cut off the top of the weeds first, and then work your way down. Attacking tall weeds at ground level can stall even the most powerful trimmer.

Edge around garden beds and walks by turning the trimmer so that the strings are spinning perpendicular to the ground. Guide the cutting head along the line you want to cut to sever the leaves and roots and rhizomes that the grass uses to spread.

Stay away from trees and shrubs—the line can cut through the bark and kill them.

SAFETY ALERT

SMALL BUT FIERCE

At top speed, string trimmers are spinning at nearly 400 miles per hour, and the engine makes a lot of noise in the process. Always wear eye protection, ear protection, boots, and long pants when operating your string trimmer. Keep away from tree trunks and shrub branches, and be aware that the spray of cut grass put out by the trimmer may also contain small stones.

▲ Use a string trimmer to cut grass in places the lawn mower can't quite reach, such as under bushes, around signs and trees, and against the house.

CLOSER LOOK

WHAT'S MY LINE?

String trimmer line comes in at least five different diameters. Use the diameter recommended for your trimmer—putting a heavier line on a trimmer will stress the motor. Putting a lighter line on a trimmer can affect performance.

You'll also have to choose between serrated line and smooth line. Either will work fine, but serrated line cuts better.

Wrapping line around the spool that holds it can be a nuisance. If you'd like to avoid this task, ask about rapid loading heads, which hold a single, short, precut piece of line that slips into the head. When it wears out, remove it and slip in another.

Loading line in your string trimmer

Wrapping line on the spool of your string trimmer can be frustrating. Here's an easy way to do it: Hold the spool in one hand, and the line in the other. Load by turning the spool instead of trying to wrap line on it with your hand. Put your thumb over the leading edge of the line on the spool as you work to keep the line from unraveling.

If the job is still frustrating—and it may be—look into a rapid-loading head, which has no spool. You can buy an after-market rapid loader to fit almost any string trimmer.

Buying a leaf blower

L eaf blowers do the laborious jobs that were once the province of rakes and brooms. They blow autumn leaves into a pile for collecting or turning into mulch and they sweep stray grass clippings off the sidewalk. Some can even work like a vacuum and are perfect for sucking up and mulching leaves and debris caught between bushes or along the edge of a fence.

When buying a leaf blower, the first decision you'll have to make is whether to get an electric or a gas-powered model. In lawn equipment, gas usually means power and electric means convenience. But when it comes to leaf blowers, electric blowers are competitive with handheld gas-powered units.

▶ Leaf blowers—the power-equivalents of rakes and brooms—push leaves, grass clippings, and similar things out of the way. Some are reversible and will vacuum up and lightly mulch debris.

Electric blowers

Electrics can accommodate a fan design that creates wind power equal to—or greater than—that of a gas unit. An entry-level electric can create winds of up to 225 miles per hour, as compared with the 145 miles per hour of a similar gas unit. While either wind speed qualifies as a hurricane-force wind, the stream of air is very small—neither blower creates enough pressure to knock you over or do damage. If you're interested in electric blowers, look to their obvious advantages: They cost less. They weigh less, are easier to start, require less maintenance, and emit no exhaust. If you're considering a battery-operated model, compare it with a plug-in model in the same price range. You're likely to find that the plug in generates nearly twice as much wind speed, weighs less, and runs far longer. Some battery-operated models run for less than 10 minutes on a charge.

Gas-powered blowers

Once a job gets out of the range of an extension cord, however, it's time to consider a gas unit. Choosing a gas unit is a matter of choosing between weight and power. The more powerful the fan, the heavier the blower. Handheld units can weigh between 8 and 10 pounds, and your arms bear the bulk of the weight.

Backpack blower

Backpack units take the weight off your arms and put it on your back. Because backs are generally stronger than arms, backpack units have bigger motors and create more wind power. Whether the unit is handheld or mounted on a backpack, however, extra power comes at an extra cost.

Using the blower as a vacuum

Some handheld blowers can be run in reverse to act as vacuum cleaners. In the process of sucking up leaves and grass clippings, vac/blowers use their metal impellers to mulch the material and shoot it into a collection bag. This cuts down on the space the material takes up. Some vacs will take 16 cubic feet of leaves, chop them into bits, and pack them into a single cubic foot. Vacuuming up all the fall leaves is a lot more work than using the machine as a blower, but for small areas and trouble spots, the vacuum feature of a vac/blower is ideal.

Buying an edger

With time, organic matter and soil collect where the sidewalk meets the grass. With more time, grass grows in the buildup, and your once tidy yard begins to look a bit ragged.

Edgers solve the problem by cutting a narrow strip between the pavement and lawn, separating the grass growing over the sidewalk from the grass in the lawn. Once you've edged, you can sweep away the unwanted grass and the organic buildup. Usually trimming once in spring takes care of the problem.

Hand edgers are no more than a rolling blade mounted on a handle. They'll do the job, but edging with them requires a lot of muscle. The more often you edge, the less debris builds up and the easier the job.

String trimmers are fine for many edging jobs. Turn the trimmer so that the strings are spinning perpendicular to the ground and lower the head until it begins cutting into the soil. String trimmers can be used to cut either straight or curved edges. Because it can be hard to keep the edge as straight as you might like, some string trimmers have guides that make it easier to cut in a straight line.

Lawns that grow aggressively may need to be edged frequently, and for this, you'll want to consider a power edger. Electric- and gas-powered edgers use their power to cut through the lawn for you. This saves your muscles for guiding the edger and pushing it along its path. Power edgers can be used to cut straight or curved lines but are better at making straight cuts. As is almost always the case, a gas unit more powerful than an electric one.

▲ Edging trims off the grass growing in the organic matter that builds up at the edge of your sidewalk. Edging is hard work when done by hand. A power edger requires very little muscle.

▶ An electric edger is less powerful than a gas-powered edger. A hand edger is only as powerful as you are.

Hand edger

Electric edger

▶ When turned on edge, a string trimmer becomes a lightweight power edger.

Watering

I t's no secret that grass needs water to live. The secret is in getting the details right. How much water? When? How often?

There are two rules of watering lawns. The first: Water infrequently. The second: Water deeply.

If you water deeply and infrequently, you will have healthy grass. Healthy grass has a dense root system that grows deep into the soil and spreads widely. The roots are able to reach far into the soil for nutrients. And even if the soil surface dries out during a drought, the roots remain in moist soil.

Water deeply and the roots will follow the water down into the soil. Frequent light waterings, on the other hand, concentrate water in a narrow band near the top of the soil. Roots have no incentive to extend below this band. They remain short, tap into fewer nutrients, are less healthy, and when the moisture disappears during the first drought, so does the grass.

Chapter 3 highlights

Watering basics

Rule #1: Water infrequently

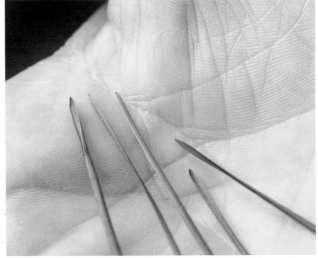

In most places the conventional wisdom is that you should let your grass begin to wilt before watering it: Don't ignore the grass, but wait for leaves to just start to roll or fold up and for the lawn to take on a somewhat gray or purplish cast. You can also test your lawn by walking across it. Wilting grass is less resilient than grass that has plenty of water, so your footprints remain after walking across the lawn. When that happens, it's time to water; some experts say you have waited too long. Your county extension service can help you sort out specific regional questions.

Rule #2: Water deeply

Ideally, you want roots to grow at least 6 inches deep and closer to 8 inches deep. So you want to wet the soil that deep. A general rule is to apply 1 inch of water at a time. In practice, the amount of water you need to apply and the length of time the sprinklers need to run depend on the type of soil you have. Given the variables, the best way to find out how deep the water and the roots go in your yard is to dig up a bit of lawn somewhere inconspicuous and measure both the roots and the depth of the wet soil after you water.

When deciding if the soil is wet enough, take rain into account as well as irrigation. Here again, the type of soil plays a role as well as the amount of rain. As a general rule, a half an inch of rain will soak 6 to 8 inches into sandy soil. It takes an inch of rain to soak that deeply into loam. For clay, you need to apply 1 to 1³⁄₁₀ inches of rain to soak the soil 6 to 8 inches deep.

▶ Wet soil is darker colored than dry soil so you can tell how deep water has soaked in. Ideally, the wet-dry line should extend as deep as you'd like the roots to grow.

SANDY SOIL

Sandy soil is a loose soil. Rarely will sandy soil be pure sand; rather it is likely to have some clay or organic matter mixed in. Water readily penetrates deep into sandy soil. For example, ½ inch of rain will soak to a depth of 6 to 8 inches in 30 minutes. But with little clay and organic matter in the soil to hold water, sandy soil dries quickly, so you must water more often. Apply ½ inch of water two or three times a week.

LOAM

Loam is a loose mixture of sand, clay, organic matter, and silt. Water readily penetrates deep into loam (1 inch of water will soak 6 to 8 inches into the soil within two hours). The soil remains moist but not waterlogged for long periods. Healthy roots can grow 6 to 8 inches deep in loam. Apply 1 inch of water every five to eight days.

CLAY

Clay is a tight, heavy soil. It takes a long time for water to soak into clay (at least five hours are needed for 1 inch of water to soak 6 to 8 inches deep). Grass roots end up in a shallow layer near the soil surface unless you adjust the way you water. With clay soil, you want to run the sprinklers until water begins to either run off or build up on the soil surface, then turn them off. Let the water soak in, then turn the sprinklers back on. Continue in this manner until you've soaked the top 6 to 8 inches of soil. Water again in five to eight days.

Checking water depth

With a 10-inch-long screwdriver, a sprinkler, and a few cans, you can ensure you're watering deep enough. Use the cans to collect water as the sprinkler is running, and determine how much it puts out in an hour. If it puts out ¼ of an inch—which is average—you'll know that you need to run the sprinkler for four hours to get the inch of water needed to reach the bottom of the roots, stopping and restarting as required to let built-up water soak in.

When the four hours are up, push the screwdriver into the ground. You've reached dry soil when the screwdriver stops. Measure how far the screwdriver traveled into the soil, and you'll know how far the water has reached. Compare this with the root length you discovered by digging, and you'll know if the water is getting down far enough. For step-by-step directions on matching sprinkler output to root depth, see page 64, "Watering to the Right Depth."

Water in the morning

The best time to water is early in the morning. It's cool then so little evaporation occurs, and usually there's less wind so all the water gets to the lawn. And generally speaking, because there's less demand for water in the morning, water pressure is higher. That means more water flows per hour so you'll be able to water in less time.

In the afternoon, conditions are reversed. The temperature is higher so water evaporates more quickly. Lower water pressure results in slower water flow. And because the day tends to become breezier as the hours pass, the water is easily blown off target when you water in the afternoon.

Watering in the evening leaves the lawn damp overnight, and when dampness lasts for long periods diseases find the conditions they need to move in.

Watering to the right depth

3

WATERING

 PROJECT DETAILS

SKILLS: Watering, measuring
PROJECT: Measuring sprinkler output and soil absorption.

 TIME TO COMPLETE

EXPERIENCED: 1 hr.
HANDY: 1 hr.
NOVICE: 1 hr.

STUFF YOU'LL NEED

TOOLS: Sprinkler, 10-inch-long screwdriver
MATERIALS: 10 soup cans or coffee cans

Watering the lawn does little good if you don't know how much water the grass is actually getting. The best way to find out is to collect an hour's output in several cans, measure, and take the average.

The next task is to find out how far the water has soaked in. An easy way to do this is to stick a long screwdriver into the ground and see how far it reaches. When it stops, it has hit dry soil.

Calibrating your sprinkler

1 WATER LAWN

Turn the sprinkler on full force and run it for an hour or until water begins to run off, whichever comes first. Time how long it takes for the water to puddle or run off. This will tell you how fast your soil can soak up water. Next, time how long it takes for the puddles to soak in.

2 SET UP CANS

Spread 10 coffee cans randomly across the area that the sprinkler will water. The cans should all be the same diameter and height.

3 RUN THE SPRINKLER

Turn the sprinkler on full force and run it for either an hour or the amount of time it takes for water to begin to run off or puddle.

4

MEASURE THE ACCUMULATION

Turn the water off. Some of the cans will be fuller than others; you can take care of that problem when you're actually watering by adjusting the placement of the sprinklers. (The sprinkler descriptions in "Choosing the Right Sprinkler," page 68, explain how much to overlap each type to ensure your lawn is uniformly watered.) Pour all the water into one can and measure the depth. Divide this measurement by 10 to get the average amount the sprinkler applied. (Most sprinklers apply in the neighborhood of ¼ inch per hour, in which case it would take four hours to apply 1 inch of water.)

5

APPLY 1 INCH OF WATER TO THE LAWN

Once you know how much water your sprinkler applies per hour and how long it takes for the soil to soak it up, run the sprinkler long enough to spread an inch of water. If your soil is slow to accept the water, turn the sprinkler off when the water begins to puddle and back on again when the water has soaked in. Keep track of the sprinkler's actual running time and continue turning the water off and on until you've applied an inch of water.

6

SEE HOW FAR THE WATER HAS PENETRATED

Stick a long screwdriver in the ground—it will stop when it reaches dry ground. Measure how far the screwdriver traveled to see the depth the water has soaked in. The water should penetrate 6 to 8 inches. (If you want to find out how deep your roots actually are, turn over a few spadefuls of dirt in various places and measure.)

7

WATER LAWN

If water hasn't yet reached a depth of 6 inches, turn the sprinklers back on, running them in 15-minute increments, testing with the screwdriver in between. If you've applied too much water, run the sprinklers for 1 hour less the next time you water. Test the depth with your screwdriver, then adjust the timing in 15-minute increments.

Watering made easy

1 t's not that watering is *hard,* actually; it's that watering a lawn is a lot easier and a lot cheaper if you approach it the right way. These tips ease the task of watering and ensure that you do it right.

Water at a rate the soil can absorb. Experience is the best teacher—if water puddles on the soil, you're applying too much too fast. Follow the steps on pages 64 and 65 to learn how fast your soil soaks up water, then adjust sprinkler running times to match.

Get a timer to regulate how long the sprinkler runs. Timers take some of the guesswork out of watering. They are available for hose-end sprinklers as well as for inground systems and in manual and electronic models. Manual models screw to the spigot and count down the amount of time you set, then shut off the water.

If your lawn is on a hillside or growing in clay soil, get a more complex timer. Electronic timers can be programmed to turn on and off at various times during the day or week. Set it to turn off sprinklers before any runoff occurs, and then to turn them back on after the water has soaked in. Set repeated on-and-off cycles until the roots have been watered.

Improve your soil's structure. Soil accepts water slowly if it is compacted or consists of clay, or if the lawn has a thick thatch layer. Aerating and topdressing improve compaction and reduce thatch.

To topdress Spread a thin layer of high-quality topsoil over the lawn (above left). Over time, this builds the soil so that the roots eventually have a better, looser growing environment. In addition, topdressing deposits healthy microbes

into the soil, which help improve soil structure.

To aerate Core aerators (above right) pull up cylinders of soil and leave them on the grass to work their way back into the ground, achieving much the same results as topdressing. More important, the holes the aerator leaves when it pulls out the cylinders create openings for water to work its way into the soil. For more on topdressing and aerating, see pages 152–157.

A permanent sprinkler system takes the worry out of watering. Properly designed, an inground system waters each part of a lawn equally. A timer turns the water off and on, and a rain sensor turns the system off if it rains. The initial expense is more than that of a hose and sprinkler, and you will have to dig trenches in your yard, but once set up, most of your watering problems are over.

You can do the installation yourself or hire a contractor to do the work. If you do it yourself, work with the manufacturer or sales company to make sure the system is designed right. Many companies have websites to help with design.

Avoiding runoff

Water that runs off the lawn wastes resources: Because the water isn't getting into the soil, it isn't doing your grass any good. Controlling runoff not only helps get water to where you need it, but also helps keep fertilizers and pesticides from washing out of the grass and into lakes and streams, where they can do environmental damage.

The first step to controlling runoff is both the most obvious and the simplest: Apply the water more slowly. Water runs off because the soil can't absorb it as quickly as the water is being applied. The rate of absorption varies with the soil—sand can absorb about ½ inch of water an hour; clay can absorb only about ²⁄₁₀ inch per hour. Let the yard be your guide.

To apply water more slowly you can turn down the water pressure, using a sprinkler that puts out water at a slower rate, or cycling the sprinkler off and on until the lawn has received a full inch of water.

To adjust water pressure, turn your sprinkler on high and check it every 15 minutes. If the water is puddling or running off, lessen the flow, move the sprinkler, and start checking every 15 minutes again. Keep turning down the water flow and moving the sprinkler until you find the right setting for your lawn. When you turn the water off, count how many full and partial turns it takes, so you can find the setting again when you turn the water on. If you're considering this option, be aware that many sprinklers will not run correctly if the water pressure gets too low.

Water also starts to run off after soil becomes saturated, and some soils saturate more quickly than others. There can be any number of reasons—a high water table, a hidden spring, a low spot, poor drainage, or an impermeable layer of clay soil underneath the surface. Whatever the reason, the best strategy is to know how long it takes for the soil to reach its limit and turn off the water before runoff begins.

The sprinklers you use can also affect runoff. In the simplest case, consider a long, narrow strip between a house and driveway. Any sprinkler you can imagine—oscillating, stationary, revolving—is going to water as much house and driveway as it does grass. A soaker hose, while designed primarily for gardens, would work well along a narrow strip of grass.

Each type of sprinkler sprays water in a different pattern. Try to choose one that matches the shape of your yard.

Local ordinances often play a role in watering practices as well as in controlling runoff. Check with your city water department to learn whether there are other rules you should be following.

▲ Runoff doesn't just waste water and cost money. It also washes fertilizers and chemicals out of your lawn and into lakes and streams where they can do a lot of damage. Choose a sprinkler where the pattern matches the shape of your yard, and place it carefully.

▶ Water long, narrow spaces with soaker hoses, which ooze water rather than spray it. Soaker hoses let you control exactly where the water goes. While slower than watering with a sprinkler, the pattern is very compact, and there's no problem with wind blowing water droplets off course.

CLOSER LOOK

WATER WHERE YOU NEED IT
Water that inadvertently hits your patio or sidewalk is guaranteed to run off. Runoff is a waste of a valuable resource, and as your water bill will testify, a waste of money. When you set up your sprinkler, watch it while the spray pattern stabilizes to see where the water lands. Adjust the spray pattern or move the sprinkler as needed, and watch again to make sure you made the right adjustments.

Choosing the right sprinkler

Each type of sprinkler—stationary, revolving, impulse, oscillating, and traveling—puts the water onto your yard in a specific pattern. Some spray water in a square pattern, others in a circle. With some, most of the water falls near the sprinkler; with others, most of the water lands at the outer edge of the pattern. The best sprinklers have a uniform pattern, a slow flow rate to prevent puddles and runoff, and a pattern that matches—or can be adjusted to match—the shape of your yard.

Stationary sprinklers

Stationary sprinklers are the simplest and cheapest. Water shoots up through a nozzle on top of the sprinkler and hits the yard in any of several patterns—square, rectangular, or circular, depending on the model. Some sprinklers have three or four heads mounted on a turret, which you can turn to get the pattern of your choice—a helpful feature in an irregularly shaped yard.

No matter which pattern you choose, however, the water distribution is very uneven. The outside edge of the pattern may get as much as five times more water than the area close to the center. Because stationary sprinklers put out lots of water over a small area, you need to move the sprinkler frequently to avoid runoff and wasted water and to ensure the lawn is evenly watered. It is difficult to cover a large area uniformly when using stationary sprinklers. They are best for spot-watering small areas.

▶ Stationary sprinklers are cheap and reliable, but the spray pattern is very uneven with far more water falling on the edges than in the middle. If you use a stationary sprinkler, plan on moving it frequently to get an even application of water.

🔍 CLOSER LOOK

WHEN SPRINKLER MEETS TREE

Trees and other large objects in your landscape, such as light posts and mailboxes, can wreak havoc on sprinkler patterns. Tree trunks and similar structures block the water, leaving dry "shadows" behind the tree. Low-hanging tree branches, meanwhile, interfere with the spray pattern of sprinklers that shoot their water high into the air, such as oscillating sprinklers. (Branches aren't a problem for sprinklers with patterns that hug the ground.) Work out a watering plan that takes your trees into account and choose a sprinkler with a pattern that works to your advantage.

3

WATERING

Revolving sprinklers

Unlike stationary sprinklers, revolving sprinklers deposit the largest amounts of water closest to the spray head. Most revolving sprinklers have two or three arms mounted on a pivot. Water shoots out the end of the arms, spinning them and spraying the water in a circular pattern. (Some also have a center geyser.)

The resulting pattern is low—low enough that tree branches generally don't interfere with it unless the sprinkler has a center geyser. In addition, the water drops are large and aren't easily blown off course by the wind. Revolving sprinklers deliver lots of water quickly and are best in small yards where runoff isn't a problem. For uniform coverage, plan ahead so that as you move the sprinkler, the pattern overlaps half of the previously watered spot.

▶ Revolving sprinklers deposit more water near the sprinkler than at the edge of their spray pattern, and must be moved frequently to get an even application of water. One advantage: They spray water low to the ground where tree branches won't deflect the water.

Impulse sprinklers

These sprinklers shoot a horizontal jet of water into the air while a spring-loaded arm breaks the jet into droplets and scatters them across the lawn in a pattern that ranges from a full circle to a sliver of a circle.

A great advantage of impulse sprinklers is that the pattern is uniform—the water is equally distributed over the area being watered. The droplets are large, like those of a revolving sprinkler, and the pattern is low to the ground. Neither wind nor overhanging branches present much of a problem as a result.

Some newer impulse sprinklers have gears that turn the sprinkler in a circle and operate more quietly and more smoothly than traditional models in which the force of the water jet hits the arm and moves it. Coverage and pattern, however, are about the same.

▶ Impulse sprinklers spread water evenly over the area they cover. Because the water droplets are large, they aren't scattered by the wind.

3

WATERING

Oscillating sprinklers

These sprinklers swing back and forth, shooting water high into the air and spreading it in a rectangular pattern. The arched arm, which moves back and forth to spread the water, can be adjusted to make a partial sweep. Because the water is shot high in the air, wind readily distorts the pattern, as can overhanging trees. Oscillating sprinklers apply water slowly, making them good for clay soil, for seedbeds, and for areas where runoff is a problem. Because most of the water is deposited near the sprinkler, areas close to it may experience puddling before enough water is deposited at the outer edges of the spray pattern.

▶ **Oscillating sprinklers shoot water high in the air, and wind can easily push the water where it isn't wanted. Because they apply water slowly, they're good in areas where runoff is a problem.**

Traveling sprinklers

Sometimes known as tractors because of their appearance, traveling sprinklers move around the yard on wheels driven by water power. The hose that feeds the sprinkler guides it as it moves across the lawn, and the traveling action makes it good for large yards. The spray pattern is very uniform; lay out the hose so that the spray patterns overlap by 50 percent. The downside of tractors is that the wheels often don't have enough power to go uphill or overcome irregularities in the yard. If the grass is thin, the sprinkler may get stuck in the mud it creates. Any of these problems can create a big mess unless you catch it early.

▶ **Traveling sprinklers apply water evenly and guide themselves across your lawn on the hose that feeds them.**

Permanent systems

A permanent system feeds water through a control box and timer and into a series of underground pipes. From there, the pipes run to a series of sprinkler heads. The heads include pop-ups, which spray in circles or fractions of circles, impulse sprinklers, and even something similar to a soaker hose. Properly arranged, the heads provide the lawn full and equal coverage. The timers that come with the system help you control the amount of water getting on your lawn. Some timers are very simple; others interface with the Internet to establish the best schedule for your location. Some systems have rain sensors, which turn the system off in the event of rain.

If your lawn is large, there probably isn't enough pressure for you to water it all at once, so the system is designed with more than one series of pipes, allowing you to water different parts of the lawn at different times. Permanent systems need to be drained during winter in cold climates. Regardless of where you live, the system should have an anti-siphon valve (also called a vacuum breaker) to prevent yard water from backing up into the house water.

▲ **Built-in sprinkler systems, which combine several types of sprinkler heads, often give the most uniform watering pattern.**

How to handle water restrictions

During periods of drought, water deeply and infrequently when the grass calls for it or don't water at all. Grass protects itself by going dormant during drought, then reviving when the dry spell ends. Your strategy for taking care of your lawn during a drought has to strike a balance between keeping the grass green and letting it go dormant. Watering deeply and infrequently will keep the lawn green, the roots deep, and the soil damp in preparation for the days ahead when watering may be banned. Irregular watering, on the other hand, may stress your grass by repeatedly bringing it in and out of dormancy. Far better to let it go dormant and stay dormant.

In the early stages of a drought, it usually isn't clear how serious the dry spell may be or whether restrictions will be imposed. Continue watering normally. If the dry spell persists, your city may restrict irrigation to hand watering. When this happens, check daily for stressed areas; water them until the root zone is replenished.

Use a shower or fan-type nozzle and let the water flow until it either puddles or runs off. You're still trying to water to the bottom of the root zone, so once the water soaks in, test with the screwdriver, and keep watering as necessary. Stop when the root zone is wet.

If a large lawn or a busy schedule makes this difficult, water only high priority areas. These may be highly visible areas in the front yard; they may be the areas you see when eating at the kitchen table. Wherever they are, water them and forget about the rest. Continue mowing, taking off no more than one-third the total height of the grass. Do not fertilize, as fertilizer can burn a dry lawn.

If the drought continues, all outdoor water use may be prohibited. At this point, you have no choice. Stop watering, and let the grass go dormant. The leaves turn tan and the grass looks dead, but the crowns and roots are still alive. Most warm and cool season grasses can remain dormant for quite a while and come back to life

after the first good rain. Perennial ryegrass can recover in as quickly as four days after a rainfall, though most grasses take longer.

Steps to prepare for drought

Properly mowing, fertilizing, and aerifying before a drought help the grass survive better.

Mowing Always cut the grass to its maximum recommended height. Longer grass equals longer roots that can obtain water from deep within the soil. It shades the soil, which helps prevent evaporation and thus more water for the plants. It also regulates soil temperature and keeps the crown of the grass plant from sunburning.

Fertilizing A lawn that is healthy and well fed going into drought stays greener longer than starved grass. Avoid fertilizing excessively, which results in tall, succulent grass with shallow roots.

Aerating Aerify with a core aerator as needed to loosen the soil, so that roots can grow deeper and water can penetrate more easily.

Installing a sprinkler system

PROJECT DETAILS

SKILLS: Digging, basic plumbing, simple wiring
PROJECT: Installing an automatic sprinkler system

TIME TO COMPLETE

EXPERIENCED: 10 hrs.
HANDY: 15 hrs.
NOVICE: 20 hrs.
Time varies with size of system.

STUFF YOU'LL NEED

TOOLS: PVC pipe cutter, screwdriver, pipe wrenches, hammer, trenching shovel, 1" pipe clamps, tape measure, pressure gauge
MATERIALS: PVC or poly pipe, elbows, T-fittings, pipe clamps as required, Teflon tape, marking paint or lime, sprinkler heads, anti-siphon valve, solvent weld

A sprinkler system can make all your watering worries go away. You can program it to meet the needs of your yard. For example, some systems let you download an automatic watering program based on localized climate information. Others have built-in rain sensors that turn the system off if rain starts to fall while the system is running.

Whatever system you settle on, plan it carefully. To begin with, make sure your plumbing can supply enough water pressure to operate the system. You also need to choose the right type of sprinkler heads for your yard, place them correctly, and at the same time make sure that the underground pipes you install are large enough to feed the sprinklers you've chosen.

Most yards are too big or too irregularly shaped to be watered all at once, so you'll need to divide the job into zones, each of which is watered separately. Timers are designed for a limited number of zones. Once you've made your decision about how many zones to set up, then you can pick a timer to match.

Fortunately, most companies that sell sprinkler equipment have design services that can do much of the planning for you. The project here, which shows how to install a basic system, will help you compile the information that an irrigation designer will need.

Once the system is installed, avoid the temptation to turn it on simply because you can or to let the timer do all the thinking for you. Having a sprinkler system doesn't free you from observing the rules about watering. If not used correctly, a sprinkler system will waste water.

Supply pipe ID

	INSIDE DIAMETER OF SUPPLY PIPE					
Length of string	2³/₄"	3¹/₄"	3¹/₂"	4"	4³/₈"	5"
Copper pipe	³/₄"	—	1"	—	1 ¹/₄"	—
Galvanized or PVC pipe	—	³/₄"	—	1"	—	1¹/₄"

Gathering statistics

Sprinkler system designers need to know how much water your system can deliver. Three things in particular are important to them—the inner diameter (ID) of your water line, the pressure at which the water is delivered, and the water flow in gallons per minute.

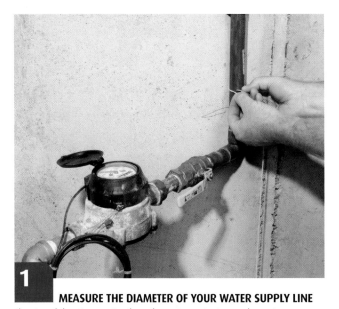

1 MEASURE THE DIAMETER OF YOUR WATER SUPPLY LINE
The size of the pipe running from the water meter to your home is a measure of its capacity. Wrap a string around the pipe and measure the string. Then check the chart "Supply Pipe ID" on the opposite page to find the inner diameter of the line.

2 MEASURE THE WATER PRESSURE
Put a pressure gauge on an indoor faucet, turn it on, and record the pressure. Turn the outdoor faucet closest to your water meter on all the way and record the reading on the gauge.

3 MEASURE THE WATER FLOW
Adjust the outdoor faucet until the water pressure reads 40 PSI (pounds per square inch). Put a 5-gallon bucket underneath the outdoor faucet and time how long it takes to fill the bucket. Write down the time. Repeat at 45 and 50 PSI. Check the chart "Gallons per Minute (GPM)," above, to convert your measurements.

Gallons per minute (GPM)

Seconds to fill a 5-gallon bucket	Gallons per minute
15	20
20	15
25	12
30	10
40	7½

WORK SMARTER

DON'T BREAK YOUR BACK
A couple of days before you dig trenches for the piping, water the area to make the job easier.

SAFETY ALERT

LOOK BEFORE YOU DIG
Check with local utility companies before you stick the shovel in the ground for the first time. You don't want to cut into water, electric, telephone, or gas lines. Each utility can tell you if its pipes or lines cross your property. Most states have a "One Call" or "Miss Utility" call-in service, where a single phone call can get you information about all the utility lines on your property.

WORK SMARTER

RENT A DITCH DIGGER
Even a small sprinkler system requires lots of ditch digging. If you want to do the job in a reasonable amount of time, and without unreasonable wear and tear on your back, rent a trencher, also called a ditch digger, to help you do the job.

1

INSTALL A SUPPLY LINE
Once your sprinkler provider has designed your system, have a plumber install the supply line. The supply pipe system should be connected to the pipe coming out of the meter before the pipe splits off into other branches. Although you could do this yourself, have a plumber do the work—it often involves drilling a hole through the foundation wall. This job may be simple enough for a plumber, but it's hard for a do-it-yourselfer.

2

DIG A TRENCH
Lay out the path of the pipes with landscapers paint or lime and mark the location of each sprinkler head with a flag or a large nail driven through a piece of paper. Dig up the sod with a spade and set it to one side of the trench. Rent a ditch digger, and dig a trench 8 to 12 inches deep or below the frost line, as required by local codes.

3

RUN PIPE TOWARD THE CONTROL VALVES
The design will call for one or more electrical control valves, which the system timer will turn on and off. Connect schedule-40 PVC or poly pipe, as allowed by code, to the line the plumber installed and run it toward the control valves, stopping where the plan says the pressure vacuum breaker goes.

4

INSTALL A PRESSURE VACUUM BREAKER
Pressure vacuum breakers are required by most building codes. The valves keep the water from your sprinkler system from backing into your drinking water. Attach an elbow to the line you just installed and put a pipe in the elbow that will put the valve at the right height. Return the pipe underground, attach an elbow, and run pipe to where the control valves will be.

5 **INSTALL THE CONTROL VALVES**

If there is more than one zone in your system, there will also be more than one valve. Connect a control valve for each zone, putting it in a protective valve box sold by the manufacturer.

6 **RUN PIPE FOR THE SYSTEM**

Assemble the system above ground before you put it in its trench. Start with pipe next to each valve and run it along the proper trench. Use PVC pipe in warm areas, connecting the fitting with a piping glue called solvent weld. PVC might crack in colder areas, so use polypipe, barbed fittings, and hose clamps in colder climates.

7 **CONNECT THE FITTINGS FOR THE HEADS**

At each flag or nail marking the location of a sprinkler head, attach a T-fitting to feed the head and attach the pipe that continues down the trench.

8 **FLUSH THE SYSTEM**

Put the pipe in the trench and connect it to the valve. Turn on the water and flush the system to clean out any dirt.

9 **ATTACH THE SPRINKLERS**

Some systems, including this one, use flexible pipe to connect the sprinklers to the pipe. Others have a pipe that snaps off at the desired height, and some simply angle the pipe to get the sprinkler to the right height. Follow the directions that come with your system.

10 **ATTACH THE TIMER**

Install your timer as directed. Run wires from the valves back to the timer and connect them.

Fertilizing

You can tell people are serious about their lawn when you see them fertilizing it. However, so many myths exist about fertilizing that even they may not know for sure if they're doing what they should when they should.

Here's a quick look at the basics:

■ How often you fertilize depends on the lawn you want. A lush lawn requires several applications per year; a decent lawn needs at least one. When you make those applications depends on the type of grass you have, and that, in turn, depends on which part of the country you live in.

■ Fertilizer not only makes your grass green, but it also helps grass grow and edge out competing weeds. Overfertilizing, on the

Chapter 4 highlights

78 **WHY YOU SHOULD FERTILIZE**
Fertilizing is the only way to ensure
your grass has the nutrients it requires.

79 **WHEN TO FERTILIZE**
Feed your lawn at the correct times of the year to
ensure healthy growth.

81 **WHAT FERTILIZER IS**
Learn what all those numbers and hard-to-pronounce
words on the label mean.

84 **HOW TO FERTILIZE**
Follow these steps to avoid those tell-tale stripes
that result when you aren't paying attention.

other hand, can be as bad as not fertilizing at all. The best way to find out
how much fertilizer to apply is to work with your county extension service to
do a soil test.

■ Fertilizer is more like a vitamin than a food. A plant's food is created by
photosynthesis. Fertilizers simply provide the raw ingredients—the nitrogen,
phosphorus, and potassium—that help photosynthesis along.

■ Fertilizing at least once a year is better than never fertilizing.

Why you should fertilize

The only way to ensure your lawn is healthy is to fertilize it. Mowing and watering correctly contribute to lawn health, but fertilizer alone provides grass with the ingredients it needs to survive and thrive.

A lawn that has all its nutritional needs met forms a thick, uniform turf. It has a deep, dense root system, and its color is a healthy green. A dense turf crowds out weeds and provides no room for new weeds to move in. With its healthy root system, the lawn is able to tap into deeper water stores so it suffers less during periods of heat and drought. In addition, a well-fertilized lawn easily shrugs off diseases and insects. Pests are less likely to attack a healthy lawn, but if they do, the lawn soon heals by growing out of the damage.

Your goal when fertilizing is to aim for balanced nutrition that results in uniform growth throughout the season. A lawn that receives too little fertilizer will be thin and thus weedy, and its color will be pale green to yellow. It grows more slowly than healthy grass, and if pests attack, it is less able to recover from the damage.

Lawns receiving excess fertilizer, on the other hand, have shallow roots and soft, succulent leaves that almost beckon for insects and diseases to move in. Using water-soluble, quick-release nitrogen for these applications also tend to create a sort of feast-or-famine cycle: You fertilize, the grass turns deep green, grows rapidly, then becomes pale and stops growing when the fertilizer runs out. So you fertilize again and start the cycle all over.

Providing balanced nutrition is a matter of fertilizing at the right times and choosing a high-quality fertilizer.

▲ Fertilizer provides nitrogen, phosphorous, and potassium, each of which are necessary to create a green lawn like this one.

▶ The difference a fertilizer makes can be huge. The lawn in the background was fertilized on a regular schedule. The lawn in the foreground received no fertilizer.

When to fertilize

Figuring out the best time and how often to fertilize your lawn may seem like rocket science. There are many different approaches, depending on whether your lawn is a warm-season grass or a cool-season one and on the quality you desire for the lawn. If you don't care about having a perfect lawn, fertilizing once a year will provide an acceptable result. But if you want a beautiful lawn, or if your lawn is used a lot or suffers from other stresses, fertilizing up to four more times a year will give you a healthier lawn that can stand up to abuse.

The best time to fertilize is when the grass is actively growing and not under stress. That time varies for the different grasses.

Cool-season grasses

Cool-season grasses grow the most during spring and fall and very little during summer. In winter, their shoots may stop growing, but their roots are still active as long as the soil is not frozen. The ideal times to feed cool-season lawns is in late summer, again 30 days later, and once in early to mid-spring.

Fertilizing in fall encourages the grass to make more carbohydrates than it uses for growth because the weather is cool. The grass plant stores the excess in its roots and crown. Over winter, it will dip into these reserves to sustain itself. A lawn that's fertilized in fall has better color throughout the winter and spring than one that is fertilized only in spring.

Use a combination of quick- and slow-release fertilizers in late summer and fall, but use only slow-release fertilizer in spring. Too much fertilizer in spring spurs excess growth that uses up all the reserves, which puts the grass at the mercy of heat, drought, fungus, and pests in the summer.

If you plan to fertilize your cool-season lawn only once a year, make the application sometime between late summer and early fall, after the heat and stress of summer are over but before freezing weather arrives. If you will fertilize twice a year, the best times to do so are in late summer and in fall.

Warm-season grasses

Warm-season grasses grow while the weather is warm from mid- to late spring until weather cools in fall. The ideal times to fertilize warm-season grasses are mid-spring, midsummer, and again in late summer.

How early in spring to fertilize warm-season lawns can be a bit tricky to predict in some regions, especially the Transition Zone. Fertilizing too early can encourage the grass to grow, and the succulent new shoots are susceptible to damage from late frosts.

Cool-season grass fertilizing calendar

	EARLY FALL	LATE FALL (AFTER LAST MOWING)	SPRING (AFTER INITIAL GROWTH SPURT)	MIDSUMMER
Low-maintenance schedule	Apply slow- or quick-release fertilizer			
Moderate-maintenance schedule	Apply slow- or quick-release fertilizer	Apply quick-release fertilizer	Apply slow-release fertilizer	
Ideal-lawn schedule	Apply slow- or quick-release fertilizer	Apply quick-release fertilizer	Apply slow-release fertilizer	Apply slow-release fertilizer

Shoot growth · Shoot growth
Winter · Spring · Summer · Fall · Winter
Root growth · Root growth

Warm-season grass fertilizing calendar

	AFTER THE SECOND MOWING	ONE MONTH AFTER THE FIRST APPLICATION	TWO MONTHS AFTER THE FIRST APPLICATION	THREE MONTHS AFTER THE FIRST APPLICATION
Low-maintenance schedule	Apply slow-release fertilizer		Apply slow-release fertilizer	
Moderate-maintenance schedule	Apply slow-release fertilizer	Apply slow-release fertilizer		Apply slow-release fertilizer
Ideal-lawn schedule	Apply slow-release fertilizer	Apply slow-release fertilizer	Apply slow-release fertilizer	Apply slow-release fertilizer

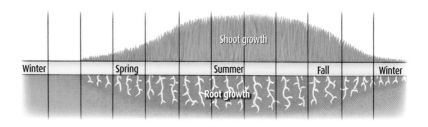

Shoot growth
Winter · Spring · Summer · Fall · Winter
Root growth

▲ Whether you've got warm-season or cool-season grass, fertilize when the grasses are at their peak of growth and not under heat or drought stress.

As a guideline, either fertilize warm-season grasses when they have greened up so that you can see that they are growing, or fertilize when you have mowed the lawn once or twice. Unlike cool-season grasses, it's OK to use a quick-release fertilizer on warm-season grasses in spring.

If you plan to fertilize your lawn more than once a summer, make the other applications one, two or three months after the second mowing, as shown in the chart, Warm-Season Grasses Fertilizing Calendar, on the previous page.

Fertilizing St. Augustinegrass, bahiagrass, and centipedegrass in midsummer can result in insect and disease problems. If these grasses begin showing signs of needing fertilizer in midsummer, an application of iron instead of fertilizer often helps to green them back up.

Scheduling by the frost dates

When to fertilize warm-season grasses depends partly on when the first and last frosts occur in your area. The first spring feeding should come after the last frost. If you fertilize before the last frost occurs, the emerging leaf blades could be damaged, plus much of the fertilizer goes to cool-weather weeds.

Your final fertilization of the year should come four to eight weeks before the last frost, so that the new growth will have time to mature before winter arrives. Fertilizing a warm-season grass too late in the season can result in a winterkilled lawn.

Fertilizer timings for cool-season grasses have little to do with frost dates. Cool-season grasses start to grow before the last spring frost occurs. They are hardy enough that frost won't harm the new growth. So, watch the lawn. When it starts to grow in spring, fertilize. Make the second application about three months after the first. Because the ground stays warm for several weeks after the first fall frost, the last application can be made as late as November.

The frost maps (below) give you the range of when you might expect first and last dates. The best gauge, however, it to keep your eye on what your grass is doing in your yard.

AVERAGE FROST DATES

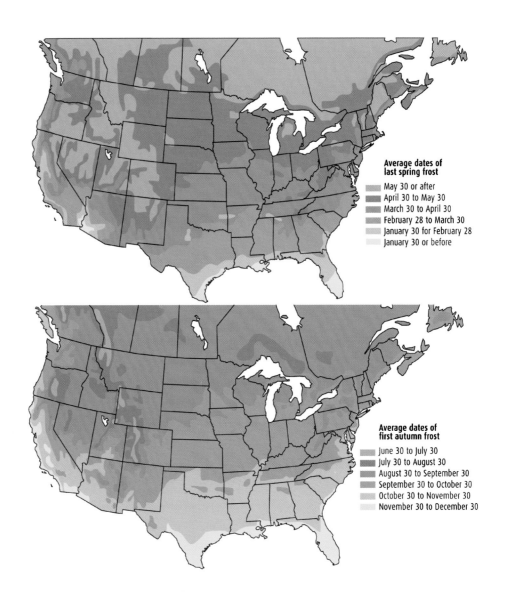

Average dates of
last spring frost

- May 30 or after
- April 30 to May 30
- March 30 to April 30
- February 28 to March 30
- January 30 for February 28
- January 30 or before

Average dates of
first autumn frost

- June 30 to July 30
- July 30 to August 30
- August 30 to September 30
- September 30 to October 30
- October 30 to November 30
- November 30 to December 30

4

FERTILIZING

What fertilizer is

Fertilizer delivers the raw ingredients that grass uses to create carbohydrates: nitrogen, phosphorus, and potassium. All fertilizers are based on these three nutrients, which are so important that their content is displayed prominently on the fertilizer bag by a series of three numbers—24-5-10, for example.

The numbers—called the analysis—tell you what percentage by weight each of the three nutrients accounts for in the package. The percentage of nitrogen is listed first, followed by the percentage of phosphorus and then the percentage of potassium. Translated, a 24-5-10 bag is 24 percent nitrogen, 5 percent phosphorus, and 10 percent potassium. The remaining 61 percent of the bag is sand, ground corncobs, limestone, or other fillers. Without fillers, the chemicals would be difficult to spread.

Nitrogen

All fertilizer recommendations are based on the amount of nitrogen required because it's the nutrient plants use the most. It's a key ingredient in chlorophyll, the green pigment that changes light, carbon dioxide, and water into carbohydrates. When nitrogen is lacking, the grass has less chlorophyll, makes less food, and isn't as green. In addition, nitrogen is one of the components making up proteins—and, therefore, it's a part of all plant cells.

Applying nitrogen encourages dense growth of leaves and roots and strengthens the grass against disease and damage from heat, cold, and drought. Too much nitrogen, however, results in shallow roots and fast-growing, succulent shoots. You then need to mow more, and the grass is more susceptible to heat and drought stresses and to insects and diseases.

Phosphorus

Phosphorus encourages root growth and is a primary component of the cells that store food as well as the membranes that surround cells. Starter fertilizers—those formulated for use on newly seeded or sodded lawns—are rich in phosphorus in order to improve seed germination and the establishment of new sprouts.

Like nitrogen, too much phosphorus brings problems. Excess phosphorus inhibits the absorption of the other nutrients that lawns require. One such nutrient—iron—is another ingredient needed for producing chlorophyll. If a buildup of phosphorus keeps your lawn from absorbing iron, the grass will turn yellow.

Potassium

Lack of potassium creates few visible problems. About the only thing you're likely to see is a little yellowing around the edges of the leaves. Nonetheless, potassium plays a critical role in lawn health. It makes for a hardier grass—one that wears better and has better resistance to temperature extremes, drought, disease, and insects. It also helps grass survive through winter.

Grass not only needs these three nutrients but needs them in the proper balance— and what that balance is depends both on the type of grass you have and where you live. In Utah, for example, there is generally enough potassium and phosphorus in the soil, and all you might need to apply would be nitrogen. In Michigan or New Jersey, where the soils are sandy, you might need to apply a fertilizer that supplies nearly as much phosphorus as nitrogen.

▶ **A fertilizer that greens in 72 hours contains quick-release nitrogen. As here, such a fertilizer is often blended with slow-release nitrogen to provide long-term feeding.**

Types of nitrogen

Quick release

Quick-release nitrogen fertilizers (also called water-soluble synthetic fertilizers) offer predictability. Water triggers the release of the nitrogen; the release is immediate so the grass quickly greens up, and the effects last for four to six weeks. Because this type of nitrogen is water soluble rather than broken down by microbes, it is effective even when soil is cold and microbes are inactive.

Quick-release nitrogen is inexpensive to manufacture, making it an affordable fertilizer ingredient. But affordability comes at a price. The effects of these fertilizers are short-lived and the grass goes through periods of feast and famine. The grass grows rapidly after application, requiring frequent mowing; then it goes through a slump as the fertilizer runs out. Also, the materials that comprise quick-release nitrogen are largely salts and so this type of nitrogen can burn the grass if improperly applied.

During rainy periods or in well-watered areas, quick-release nitrogen can leach through the soil beyond the reach of the grass's roots. Once it gets below the root zone,

CLOSER LOOK

COMPLETE FERTILIZERS
Any fertilizer that contains nitrogen, phosphorus, and potassium is called a "complete fertilizer" because it contains the three main nutrients all plants require. However, a complete fertilizer may lack some of the nutrients that your lawn needs such as iron and sulfur, and it may not be properly balanced for your lawn. Read the label thoroughly to make sure you're getting what your lawn needs.

BUYER'S GUIDE

TWO-FER ALERT
St. Augustinegrass is very sensitive to most herbicides, including the widely used 2,4-D. If you have St. Augustinegrass, read the bag label to make sure the fertilizer combo is safe to apply on your lawn.

it not only does the plant no good but is also likely to work its way into the water table. From there it eventually ends up in lakes and streams, where it does exactly what it was designed to do—promote plant growth, causing weeds and algae blooms that choke the water.

If you're using a quick-release nitrogen fertilizer, apply it to dry rather than wet grass to prevent burning. Never use a fertilizer that contains more than 20 percent quick-release nitrogen. After fertilizing, water immediately to wash the fertilizer into the soil.

Slow release

Also called controlled-release, timed-release, and continuous-release, slow-release fertilizers provide nutrients at a predictable rate over three to six months. They ensure uniform turf growth throughout the season. You can apply them heavily without fear of burning your lawn. The main disadvantages of slow-release fertilizers are that the lawn greens up slowly after their application, and they can be more expensive than quick-release fertilizers.

Some slow-release fertilizers are complex nitrogen compounds that slowly break down in the soil into plant-usable nutrients. Some are designed to be broken down by microbes, which means that they are not effective until the soil warms enough for the microbes to be active. Others are composed of quick-release nitrogen particles coated with a material that lets the nutrients ooze out at a set rate, usually

only when the material is wet. Still others are made up of a mix of coated pellets that vary in the thickness of the coatings, which break down at different rates.

Many manufacturers combine quick- and slow-release nitrogen in the fertilizer to avoid the disadvantages. The result is a balanced turf fertilizer that provides a quick greenup and uniform growth throughout the summer.

Organic

The term *natural organic* refers to any fertilizer that is made of dried or composted plant or animal waste. A wide variety of natural organic fertilizers can be found on the market. Among those most suitable for use on turf are ones made from sewage sludge or from poultry waste.

Organic fertilizers release nutrients slowly. They contain valuable micronutrients and can help improve soil structure. Because their nutrients are released as soil microorganisms break them down, the effectiveness of natural organic fertilizers is weather dependent. They work only if the soil temperature is above 50°F (10°C).

These fertilizers contain low amounts of nutrients (typically they are around 6 percent nitrogen) so they are an expensive option. However, they rarely burn the lawn and are a good choice for dormant-season applications.

Some fertilizers are synthetic organics, as opposed to those made from sludge or animal waste. They often contain urea, which is a salt that can burn your lawn. Read labels carefully, so you know what you're buying.

Special formulations

Countless fertilizer formulations are available, including starter fertilizer, winterizer, and fertilizer mixed with herbicide, pesticide, or fungicide. Each is usually labeled in large print on the bag, but you can always ask for information from the garden center staff.

Starter fertilizer is applied when you plant a new lawn (whether from seed, sod, or sprigs) or overseed an existing lawn. Starter fertilizer is rich in phosphorus, which promotes root growth, and in nitrogen, which promotes leaf growth. A typical formulation (but by no means the only one) is 20-27-5—20 percent nitrogen, most of it slow-release, 27 percent phosphorus, and 5 percent potassium.

A winter fertilizer or "winterizer" is applied during the late summer to late fall, depending on climate. Its purpose is to strengthen the grass for the coming cold weather. It is rich in slow-release nitrogen and potassium. The potassium helps create a hardy, disease-resistant grass with good ability to recover from injury. The slow-release nitrogen remains dormant through the winter. In

the spring, when the soil warms up, the nitrogen is released, greening up the lawn and encouraging leaf growth. A typical formulation is 22-3-14.

Two-fer fertilizers. These provide broad-spectrum control of pests while feeding your lawn. Weed-and-feed fertilizers in which herbicides have been added may be the most common. But there are also fertilizers combined with either fungicides or pesticides.

Weed-and-feed is a fertilizer to which herbicides have been added. The herbicides generally control broadleaf weeds, but some also control grassy weeds. Some weed-and-feeds contain a preemergence herbicide, which prevents weeds from germinating or emerging from the ground. Most weed-and-feed fertilizers are "broad spectrum," killing a wide range of weeds—the labels of some products say they'll control 50 to 70 different weeds.

Two-fer fertilizers can save you time and effort when used properly. They are a good choice when it is time to fertilize *and* your lawn is having

problems with weeds or pests *and* the pesticide is one that will actually control the problem. If your lawn isn't having problems and doesn't have a history of problems that the two-fer controls, then you are wasting money as well as effort. In addition, these products may also result in the overapplication of the fertilizer, herbicide, pesticide, or fungicide.

Reading the label

Most fertilizers contain a mixture of fast- and slow-release nitrogen—a combination in which each fertilizer offsets the disadvantages of the other. A properly balanced fertilizer will have enough quick-release nitrogen to green up the lawn quickly, but not enough to leach. As the quick-release nitrogen is depleted, the slow-release nitrogen begins to kick in, and the grass stays green.

Formulas to jump start the lawn may contain a mix of 25 percent slow-release nitrogen and 75 percent fast release. Ones designed to prevent leaching average 50:50 slow- and quick-release nitrogen.

Unfortunately, not all fertilizer bags are clearly labeled quick or slow release. Price will give you some inkling. Generally speaking, the lower the price, the higher the quick-release nitrogen content. For a more exact reading of the contents, look at the "Guaranteed Analysis" label on the back of the bag, then see "Determine the amount of slow-release nitrogen" below for directions on how to convert the amounts listed on the label.

CLOSER LOOK

TURFGRASS FORMULAS
Turfgrass fertilizers contain more nitrogen than either phosphorus or potassium. Usually, they contain three to five times as much nitrogen as phosphorus, and one and a half to two and a half times as much phosphorus as potassium. A 24-5-10 or a 15-5-10 fertilizer is a turfgrass formulation, while a 10-10-10 fertilizer is not.

4

FERTILIZING

The percentage of nitrogen, phosphorus, and potassium in the fertilizer, in that order

Guaranteed Analysis

Turf Builder® Lawn Fertilizer With 2% Iron 29-3-4 F643
Total nitrogen (N). 29%
    6.6% ammoniacal nitrogen
    12.3% urea nitrogen
    9.3% other water soluble nitrogen*
    0.8% water insoluble nitrogen
Available phosphate (P_2O_5). 3%
Soluble potash (K_2O). 4%
Sulfur (S). 8%
    8.0% combined sulfur (S)
Iron (Fe) (Total)**. 2%
Derived from: methyleneurea, ammonium phosphate, potassium sulfate, ammonium sulfate, iron oxide.

*Contains 6.8% slowly available methylenediurea and dimethylenetriurea nitrogen.

**No claim for iron in Colorado.

Quick-release nitrogen, which is immediately available to the lawn

Slow-release nitrogen, which is available to the grass over time

Important micronutrients for turfgrasses

The source of the nutrients in the bag

The percentage of the total nitrogen that is slowly available

CLOSER LOOK

MICRONUTRIENTS
In addition to nitrogen, phosphorus, and potassium, grass needs small amounts of other nutrients, including iron and sulfur. They're called micronutrients. While the amount of micronutrients that grass needs is small, they're still important. Iron is necessary to make chlorophyll. A lawn lacking adequate iron will turn yellow. Sulfur makes the soil more acidic, helping prevent some diseases. Fertilizers often include sulfur and iron in the mix. The amount is usually listed in the guaranteed analysis.

Determine the amount of slow-release nitrogen

Take a look at the label on the back of the bag. Two items will help you figure out the amount of quick- and slow-release nitrogen it contains. First is the first number in the guaranteed analysis (29-3-4), which tells you that 29 percent of the contents of the bag is some form of nitrogen. The second is the asterisk at the bottom telling you that the bag "contains 6.8% slowly available nitrogen"—the slow release nitrogen. While 6.8 percent is the amount of slow-release nitrogen, it is 6.8 percent of the *bag,* not of the nitrogen. To learn what percentage of *nitrogen* is slow release, you have to do a little math. Divide the percentage of

slow-release nitrogen (6.8%) by the percentage of total nitrogen (29%), or:

$$\frac{6.8\% \text{ slow-release nitrogen}}{29\% \text{ total nitrogen}} = 0.23 \text{ or } 23\%$$

The slow-release nitrogen in this case accounts for 23 percent of the total nitrogen. (To convert from a decimal to a percentage, multiply your answer by 100. In this case, 0.23 × 100 = 23%.) A fertilizer with 23 percent slow-release nitrogen will green up your lawn quickly and feed it over a long period.

How to fertilize

Short of hiring someone to do the work, there is little you can do to make fertilizing easier than it already is. Know how much fertilizer your grass requires and the size of your lawn, fill the hopper, set the dial, and go.

For the best results, start with a soil test, which will tell you how much fertilizer you should apply and which formulation to use (see page 148). Soil tests are cheap, easy, and the best way to make sure you're giving the lawn what it needs. Without a soil test, follow the directions on the fertilizer bag; most fertilizers are geared to supply about ½ to 1 pound of nitrogen per feeding.

Choose a spreader

There are three types of fertilizer spreaders: drop, rotary or broadcast, and handheld.

Drop spreaders apply fertilizer in a uniform pattern, simply dropping it between their wheels. This makes the applications precise, so this type of spreader is a good choice to use around areas where you don't want lawn fertilizer to go, such as gardens, shrub beds, and pavement. The precise application rate also means you'll need to pay particular attention to how much you overlap each pass to avoid stripes showing up in the lawn. Aim to follow the wheel track from the previous pass. Some of the newer spreaders on the market have an arrow on the hopper to help guide you.

Because most drop spreaders are only about 18 inches wide, it takes more time to cover your entire yard with one than with a rotary spreader.

Rotary spreaders, which are also called broadcast spreaders, fling fertilizer well beyond their wheels. They're great for large properties where precision is not important. More fertilizer lands near the spreader than farther out. To ensure fairly even application, run the spreader so the fertilizer at the outer edge of the pattern falls along the tracks left by the wheels in the previous pass. Starting the next pass about a foot from the wheel tracks of the previous pass should just about do it. Some of the newer rotary spreaders have guards that prevent the fertilizer from getting into shrub and flower beds.

A **handheld spreader** is basically a crank-operated rotary spreader. Getting a precise application pattern with these spreaders is very difficult. The hopper holds only a small amount of fertilizer and requires quite a bit of cranking. It's best for use in small areas and by people with strong arms. It's worst for applying combination fertilizers, since the dust from the material readily billows up into your face.

Read the label

The label has all the information you need to know to do a good job. It will tell you how much fertilizer to apply, whether you should wear a dust mask or other safety equipment, and whether to water after fertilizing.

◄ Pros prefer drop spreaders because the fertilizer falls uniformly between the wheels. Follow the wheel marks in the lawn to keep track of where you've been.

▼ Handheld rotary spreaders are the least reliable because the rate of application varies with the speed at which you turn the crank.

▼ Rotary, or broadcast, spreaders cover large areas quickly because they spread material well beyond their wheels. The application pattern is uneven, however, with the spreader dropping more material near the wheels and less at the outer edge of the pattern.

Applying fertilizer

Here are a few tips to ensure even application that won't leave stripes in your lawn.

Follow the directions on the bag carefully. Measure the size of your yard, and measure out the right amount of fertilizer for it. Depending on the size of your yard, applying the entire bag may be way too much or way too little.

Fill the spreader while it is standing on pavement so you can clean up any spills. Be sure to clean up if you do spill so the nutrients don't end up down the drain.

Make a pass with your fertilizer spreader along each end of your yard. (To work most efficiently, choose the ends that are farthest apart.) These header strips provide a convenient starting and stopping point for each pass and keep fertilizer away from areas that need no fertilizer. If your lawn is irregularly shaped, make header strips around its entire perimeter.

Once the header strips are down, walk back and forth between them, spreading the fertilizer. Begin walking before you open the chute and close it when you reach the far header but before you stop walking to avoid leaving piles of fertilizer at your starting and stopping points. Shut off the spreader if you travel over pavement.

Walk at a steady pace. Your speed affects the rate at which the fertilizer is applied. Moderate speed is best. Watch for dips in the ground, which can cause the fertilizer to spill out. Walk in a straight line so that the wheel tracks from the first pass give you a guideline to follow on the next pass.

Turn the spreader, shutting it off while you turn, then walk back. If using a rotary spreader, move about 1 to 2 feet away from the previous pass, turn and begin spreading. If using a drop spreader, line up the spreader's wheel with the wheel track of the previous pass.

Unless you're using a combination fertilizer, water after you fertilize so that the fertilizer moves down into the soil where the roots can access it. Check the label before watering in combination fertilizers.

▲ First make header strips on each end of your yard. The driveway can be a good starting point.

▲ Slightly overlap each pass for uniform coverage. With broadcast spreaders, move 1 to 2 feet over from the previous pass.

 WORK SMARTER

DON'T GET BURNED

Quick-release fertilizers don't have to burn your lawn. Here are some tips for avoiding problems:

- Always read and follow all directions on the fertilizer bag.
- Apply ¼ to ½ inch of water after spreading most fertilizers. Some combination fertilizers should not be watered after application, however, so read the label before pulling out the hose.
- Never apply more fertilizer than the soil test or fertilizer label calls for.
- Pay attention to how much you are overlapping each pass to avoid "double-dosing" the grass.

Minimizing fertilizer runoff

A healthy lawn filters out pollutants as rainwater seeps into soil, replenishing groundwater. Overfertilizing with nitrogen can tax this natural filter. Because some of that nitrogen is water soluble, rain can wash it into the water table. The result: The nitrogen you spent good money for isn't working on your lawn—it's making its way to streams and lakes where it causes algae and weed growth.

When you fertilize properly, only about 3 percent of the nitrogen will end up in nearby bodies of water. If you overwater, overfertilize, or are careless when spreading fertilizer, some 15 percent of the nitrogen can end up there. Here's what you need to do to fertilize properly.

- Sweep any fertilizer that lands on your walk, driveway, or patio back onto the grass. Remember that 100 percent of any fertilizer that remains on a hard surface will end up down the storm drain, where it eventually winds up in streams and rivers.
- Sweep clippings back onto the lawn after mowing. Clippings contain nitrogen and phosphorus, which will feed your lawn as they break down. In addition, clippings washed into a body of water will use up oxygen as they decompose.
- Leave a 20-foot safety zone around wells and streams where you apply no fertilizer.
- When you come to the end of a row, close the chute on the spreader, shutting off the flow of fertilizer.
- Use fertilizer in which 50 percent or more of the nitrogen is in a slow-release form. This is less likely to leach into groundwater.

4

FERTILIZING

Solving problems

Lawns do not have an easy life. They are trampled on, run over, and cut down in their prime. Diseases attack them, bugs feed on them, and droughts send them into dormancy.

Yet of all the things that can happen, of all the bugs and diseases that could attack your lawn, only a handful ever will. The trick is in knowing which handful will be the ones. This chapter will help you identify the problems that plague lawns.

Projects later in the chapter will give you step-by-step directions for solving them. Before you get to the projects, though, keep one key idea in mind:

A healthy lawn that receives adequate fertilizer and water and that is mowed high will be better able to ward off pests. If an insect or disease does move in, a healthy lawn will suffer less damage and recover more quickly than one that is stressed from lack of water or nutrients.

Chapter 5 highlights

Look for problems

The best way to prevent problems from getting out of hand is to stay on top of them, noting their onset and the pattern of the development of their symptoms. Even though you're out there mowing your lawn every four or five days, it's easy to become blind to what is going on with the grass. You're listening to your mp3 player, thinking about an upcoming presentation, or just letting your mind wander. By the time you notice a problem cropping up, a disease or insect could be thoroughly settled in.

The next best way to deal with problems, then, is to dedicate a time every three or four weeks to walk across the lawn and see what's going on. You'll want to take a good, close look at the grass. You'll also want to look at what else is going on in your yard—for example, whether a tree has gotten so large or its canopy so dense that the grass no longer receives enough sun, or whether the kids have set up a new play area that's tearing up the lawn. Weeds can tell you quite a bit about your lawn. Dandelions, for example, are an indication of acidic soil; white clover is a sign of moist, infertile soil; and ground ivy and speedwell flourish where drainage is poor.

First impressions

Start with the simple stuff on your trek across the lawn. Take a general look at the lawn's color and health while watching for problem spots. You'll want to examine these more closely.

Pay attention to the insects you encounter. White or brown moths flying up out of the grass as you walk across it are probably adult sod webworms. Beetles that gather by yard and porch lights are the mature form of the grubs that nibble the roots of your grass.

When you find problems, note their nature. Is the entire lawn affected or only a few spots? Do you see yellow grass, brown patches, or thin areas? Or does the grass just seem to be off-color in some way?

Check the size and shape of the problem area. Note its color and whether the color is uniform throughout or varied. A lawn that is yellow all over, for example, suffers from a different problem than a lawn that only has yellow spots. A spot that is yellow in the center and gray along its edge is often caused by a disease. A lawn that is yellow all over may be suffering from a simple lack of iron.

Take a shovel to the problem. If you dig up a chunk of grass and see white hairs, it's probably a fungus. The only way to be sure, however, is to send a sample to the extension lab of your state university. It's impossible to positively identify a disease without culturing it in a lab.

If the problem seems to be spreading, note the speed at which it spreads. Diseases *tend* to spread very rapidly. Insect damage *tends* to spread more slowly. Note the direction in which the damage spreads: Armyworms, for example, often start at the south end of a lawn and move north; many diseases grow outward from a central point.

Keep track of when the problem first shows up. The timing of its appearance is often a clue to its cause.

Also consider recent activities and weather. For example, did you have a backyard party that gave the lawn a heavy workout it's not used to? Or has the weather been unusually hot? Hotter-, drier-, cooler-, and wetter-than-normal weather all can provide the right conditions for pests you wouldn't normally see in your region, while heavy use can physically damage the grass plants as well as compact the soil they're growing in.

▶ **The best way to find problems is to look for them. Take a walk across your lawn. If you notice any dead or discolored spots, get down and check them out. Look for their identifying characteristics. The pages that follow will help you identify and treat the problem.**

Take a closer look

CHECK WHAT'S GOING ON IN THE SOIL

Once you've done a once-over of the lawn, get out a shovel or trowel and slice into the ground in the problem area. Work the shovel back and forth so you can see a cross-section of soil. Check for everything from worms (good news) to thick layers of thatch (bad news). Problems with roots and soil don't show up as "a-ha!" clues. Taking a look at them, however, can help you figure out whether the problem results from pests, or from something you have or haven't done to the lawn.

EXAMINE THE ROOTS

Start with the depth of the roots. Grasses with short roots are easily stressed. Hot, dry, windy weather will be especially hard on them, quickly turning the lawn brown and dry. Watch for rocks or construction debris, which will limit the depth of the root system in localized spots.

SIZE UP THE THATCH

Measure the depth of any thatch—a buildup of organic matter between the grass plant and the ground. A layer up to ½-inch thick is good for the lawn, protecting the plants' growing points. Thicker layers, however, can interfere with grass growth. Thatchy lawns tend to scalp easily when you mow, their roots are shallower so the grass is more susceptible to drought and other stresses, and they need frequent fertilizing.

DETERMINE THE TYPE OF SOIL

If you feel a lot of resistance when you put the shovel in the soil, the soil may be compacted or heavy clay. Both conditions will limit the depth of root growth and the movement of water and air through the soil to nourish the roots. If the soil is loose and light colored, it may contain a lot of sand, which tends to be infertile and dry. Tests described on pages 144 to 147 will help you determine your soil type.

Is it a bug, a disease, or something you've done?

Because it's as likely for a problem to be caused by environmental and cultural conditions as it is for insects or diseases to be the culprits, you won't be able to treat a problem adequately until you know what's going on. To help you sort this out, get on your hands and knees and look even more closely at the problem area.

Now you want to find real evidence of the cause. For example, hard dots on leaf blades are most likely the spores from a fungus; a fuzzy coating is the actual fungus. Chewed leaf blades, tunnels in the plant's crown, and stippling on the leaves are only some of the signs of insect damage.

Look for insects in the thatch or root zone and among the leaf blades. Not every one you see will be a problem. Some of the insects in a lawn are beneficial predators—rove beetles, ground beetles, spiders, and ants eat harmful insects, for example. So you will find it helpful to get to know which ones mean trouble.

A drench test will bring yet more bugs out into the open. It's especially good for flushing out insects that feed on the crowns of grass plants, such as chinch bugs, cutworms, mole crickets, armyworms, sod webworms, and billbugs. This is a standard test for professional turf managers and one of the simplest to do.

▲ Grass leaves tell you a lot about the type of problem your lawn may be facing. Leaf spots, as here, or stippling indicate disease. Chewed or cut leaves are the work of insects.

🔍 CLOSER LOOK

IDENTIFYING BUGS

All told, only about a dozen insects create problems in lawns. Combining the various forms of beetle grubs into one group narrows the number down to about 10 insects you really need to be able to identify. You can become familiar with them by checking the profiles that start on page 95, which have a photo, a description, and advice on controlling each insect.

▶ Soaking the lawn with soapy water brings many insects to the surface where you can identify them and determine if there are enough of them to cause a problem.

Checking for insects with a drench test

▲ A drench test involves applying soapy water to the lawn to force insects to the soil surface. Mark off a square yard of lawn so you can see if they are plentiful enough to cause a problem.

Lawn insects have a way of keeping out of sight. Many live underground, either as the immature form of a beetle or other insect; others crawl around in the grass where they're hard to see. A few clues, however, can tip you off to their presence. Lights attract some beetles (the adult form of the grubs that eat your lawn's roots); you may find beetles gathered by a porch light or other landscape lighting fixture in the morning. And those metallic-green Japanese beetles eating holes in your roses started out as white grubs in the lawn.

Some of the butterflies or moths flitting through your yard were once larvae feeding on your lawn. Gray-brown moths that rise up around your feet as you walk across the lawn, for example, began their lives as cutworms, which chew grass plants off at the base. Orangish butterflies with clublike antennae are adult fiery skippers, which leave 1- to 2-inch brown spots of damaged grass in the lawn.

One of the easiest ways to find out what's in your lawn is to do a drench test. The drench test is a low-tech way of getting some subterranean insects to come out in the open. All you need is some water, dishwashing liquid, and a willingness to look a few bugs in the eye.

All yards have some bugs, and you may be surprised at how many surface. The only way to tell if you've really got a problem is to mark off a square yard of lawn and count how many insects you find there. Any more than five armyworms per square yard is a problem, for example, but your yard can tolerate up to 15 fiery skippers per square yard. The chart on page 93 tells you the threshold for all the pests you may find.

1 **MOW THE TEST AREA**

Bugs will be hard to find in grass that's long enough to be mowed. Mow the lawn and pick out a spot for the test that has both healthy and damaged grass.

2 **MARK IT OFF**

Measuring and marking a small section of lawn lets you calculate the number of bugs per square yard and determine whether their presence is a problem. To mark off the spot, drive four stakes partway into the ground at 1-yard intervals to create a square. Wrap string around them to mark the test area.

3 **PREPARE A MIXTURE OF WATER AND DISH SOAP**

Mix 2 to 4 tablespoons of dishwashing liquid into 1 gallon of water. Fill the can first, then add soap.

4 **DRENCH**

Pour the soap-water mixture onto the test area. The liquid irritates the insects, and they'll surface like earthworms after a rain.

5 **COLLECT THE SAMPLES**

Collect the bugs, sorting them into like groups and putting them into jars. Identify them using the profiles starting on page 95. Count the number of each. If you have more bugs per square yard than the threshold amount, take one of the actions listed in the chart.

WORK SMARTER

USE A WATERING CAN

The easiest way to apply the soap and water mixture is with a watering can. The place to mix the soap and water is right in the can. Make sure you use dishwashing liquid, not dishwasher soap.

Drench test results: The numbers tell you when to treat

PEST	DESCRIPTION	GRASSES COMMONLY AFFECTED	DAMAGE	THRESHOLD POPULATION REQUIRING CONTROL	CULTURAL CONTROLS
Armyworms	Gray to black worm with a yellow stripe on its back and wider yellow stripes down each side.	All grasses	Grass blades may initially appear skeletonized. Mature larvae eat the entire leaf. Their feeding forms irregular brown patches that can quickly spread over an entire lawn.	5 per square yard	Dethatch lawn; overseed; drain soggy areas.
Chinch bugs	Small black bugs, less than ¼ inch long, with whitish wings folded flat across their backs.	Prefers St. Augustinegrass	Their feeding causes irregular patches of yellow grass that turn brown. Patches die during hot weather.	135 per square yard	Dethatch; apply less nitrogen, water well.
Cutworms	Fat larvae, 1½ to 2 inches long, dull yellow to gray, with stripes running down their sides. Adults are 1¼-inch-long gray to brown moths that gather at lights.	All grasses except bluegrass	They cut off grass blades near the soil surface, forming fingerlike brown spots in the lawn. The cutworm's feeding path is often visible in the morning dew.	5 per square yard	Dethatch lawn; overseed; drain soggy areas.
Fiery skippers	Larvae have a pink-green body and a red-and-black head. Adults look like butterflies and are either orangish or brown.	Bentgrass, bermudagrass, St. Augustinegrass	Look for chewed or missing leaves. Lawn turns brown in 1- to 2-inch patches, which can coalesce into larger, irregular patches.	15 per square yard	Dethatch, apply a low-nitrogen fertilizer; water correctly; overseed with fiery skipper-resistant grasses.
Mole crickets	The drench test reveals wingless crickets with velvety, grayish-brown bodies, large beady eyes, and spadelike front legs. The adults, which congregate around lights at night during the spring, are similar but have wings. They are 1 to 1¼ inches long when fully grown.	Bentgrass, bahiagrass	Their tunneling uproots grass plants and kills lawns. Feeding girdles the stems of seedlings at the soil surface.	The size of mole crickets varies greatly during their life cycle, and the amount of damage a single cricket can do varies greatly. Because of this, there is no reliable threshold.	Fertilize and water properly.
Sod webworms	Thin, cream-colored larvae up to ¾ inch long have two rows of brown or black spots with bristles growing out of them. White or brown moths will fly out of the lawn in front of the mower or as you walk across the lawn.	All grasses, but especially bentgrasses and bluegrasses	Sod webworms form a silken shelter in which they live and eat grass blades. Grass blades are clipped off close to the ground, but these may not be present in the damaged area. Damage appears as softball-size spots of brown lawn that enlarge as infestations become severe.	15 per square yard	Control by dethatching, watering, and fertilizing properly.

Lawn pests

O n the following pages, you'll find profiles of the most common problems you might encounter as you walk across your lawn. They're divided into three general groups: diseases, insects, and climate and care problems. Check the general description for symptoms that match the ones you see in your lawn. Then read further for more diagnostic clues as well as advice on controlling the problem. You'll find that the descriptions fall into a few broad categories:

Spots

Spots in the lawn are often the first sign of trouble, and the damage symptoms you see from many insects and diseases start out as spots. Looking closely at the spots, you'll see that they can be further categorized by their size, shape, color, and the type of damage within the spot.

Rings

Here, the spots are simply circular rings in the grass. They vary from bright green rings that stand alone to brown or tan rings encircling a dark green area; these are known as "frog eyes." Note the pattern of the ring and check the leaves within it for lesions.

Patches

Patches are larger than spots. They can start out brown, pinkish, gray, white, or orange—almost any color you can imagine. The color is a clue as to what the problem might be. Patches may be circular or irregular in shape, another clue to identification. You'll want to look for spots on the leaves, for weblike coverings visible in the dew, for patterns that the patches may form, and for variations in color between a patch's leading edge and its center.

Cut leaves

Leaves that weren't cut by the lawn mower were almost certainly cut by insects. Look to see if the cut is smooth or ragged and whether it is at the leaf tip, along the edges of the blade, or at its base. Also look for signs of an insect nearby, such as smooth, silky tunnels or the bug itself.

Discolored grass

A lawn with the color that is simply "off" often suffers from cultural problems, such as too little or too much water, too little fertilizer, too much heat, or a dull mower blade. Disease and insect troubles also start as discolored grass, but it takes a well-attuned eye to notice them.

▲ Patches are essentially large spots. Check their shape and color, and the outer growing edge. Look for lesions on the leaf and note whether grass has begun to regrow within the patch. This is brown patch.

▲ Check the distribution of spots across the lawn as well as their color, size, and shape. Also look for lesions on leaf blades. Spots can grow or merge with other spots into large patches. This is dollar spot.

Insects

Insects will either chew leaves or roots of the grass plant or suck sap from it. When only a few pests live in your lawn, you probably won't notice their presence, but when populations build up you'll start seeing spots and patches of dead, damaged, or discolored grass. The damage may be caused by the adult insect or by its larva or immature form. Sometimes both life stages feed on the lawn.

The following descriptions start when the population has grown large enough for the damage to be noticeable. They provide identifying clues to help you separate one insect pest from another. For example, a distinguishing symptom between billbugs and white grubs is the way in which the grass pulls from the ground. With billbugs, individual leaves easily break off in your hand, while white-grub-damaged grass hangs together and pulls up like a piece of sod.

These are only a few of the insects that damage lawns. If your problem doesn't match any of these symptoms, check the descriptions of lawn diseases and cultural problems. Or see a Home Depot associate who can help you identify the insect and find a control for it.

Armyworm

Symptom:
Small patches of brown grass appear with leaf blades eaten along their edge giving a torn, ragged appearance.

As their name implies, armyworms travel in packs. They start in the South, where they are a major turf pest, and ride winds or march northward. Damage appears in late spring to late summer, depending on where you live. It begins in small, irregular patches, often on the south edge of a lawn, that can grow several feet wide when populations are large and weather is hot and dry.

Use a drench test to monitor their presence and know when to start controls. Armyworms are fat, 1 to 2 inches long, and dull yellow to gray, with stripes running down the sides of their bodies.

Remove thatch and eliminate wet spots to help prevent damage. Apply a pesticide labeled for armyworms to control the insects.

Beetle grub

Symptom:
The grass is dying in irregular patches. When you tug on it, it easily pulls away from the ground, as if you were lifting a rug off the floor.

White grubs are the larval form of several types of beetle, including Japanese beetles, June beetles, masked chafers, and European chafers. The beetles lay their eggs in late summer. After hatching, the grubs feed on the roots of grass until cold temperatures force them deeper into the soil.

Their feeding causes the grass to wilt and die from lack of water and nutrients; however, the damage often doesn't show up until the following spring. The damage frequently begins on south-facing hillsides and other areas that warm up quickly in spring. Birds, skunks, and other animals add to the damage as they dig up the lawn looking for their own dinner. Use an insecticide before eggs hatch or when grubs are newly hatched. A thick layer of thatch can interfere with the insecticide reaching its target.

Bermudagrass mite

Symptom:
Irregular patterns or streaks appear in lawn; silver tinge develops on emerging leaves.

Several types of mites attack lawns, including clover, winter grain, banks, bermudagrass, and two-spotted spider mites. All except two-spotted mites and banks mites begin feeding on grass plants in fall and continue feeding over winter. Often the first time you notice their damage is in spring. Two-spotted and banks mites are active during summer.

Mites are tiny insects almost impossible to see with the naked eye. They feed by sucking sap from the plants, creating yellow to white stippling on leaf blades. Severe infestations can kill the grass. Bermudagrass mite-infested lawns also develop witches' brooms in the grass.

Because spider mites reside on leaf blades, one way to control them is to scalp the lawn. Bag the clippings as you mow and dispose of them. You can also spray lawns with a pesticide labeled for the type of mite attacking your lawn.

Billbug

Symptom:
Grass is brown, thin, and dying in circular patches. It pulls up in handfuls from the crown.

Damage begins in small irregular spots and can spread many feet in diameter. Small, up to ⅜-inch-long, C-shape grubs with reddish brown heads and no legs do the damage, feeding on the crown of the plant. Dig around the roots to see the grubs. To identify the cause of the damage, pull on the grass. It will break away from the crown and have frass, a sandy material, at the cut ends, if billbugs are the culprit.

Control by killing the adults before they lay eggs. The adults are dark gray to brown weevils (beetles with a long, hooked snout). They are active at night; check for them around lights. You can also flush them out of the grass with a drench test. Begin monitoring for them in midspring. Use a grub control that is also labeled for billbugs, following all label directions. Water and fertilize adequately and cut the grass longer to help the lawn ward off damage.

Chinch bug

Symptom:
Along pavement and in hot sunny areas, the lawn turns yellow, then brown, and begins to die in irregular patches.

Various species of chinch bug exist in North America, attacking all types of turfgrasses. Adult chinch bugs are small, less than ¼ inch long. They may be black, reddish, purple, or gray, depending on the species. All have white wings that, when folded against the bugs' backs, form an hourglass pattern. Immature bugs are wingless and red.

Chinch bugs do their damage by sucking sap from the grass plant. Because they feed exclusively in hot, sunny areas, you may notice the damage outlining the shade pattern of a tree.

Confirm the presence of chinch bugs with a drench test or by examining affected areas closely and looking for adult and immature bugs. Control chinch bugs with an insecticide labeled for the bugs. Watering before applying insecticide will bring the bugs up higher in the canopy and ensure better control. You can also replant with a resistant grass species.

Cutworm

Symptom:
You see 1- to 2-inch-diameter brown spots in the lawn. Leaves in the spots have been chewed, but no silken tunnels accompany the damage.

Cutworms are the larvae of a number of moth species, the type that you see fluttering around street lights at night. Like sod webworms and fiery skippers, cutworms feed at night on grass blades, but their feeding is concentrated at leaf tips rather than at the base of the blade. However, in newly seeded lawns, they will cut the young blades off at their base.

Damage is most prevalent in early and late summer. It occurs in small, irregular patches that can grow several feet wide. A drench test will reveal fat, dull gray, green, or brown larvae up to 1 inch long. When disturbed, the larvae curl up into a C-shape, which is a distinguishing feature.

Control cutworms with an insecticide labeled for the pests, applying it at night when the larvae are most active.

Fiery skipper

Symptom:
You see 1- to 2-inch-diameter spots of brown, chewed leaves but no silken tunnels.

Fiery skippers are the larvae of a small, orangish butterfly. The butterflies feed on flower nectar and lay their eggs on blades of grass in lawns near flower beds. The larvae feed on the grass from May through September. If populations are large, the spots may coalesce into large patches. A drench test will reveal larvae with a greenish-brown body up to 1 inch long and a black head.

Control is not usually necessary unless the population is large. Dethatching helps to eliminate the larvae's habitat. The bacterial insecticide *Bacillus thuringiensis* (Bt) and beneficial nematodes help control the insects' population.

Fire ant

Symptom:
Red ants, up to ¼ inch long, but often smaller, build mounds up to 18 inches in diameter in the yard. The ants bite aggressively, leaving white pustules on the skin.

Fire ants, while not dangerous to the turf itself, are aggressive, biting insects that live in the lawn. Their bites can be quite painful.

The best way to control fire ants is a two-step process. Begin by applying what's known as a broadcast bait—usually a corn-based product treated with poison that the ants take back to the mound, killing the queen and workers. These baits are a granular product, applied in the same way as a fertilizer. Apply to dry grass when no rain is expected and when ants are visible in the yard.

You should also treat individual mounds. Boiling water poured over the mound will kill the ants in it about 60 percent of the time, but boiling water can also kill the grass. Liquid, granular, and powdered mound treatments are also available at home and garden centers. Take care to avoid disturbing the mound as you treat it because the ants will come out fighting.

No product, or combination of products, is 100 percent successful in getting rid of fire ants, largely because ants in adjoining areas will recolonize empty areas.

Mole cricket

Symptom:
Large areas of your lawn are brown and spongy. Grass blades are clipped off just below the soil surface, and you see small mounds of soil across the lawn.

Mole crickets are primarily a problem in the southeastern and southwestern parts of the United States. They are brown insects, roughly 1¼ inches long. Their hind legs resemble those of a grasshopper; their front legs end in feet that are shovel-shaped, like a mole's. Mole crickets live most of their lives underground, tunneling and eating roots, stems, and leaves. The tunnels, which get larger as the mole cricket grows, do more damage than feeding does.

Treat the lawn for mole crickets soon after they hatch. Use a drench test, in which you saturate a patch of ground with soapy water, to monitor egg hatching. When the young crickets are about ⅜ inch long, begin applying an insecticide labeled for these insects. Watering a day or so before applying insecticide helps ensure the insects are not too deep in the soil.

Sod webworm

Symptom:
You see 1- to 2-inch-diameter brown spots in the lawn. Within these spots, the grass leaves are cut off at the ground; silken tunnels dot the grass nearby. Light tan moths fly up as you walk across the lawn.

Sod webworms, the larvae of a beige to tan moth with a long snout, hide in a silken tunnel by day and emerge to feed on grass blades at night and on overcast days. The tunnel is often surrounded by droppings. Their feeding begins in late spring and lasts into late summer as new generations appear. If populations are large, the spots can coalesce into large patches. Adult moths fly across the lawn in a zigzag pattern, dropping eggs. You also often see them rise up in front of your mower or as you walk across the lawn.

The larvae are easy to control with insecticides. To time your applications correctly, use a drench test to monitor the number of larvae, which are thin, grayish, and up to ¾ inch long. Because heat-stressed grass is most susceptible to their damage, make sure the variety making up your lawn is adapted to its growing conditions.

Diseases

Most lawn diseases are caused by fungi, which are living organisms closely related to plants. Fungi are opportunists. They wait for the right set of weather conditions—temperature, moisture, humidity, and sunlight—before moving in for the kill. In addition, they exploit grass that is damaged, weak, or soft and succulent from excess nitrogen.

Diseases generally cause spots in the lawn, which can vary in diameter from a few centimeters to several feet. When they're bigger than a few inches, spots are called patches, and when the patches become several feet across, they're called blights. Affected plants also develop spots or other markings on individual leaf blades. These markings are one feature that will help you narrow down the cause of your lawn's problems. When insects or cultural conditions are the culprits, the spots don't develop.

As with insects, this is only a small sampling of the diseases that can affect lawns. Check with your Home Depot associate for more information on lawn diseases in your region, how to control them, and when to treat them.

Brown patch

Symptom:
Circular brown patches form, varying in size from about 12 inches to several feet in diameter. The patches may be ringed by a gray band in the morning. In tall fescue the patches may be large and irregular in shape.

Brown patch affects all turfgrasses, especially in warm, humid weather. It is a fast-developing disease that can appear overnight, especially during periods when the grass is wet for more than 10 hours at a time and nighttime temperatures remain above 65°F (18°C). Lush, tender grasses are most susceptible.

Patches can grow to several feet across. In the early morning, they often display a distinguishing smoke ring or dark halo around their outside edges. Also, new grass may grow in the center of the patch so that it looks like a doughnut.

To prevent brown patch disease, water only in the morning so that the lawn has a chance to dry during the day. Fertilize moderately—excess nitrogen from overfertilization encourages brown patch growth. Apply a fungicide labeled for the disease.

Dollar spot

Symptom:
Small, dollar- to softball-size circular spots form during moist, moderately warm weather.

Dollar spot is a fungal disease that attacks drought-stressed, underfertilized lawns. Thick thatch also contributes to its development. The disease starts as small tan spots that may join to form large blighted areas. Leaf blades often display straw-colored, hourglass-shaped lesions edged in red. A cottony growth may be visible in the grass when dew covers the lawn.

To prevent dollar spot, keep lawns healthy with proper fertilization and watering and avoid letting thatch become too thick. Apply a fungicide labeled for dollar spot as soon as the disease appears and again 7 to 10 days later.

Fairy ring

Symptom:
A large, 4- to 12-inch-wide ring of fast-growing, dark green grass forms in the lawn. Toadstools sometimes develop in the ring.

Fairy rings are caused by fungi that feed on organic debris in the soil, such as dead tree roots, buried wooden stakes, and old fence posts. The ring can grow to a diameter of 3 to 100 feet or more, and it may develop toadstools after an extended wet spell.

Fairy ring is generally harmless, though it can compete with the grass for water and nutrients and may form a coating on the grass that blocks water from penetrating the affected area. Fungi shelter the grass from rain, resulting in damage. Occasionally, fairy ring will kill the grass within the circle.

Fertilizing to improve the color of your lawn can mask the symptoms of fairy ring. Digging up the debris, if possible, will also help.

Gray leaf spot

Symptom:
Grass leaves develop gray, brown, or purple lesions; the lawn shows a general yellowing followed by a massive die-off of the grass.

Small chocolate-colored spots—$\frac{1}{16}$ inch in diameter—suddenly appear on the leaves, then the grass takes on a blue-gray appearance and starts to thin out as if it were suffering from drought. Gray leaf spot spreads across a lawn quickly and can kill the entire stand. Tips of dying leaf blades have a characteristic twist. To verify that gray leaf spot is the culprit, put a slice of suspect grass in a sealed plastic bag overnight. Spots of gray mold will develop on leaves if they are infected.

Perennial ryegrass and St. Augustinegrass are most affected; tall fescue also suffers occasionally. The disease develops in late summer, especially in hot, dry years. Overfertilized, overwatered, or drought-stressed lawns and lawns growing in compacted soil seem to be most affected. The best control is to prevent the disease with proper care of your lawn. Replacing the grass with a resistant species will also help.

Gray snow mold

Symptom:
Large, circular patches of tan grass form as snow melts in spring.

Like pink snow mold (page 100), gray snow mold develops under a blanket of snow. It primarily affects cool-season grasses, especially ones that have been under snow cover for several months. Mild symptoms develop after 40 to 60 days of snow cover. Moderate symptoms develop between 60 and 90 days. Infections that develop after more than 90 days of snow cover are usually severe.

Symptoms start out as small, yellowish-green spots. The spots grow in size and often develop a fluffy white to gray ring of fungal threads around their borders. The spots can grow to 2-foot-diameter patches, which can join into large blighted areas. Hard black bumps form on the leaf blades.

The symptoms will quickly disappear in warm weather. The disease seldom kills more than the leaf blades, but it will recur the next year unless you get it under control. You can discourage the growth of gray snow mold by mowing until the lawn stops growing in fall and by avoiding late-fall applications of quick-release fertilizer.

Leaf spot

Symptom:
From a distance you can see an irregular pattern of tan or brown spots spread across the lawn, and the spots may cover large areas.

Look at a leaf close up. If you see lesions on it, the problem is probably one of several leaf spot diseases caused by fungi. Melting out leaf spot disease is the most common. Its lesions begin as small brown spots that turn tan, gray, or white bordered with dark purplish red or black. The lesions usually form in midspring or late fall. When weather warms, the entire leaf blade may die. The disease can progress to the point that it attacks the crown and roots, eventually thinning the lawn. Overfertilized lawns and grasses stressed by short mowing, thick thatch, or over- or underwatering are highly susceptible to the disease. Control leaf spot by keeping your lawn healthy. Also avoid watering late in the day. Consider replacing your lawn with a leaf-spot-resistant grass.

Necrotic ring spot

Symptom:
Straw-colored or reddish brown frog-eye spots, in which dead grass surrounds a tuft of living grass, appear. They vary in size from 6 inches to 3 feet across.

Necrotic ring spot favors dense lawns that grow in compacted soil, have excess thatch, or are in exposed sites. Mowing short and overfertilizing will also make a grass susceptible to the disease. Necrotic ring spot is most prevalent in the cool, wet weather of spring and fall. In cool regions, the disease can afflict a lawn all summer.

Patches grow outward, eventually joining into large blighted areas. Off-yellow, tan, or reddish brown leaf lesions may be present. If you dig up a clump of affected grass, the crown and roots will be brown or black and rotted.

Control necrotic ring spot by keeping your lawn healthy, mowing at the upper end of the height range, and fertilizing and watering moderately. Eliminating thatch can also help.

Pink snow mold

Symptom:
Pinkish-white patches up to 12 inches across appear; affected leaf blades are matted and tan.

Pink snow mold is caused by a fungus that thrives in cold, wet situations. The disease often shows up as the snow melts in spring, especially if weather remains cold and snow covered the lawn for long periods. The spots start out yellowish green, then develop the characteristic pinkish white fungal threads. Patches grow outward with a rusty pink leading edge.

Cultural controls include pruning your trees to let more light onto the lawn. Avoid overfertilizing, especially in fall. Mow until winter sets in; tall grass is more susceptible to the disease. Dethatch as necessary. Lightly infected grass will recover on its own in a few weeks. Otherwise, apply a fungicide labeled for pink snow mold.

Powdery mildew

Symptom:
A powdery, white growth coats leaf blades and your lawn looks as though it's dusted with flour.

Powdery mildew is a fungal disease that affects bluegrass, bermudagrass, and some fescues. The disease is most likely to occur in shady areas of a lawn and during periods with cool nights and warm, humid days. Affected areas appear white or light gray from a distance. Looking at the leaves up close, you'll see small masses of white spores, roughly $\frac{1}{16}$ inch in diameter. Underneath the mold, the grass blade may develop yellow spots.

Powdery mildew is generally harmless. You can decrease its likelihood by pruning trees to let in more light and thinning nearby shrubs to improve air circulation. Avoid overfertilizing and overwatering in shady areas. Overseed with a mildew-resistant grass.

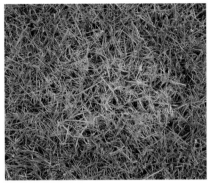

Pythium blight

Symptom:
Your lawn develops irregular light brown patches 1 to 3 inches wide that mat when you walk on them.

Pythium blight occurs during the hottest, most humid days of summer, often starting in low spots and following drainage patterns as it spreads. It attacks heat-stressed lawns and lawns in poorly drained soil. All cool-season grasses are susceptible, especially ryegrass.

The patches are initially composed of wet-looking leaves that then turn copper in color and finally become matted and tan. In the early morning you may see a cottony web around the infected areas. As the temperature approaches 95°F (35°C), affected areas can die.

Control pythium blight by limiting fertilizer applications during wet spells, by watering during the day instead of at night, and by waiting until affected areas are dry before you mow. Apply a fungicide labeled for pythium blight to treat the disease.

Red thread

Symptom:
Light pink to tan circular patches develop in cool, humid to wet weather; a pink to red webbing binds the leaves together.

Red thread is a fungal disease that thrives in cool, moist weather, so it is most prevalent in midspring and in fall. It favors lawns that are low in nutrients. From a distance, the disease appears as tan or pink patches that range from 4 to 36 inches in diameter. A closer looks reveals an antlerlike growth on the leaves. Red thread is not a serious disease, one that kills the lawn. It does not affect the roots, so the grass eventually recovers. Fertilizing will improve a mild case of the disease. A contact fungicide labeled for red thread can help in serious cases.

Rhizoctonia large patch

Symptom:
Straw-yellow to brown circular patches form on warm-season grasses in fall or spring.

Rhizoctonia large patch is a significant disease of zoysiagrass and other warm-season grasses. You see it most often in fall and spring as lawns either enter or emerge from dormancy. Rhizoctonia large patch is closely related to brown patch disease, which can be serious on tall fescue, but it only affects warm-season grasses.

Patches start as slightly matted areas of orange grass and can grow up to 20 feet in diameter. Leaves in the patch die, turning yellow-brown, while the expanding edge of the patch remains orange. The grass thins within the infected areas and weeds often move in.

The disease weakens the grass but does not kill it, and the lawn usually recovers. Bermudagrass can bounce back quickly in warm weather; zoysiagrass is much slower to recover. Thatch buildup, overfertilizing, poorly drained soil, and overwatering favor development of rhizoctonia large patch. Proper care of your lawn helps prevent the disease.

Rust

Symptom:
You see irregular, off-color to yellow-brown patches in the lawn; up close, the leaf blades sport rusty brown pustules.

In early stages, the disease occurs in localized areas of your lawn, but then it spreads. Initially the leaves develop yellow flecks that grow and connect into rows parallel to the leaf veins. The leaf surface under the spots ruptures and rust-colored pustules form. Orange or red powder brushes off on your shoes as you walk over an infected area.

Rust first appears in late summer and early fall, although an infection occasionally begins in spring. It is most common in warm, moist weather on stressed grass that is not growing. Avoid the disease by keeping your lawn growing with proper watering, fertilizing, and mowing.

Slime mold

Symptom:
Leaf blades are coated with bluish-gray, black, or white balls that feel powdery; the lawn has indistinct, irregularly-shape patches of yellow and orange or of gray and purple.

Slime mold is more disconcerting than dangerous. It is caused by a slimy but nonpathogenic fungus that feeds on organic matter in the soil. The fungus reproduces during wet periods, and that is when the powdery balls develop on the grass leaves. Affected grass occurs in patches that are 2 to 6 inches in diameter with well-defined borders. Slime mold doesn't hurt the grass, but if you object to the patches, you can hose down the spores with water to wash them away. Infection usually lasts one to two weeks.

Summer patch

Symptom:
In hot weather, you see scattered circular to crescent-shape patches of dead grass 4 to 8 inches across. Eventually the patches develop a frog eye.

Summer patch is quite similar to necrotic ring spot disease. Small spots of dead grass surround a green frog eye of living grass. The spots eventually grow into large dead patches. Roots and crowns of the affected grass look dead. The main difference is that summer patch shows up during hot dry weather while necrotic ring spot is a cool-weather disease.

The same conditions that lead to necrotic ring spot favor summer patch disease: excess thatch, short mowing, and overfertilization, especially with quick-release fertilizer. Prevent the disease by using good maintenance practices. Replace your lawn with a resistant variety that tolerates the weather stresses in your region.

Climate & care problems

Some problems have no organic or living cause, such as an insect or disease. Instead, they result from environmental extremes, like excess shade or periods of heat, cold, humidity, or damp, overcast weather. These conditions stress plants as well as make the grass more susceptible to diseases.

Your care practices can also be detrimental to lawns. Over- and underfertilizing, over- and underwatering, and scalping the grass when you mow are just a few of the things that can damage your lawn and make it more susceptible to pests. Not taking care as your work, such as letting a spreader tip over and spill fertilizer, or spilling

gasoline as you fill the mower tank or using salt to melt ice on sidewalks, can kill the grass.

The best way to avoid care problems is to mow, water, and fertilize correctly. To avoid environmental problems, choose a grass that's well adapted to your region and to the growing conditions within your yard.

Clay soil

Symptom:
Soil is hard and dense, and water runs off rather than soaks in.

This is a sign that the soil is either compacted or high in clay content. If the soil is rich in clay, topdress to add organic matter.

Dog urine

Symptom:
You see small patches of completely dead turf, surrounded by a ring of quick-growing grass.
The culprit is actually the concentrated nitrogen in the dog's urine, which burns the lawn. If you can, dilute the urine with water soon after the dog has used the spot. If, as is more likely the case, you don't discover the damage until it's done, time will repair it. Surrounding grass will eventually grow into the damaged area. If you own the dog, consider training it to use a dedicated area where the damaged grass will be out of sight.

Dull mower blade

Symptom:
Lawn has dull color with a whitish tinge.

Dull mower blades shred leaf tips. These tips turn white or brown as the shredded parts die back. Fixing the problem is as simple as sharpening your mower blade (see pages 42–44).

Lack of fertilizer

Symptom:
Grass turns yellow or pale green.

Yellowing often indicates that a lawn needs fertilizer, but some grasses are naturally more yellow, gray, or blue than green and never become deep green, even after fertilizing. Become familiar with your grass so that you know what to expect. If your goal is to have a dark green lawn, consider overseeding with a variety that is naturally the color you desire.

Lack of water

Symptom:
Lawn is bluish gray; grass remains compressed when you walk on it, leaving footprints.

See Chapter 3, starting on page 60, for detailed information on making sure your lawn receives the right amount of water.

Moss or algae

Symptom:
Grass is thin or ground is bare, with unusual green growth in the bare areas or brown or black scum on the soil.

When lack of light causes a lawn to thin, moss or algae can take the place of the grass. Moss and algae grow in soil that is either acidic, infertile, overwatered, poorly drained, or shady. Remove the conditions that encourage their growth. Cut back on watering. Apply lime to correct the acidity. Core aerate to correct compaction and improve drainage. Plant a shade-tolerant grass and apply a fertilizer containing iron, which inhibits the growth of moss.

Loose, sandy, or gravelly soil

Symptom:
The lawn is constantly dry, yet you water deeply and infrequently and the roots are deep.

Sandy and gravelly soils are infertile and don't hold water. They need organic matter. Topdress with compost or renovate the lawn entirely, tilling in compost before you plant.

Poor growing environment

Symptom:
Roots are short.

Roots that are less than 4 to 6 inches long can be a sign of watering shallowly and infrequently, excess thatch, or poor soil, as well as obstructions in the soil. Improve root growth by watering correctly, dethatching, and possibly topdressing.

Thatch

Symptom:
A dense layer of organic debris separates the grass blades and the soil.

Thatch buildup occurs when organic matter accumulates faster than soil microbes can break it down, which can result from overfertilizing or overuse of herbicides and insecticides. See "The Truth About Thatch," which begins on page 114, for more information on removing thatch.

Uneven application of fertilizer

Symptom:
Pale green strips of lawn show up in your otherwise dark green lawn.

When you're not careful about overlapping each pass of your fertilizer spreader, some parts of the grass may receive too little fertilizer while other parts may get too much. Check pages 84 to 85 for step-by-step information on spreading fertilizer.

Other problems

Gophers

Symptom:
Crescent-shaped mounds of dirt appear in the grass.

Gophers are 6- to 10-inch-long, dark brown to gray mammals, although their colors vary widely, ranging from white to nearly black. Because they rarely go above ground, however, the best way to identify gophers in your lawn is by the crescent-shaped mounds they form as they dig and push excess soil to the surface. Their borrows can cover anywhere from 200 to 2,000 square feet

There are two ways to control gophers: traps and poison. Traps should be set in the main tunnel. You can find the main tunnel by looking for a circular dirt plug near the middle of a mound. Probe the ground with a broom handle, or with a gopher probe, made especially for the task. Stick the probe in the ground, off to one side of the plug. Keep probing until the probe drops rapidly through a tunnel. Main tunnels are roughly 6 to 12 inches deep and 2 to 3 inches in diameter. Secondary tunnels are smaller and not as deep.

Dig to the tunnel and put two traps in it—one facing in each direction. Stake them in place. There's no need to bait the trap—the gopher will walk into it in the course of its travels. Cover the hole you dug with a piece of plywood, making sure it seals out all the light. If you don't catch a gopher after three days, move the trap elsewhere.

With poisons, you have a choice between granules, and blocks. Granules kill quickly but lose strength in the ground. Blocks last longer, but can take 5 and 10 days to kill. Like traps, poison should be placed in a main tunnel of the burrow.

Moles

Symptom:
Raised lines of grassless soil wind through the lawn.

Moles have large paddle-shape front feet with long toenails that they use to dig through the soil. Like gophers, moles push excavated soil to the surface. The easiest way to identify mole activity is by the raised lines in the lawn, which are the top of their tunnels; moles are the only animal that creates such tunnels. Surface tunnels are usually most prevalent in the spring and fall or after a warm rain, when the grubs and worms that moles eat are near the surface. During winter and summer, moles burrow deeper to find food.

Because moles eat insects and worms, poison baits are not effective. Using a pesticide to kill grubs and worms is also ineffective. The best way to control moles, then, is to set a trap in an active tunnel after a rain in spring or fall. Active tunnels are relatively straight, not winding, connecting two sections of the burrow. To see if a tunnel is active, flatten it gently with your foot. Check the next day—an active tunnel will have been reopened.

There are several different types of traps. With some, you flatten the tunnel and set the trap to straddle it. With others, you dig out some soil before setting the trap. If you don't trap the mole within two days, move the traps to another tunnel.

Fumigation is another possibility, but this is difficult, and unless you can fumigate the entire burrow, it will be ineffective. Given the size of a burrow—$\frac{1}{5}$ acre— you will probably need the cooperation and permission of at least one neighbor to fumigate.

Shade

Symptom:
The grass is thin or the ground is bare under a tree or near a building.

Shade is a problem for lawns, but if the shady spots in your yard receive at least four hours of sunlight daily, you should be able to grow grass in them. With care, it might even be good grass. However, it's unlikely it will be as healthy as one that receives direct sunlight for an entire day.

Some grasses deal better with shade than others. In the North, a mixture of 50 to 60 percent Kentucky bluegrass, 30 to 40 percent fine fescues, and 10 to 20 percent perennial ryegrass is a good choice for shaded lawns. In the South, the best grass for shaded lawns is St. Augustinegrass. Zoysiagrass will grow in moderate shade, and centipedegrass tolerates light shade.

To care for a shady lawn:

Fertilizing Fertilize less. Shaded grass needs one-half to two-thirds the amount of nitrogen that grass in sunny sites requires.

Watering Generally, shaded grass also needs less water than grass growing in sun. When the shade comes from trees, however, you may actually have to water more to meet the needs of both the lawn and the trees.

Mowing Mow shaded grass $\frac{1}{2}$ to 1 inch longer than the normal mowing height. Longer leaves allow grass to soak up more sun.

Cleaning up Rake up tree leaves as soon as they fall, so that they don't shade, smother, and further distress shaded grass.

Treating problems

▲ Pesticide companies have developed a wide variety of lawn treatments, ranging from chemical controls designed to wipe out everything green to biological controls for controlling grubs. Evaluate your lawn problems carefully, and select a product specific to the problem.

H aving decided what it is that's bugging your lawn, what do you do?

You could apply a pesticide, of course, which will put an end to most insect and disease problems. So why not start there and get it over with? It's a bit like driving a nail with a sledgehammer. The sledgehammer will do the job, but unless you're careful, you may put a hole in the wall while you're at it. In the case of your lawn, the beneficial insects that help control pests and the earthworms that aerate your soil are the hole. While pesticides kill the damaging bugs, they also kill the beneficial ones.

A better approach is to first determine how bad the problem is, and then develop a plan of attack. For example, if you see only one or two white grubs in your entire lawn, you don't need to treat everywhere. Squashing the ones you do see plus watering, mowing, and fertilizing correctly to keep your lawn healthy may be all that's required. If and when problems do get out of hand, then turn to pesticides.

Choosing pesticides

The most important consideration when buying pesticides is whether the product is labeled for both the pest that is damaging your lawn and the type of grass in the lawn. If the pest is not listed on the label, it's possible that the pesticide won't help to control it. And if the grass is not listed, it could be because it doesn't tolerate the pesticide. For example, 2,4-D (a broadleaf herbicide) can damage

or kill St. Augustinegrass. Read labels carefully, noting all directions and warnings. It's up to you to use pesticides safely and correctly.

Lawn insecticides and fungicides come in liquid, powder, or granular form.

Liquids are sold as concentrates and as ready-to-use sprays. Mix concentrated liquid pesticides with a hose-end or a pump sprayer following the directions on the pesticide label, then spray. Concentrated pesticides are the most dangerous because they are full strength, so be sure to follow all safety recommendations on the label as well.

Ready-to-use sprays are premixed at the correct strength, so all you have to do is spray the pesticide. Many of the sprayers for these products are as convenient and easy to use as typical pump and hose-end sprayers.

Many fungicides are formulated as **wettable powders.** Like concentrated liquids, you mix them with water in your sprayer. Unlike liquids, powders have a tendency to settle out of the water. To keep the particles suspended, agitate or shake the sprayer frequently. Again, follow all directions on the pesticide label.

Granular pesticides are meant for broad application over the entire lawn with a fertilizer spreader. Sometimes these are combined with fertilizer, allowing you to do two jobs at one time. However, use these two-fer products only when the time is right for both fertilizing and controlling the pest.

Reading pesticide labels

Get the most for your money—and get better results—by carefully reading the label of insecticides, herbicides, and fungicides, or any other type of pesticide you use. A minute or two spent reading the label can prevent many problems later on.

Problems occur when a label isn't followed exactly. For example, applying at the right time for the wrong problem or applying too much or too little or during the wrong kind of weather can result in major problems and sometimes even dead plants.

The main front label tells exactly what the product does and which plants it works on. It also lists the active ingredients in the pesticide and provides a signal word denoting how poisonous the pesticide is to humans.

A pesticide or formulation marked **"Caution"** is the least toxic.

"Warning" means that the material is moderately hazardous, and you should take greater care when using the pesticide.

Pesticides labeled **"Danger"** are the strongest and most dangerous to handle. They are poisonous and possibly corrosive.

The back label offers more detail about using the pesticide. The most important information on the label are the safety precautions you should take when using the pesticide and what to do in case of an accidental poisoning.

Next in importance are the Directions for Use. These will tell you how to mix the chemical, if necessary, and how and when to apply the pesticide.

Always use the prescribed amount: Applying an extra-concentrated mix won't kill any more pests than the right amount will. But it will dump extra poison into the environment, and it could damage your lawn. If you use a concentration that's too low, you're not likely to solve the problem. Also, because the lower concentration exposes the pests to the pesticide but doesn't kill all of them, they begin to develop resistance to the pesticide so that even higher concentrations won't kill them. Then you really have problems.

Storage and disposal information is also included on the back label. You can't just dump leftover lawn chemicals on the ground or down the sink. Not only can they damage the plumbing or the lawn where you pour them, but they also contaminate drinking and groundwater supplies.

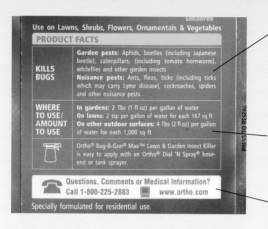

These are the pests that this product will control. If the insect feeding on your lawn isn't on the list, chances are the pesticide won't help.

General directions for how much pesticide to mix up.

Where to find information in case of emergency.

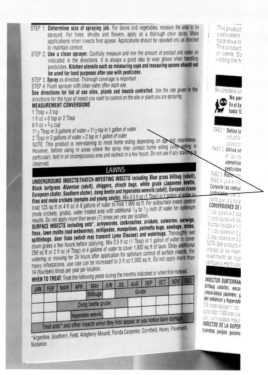

These are the active ingredients in the container. Active ingredients are the ones that do the job.

The signal word clues you to the toxicity of the ingredients. Pesticides with "warning" labels are moderately toxic.

Detailed directions for using the pesticide on a specific crop or type of plant.

A chemicals glossary

When standing in the garden center trying to find a cure for a problem, it helps to know some terms.

Fungicide: A pesticide that kills diseases caused by fungi, such as rust and leaf spot disease.

Insecticide: A pesticide that kills insects.

Systemic: A formulation that gets into the plant's system and protects it from root to leaf tip. The pest—whether fungi or insects—would not have to come in direct contact with the pesticide to be controlled.

Contact: A formulation that protects or affects the parts of the plant that the spray touches. In the case of insecticides, it also means that it kills any bugs it contacts.

⊘ SAFETY ALERT

PESTICIDE SAFETY

Insecticides and fungicides are poisonous materials, and you should be careful when handling them. Read the label before applying pesticides and follow all recommended safety precautions. The precautions vary from product to product and brand to brand, but here is a general rundown on how to protect yourself.

■ Wear a long-sleeved shirt, long pants, boots, and socks.
■ Wear neoprene rubber gloves, and wash them before taking them off.
■ Take a shower when you finish.
■ Wash the clothes you wear while spraying separately from the rest of your laundry.
■ Read the label to determine how long to keep pets and children off the lawn. With some materials you only need to wait until sprays have dried completely. With others, there's a 24-hour or longer waiting period.

Repairing your lawn

Once insects and diseases are under control, turn your attention to getting your lawn back into shape. If insects left only a few bare spots in the lawn, you can simply **patch** them using seed or pieces of sod. To learn how to patch a lawn, see pages 179–180.

When more than 40 percent of your lawn has been affected, it's better to work on the entire space. However, you don't have to start from scratch. You can cut the existing lawn very short, then **overseed** it (see pages 181–183). Overseeding allows you to invigorate the grass with pest-resistant varieties as well as restores your lawn's beauty

Three ways to apply pesticides

Depending on when and what you're applying to your lawn, you will use one of these three devices:

Spreader: Drop, hand, and broadcast spreaders apply dry granular products. They're good for covering large areas.

Pump sprayer: Ideal for spot treatments using liquid materials. For small applications, ready-to-use pesticides in spray bottles work well. For large areas, move up to a 2-gallon or larger pump sprayer. With both types, adjust the nozzle to put out the coarsest spray possible and spray only when there is no wind to prevent the material from drifting to nontarget areas.

Hose-end sprayer: Good for large lawn areas. This consists of a sprayer and a jar in which you place the pesticide. Screw on the jar and attach the sprayer to a hose, then spray. For even application, use an even, sweeping motion and follow a pattern as you move across the lawn. You may need to refill the jar more than once before finishing.

Special safety equipment

■ **Dust mask:** Keeps powdery pesticides out of your lungs. It's smart to wear one even when you're simply pouring fertilizer into the spreader.

■ **Respirator:** Few pesticides available to homeowners require use of a respirator. But if you are spraying one marked Danger, you'd be wise to wear one. Respirators prevent you from breathing the fine mist from a spray.

■ **Neoprene rubber gloves:** These won't melt when exposed to chemicals like regular rubber gloves do. Wear neoprene rubber gloves when you're pouring the pesticide into the sprayer—the most dangerous time when handling pesticides—to avoid getting the concentrated pesticide on your hands.

Using a hose-end sprayer

 PROJECT DETAILS

SKILLS: Measuring, spraying pesticides evenly

PROJECT: Applying fungicide or pesticide with a sprayer that attaches to the garden hose

 TIME TO COMPLETE

Time required depends on the area being sprayed.

 STUFF YOU'LL NEED

TOOLS: Hose, hose-end sprayer
MATERIALS: Insecticide, fungicide

 SAFETY ALERT

WASH AFTER USING

Wash your hands immediately after spraying and do not eat, smoke, or use the toilet until you have. Shower and change clothes when you are through spraying. Wash clothes separately from the rest of the laundry immediately after use. A dust mask or respirator is recommended if you're spraying trees and is a good idea when you're spraying the lawn, but most labels do not require it.

A t some time or other, you may be applying chemicals to solve a lawn problem. Chemicals come either in liquid form, which you spray on the lawn, usually after diluting, or in granular form, which you apply with a fertilizer spreader.

Hose-end sprayers are a convenient way to spray liquids. Newer sprayers eliminate the need to mix and measure concentrates. You put the concentrate into the sprayer's canister, and the sprayer mixes the concentrate at the proper rate into the water spray. Water never enters the canister, so the concentrate isn't diluted: You simply pour any excess back into the original jar when you finish spraying.

Here's how it works: Water traveling through a pipe creates a vacuum when it passes over a hole. A sprayer's nozzle assembly has a hole in the bottom that sucks the concentrate into the nozzle where it mixes with the water. By controlling the rate at which water flows through the nozzle, the sprayer controls the vacuum and the amount of concentrate added to the spray.

Hose-end sprayers work with almost all concentrated pesticides and with water-soluble fertilizers, such as Peters or Miracle-Gro. Some products, especially those designed to kill weeds, should be used only in a pump sprayer. Read the directions that come with the sprayer and the concentrate to make sure the two are compatible.

▲ **Hose-end sprayers pull chemical concentrate from a container and mix it into a spray of water at constant rate. Follow the label directions to set the sprayer at the correct rate.**

5

SOLVING PROBLEMS

1 **PREPARE THE LAWN**

Depending on what you're using, you may have to mow or water the lawn before spraying. Read the directions on the concentrate and follow them carefully.

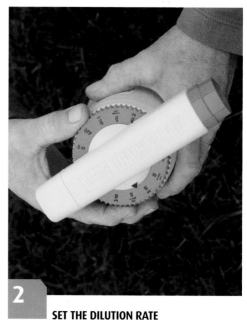

2 **SET THE DILUTION RATE**

Read the pesticide label to find the rate at which the material is supposed to be applied, then set the dial on the sprayer accordingly.

3

PUT THE CONCENTRATE IN THE SPRAY CONTAINER

Pour the undiluted concentrate into the sprayer, filling the canister about halfway. Use the concentrate full strength—the sprayer will mix it with water from the hose in the proper proportion. If the sprayer you're using doesn't have a mixing dial on top, add the amount of water specified to the canister. Read the directions on the container and on the sprayer and measure accordingly. Because you are handling the pesticide at full strength, this is the most dangerous step. Use chemical-resistant gloves as you pour and measure and follow all safety precautions listed on the label. Pour the water in first, followed by the chemical.

 WORK SMARTER

RELEASE PRESSURE IN THE SPRAYER

Pressure builds up in the canister while you're spraying. Then when you finish spraying and remove the lid to clean the sprayer, the pressure spews pesticide into your face. To avoid this mess, turn off the water and give the trigger a final squeeze to release the pressure.

4

CONNECT THE HOSE

Attach the hose to the sprayer. If the nozzle has an adjustable tip, you can rotate it to control the direction in which the chemical sprays. Some sprayers allow you to remove the tip so you can shoot a concentrated jet of pesticide-water mix some 20 to 25 feet up into trees.

5

SPRAY THE LAWN

Pull the trigger, or in some cases put your finger over an air hole, to apply the spray. Hold the sprayer at a uniform height and swing it back and forth in long, steady, overlapping swaths. Walk backwards across the lawn at a steady pace. Stop spraying at the end of each pass and move over and start spraying again. For more uniformity, consider spraying half the specified rate in one direction, then applying the second half at right angles to the first. When you have covered the entire yard, stop spraying.

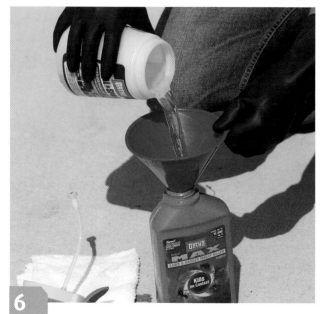

6 POUR THE LIQUID BACK INTO ITS JAR

When you're done spraying, turn off the hose and unscrew the canister. Pour any leftover chemical back into its original jar.

7 RINSE OUT THE CANISTER

A surprising amount of chemical remains inside the canister after spraying, chemical that could contaminate whatever you spray next if you don't clean it out. In some cases, flushing the canister with water for about a minute is all you need to do. In other instances, you fill the canister about 10 percent full with clean water, screw on the top, and swish to rinse the canister sides. Exactly how you clean the canister, however, depends on the pesticide product you sprayed. Read the label and follow the cleaning directions to the letter.

Be sure to work over soil or grass (not the part you just sprayed) so that the rinse water will not wash into storm sewers or drains.

8 CLEAN OUT THE NOZZLE

You'll need to clean the nozzle as well as the canister. Hook the top back up to the hose, keep the dial at the setting you used while spraying your lawn, turn on the water, then pull the trigger a couple of times to flush the nozzle. Again, work over grass or bare soil so that the water doesn't run off your property. Also avoid spraying nearby gardens so there's no chance that the pesticide residue could damage the plants. Again, if label directions differ from these guidelines, those are the ones to follow.

 WORK SMARTER

FINISH THE JOB

Instructions for some of the concentrates you spray may tell you to water the yard *after* you've sprayed. This often helps wash the spray to where it's needed most. Not all sprays require after-watering, and a given spray may require after-watering in some situations and not in others. Read the label carefully, looking for information on the problem you're treating, and follow the directions carefully.

 CLOSER LOOK

WETTABLE POWDERS

Some pesticides and herbicides come as what's called a "wettable powder." Wettable powders don't dissolve in water; they're very fine powders that are suspended in the water. The powder may settle somewhat during use. If so, shake the sprayer to redistribute it.

Using a pump sprayer

PROJECT DETAILS

SKILLS: Measuring, spraying
PROJECT: Treating disease and insect infestations with liquids or wettable powders

TIME TO COMPLETE

Mixing the chemicals will take 5 to 10 minutes. Treatment time depends on the size of the affected area.

STUFF YOU'LL NEED

TOOLS: Pump sprayer
MATERIALS: Water, fungicide, or insecticide concentrate

U nlike a hose-end sprayer, a pump sprayer is self-contained. It holds 1 to 5 gallons of diluted chemical, has a pump to build up pressure in the container, and a wand that you use to apply the spray.

The substance you're spraying comes in concentrated form either as a liquid or as what's called a wettable powder. Liquid or powder, you fill the tank, then measure the pesticide into water in the sprayer. Put on the top, then agitate—give things a good shake. Wettable powders don't dissolve, however, but stay in suspension in the water. They may well settle while you're working, in which case you simply shake the sprayer again.

Spray only the affected area, not the entire lawn. The directions on whatever you're spraying will tell you how much you'll need to mix up to cover a given area—usually in terms of hundred-square-feet per gallon. Figure out how many square feet you have to treat and mix up enough to cover it. Don't mix up an entire gallon unless you think you'll use it all. Once mixed with water, most controls don't keep for very long, and many can corrode the tank and spray nozzle.

SAFETY ALERT

KEEP IT CLEAN
Buy a measuring cup and spoon to use when measuring out chemicals. Rinse them well and store them where they won't get mixed in with household kitchenware. Make sure they are well out of the reach of children. Don't use insecticide or fungicide measuring equipment in the kitchen, no matter how well you think you've cleaned it.

WORK SMARTER

SPRAY ON A CALM DAY
Apply pesticides when there's little or no wind so that the spray won't drift into areas where it doesn't belong. If there is a slight breeze, work with the breeze at your back and back away from the area you've just sprayed.

1

TEST AND CLEAN THE SPRAYER
Pump sprayers often get clogged through use. The time to find out if your sprayer is clogged is *before* you fill it. Fill the tank partway with water, put on the lid, then pump up the pressure. Spray, checking for clogs. If the nozzle is not spraying uniformly, brush it with an old toothbrush or use a toothpick to break up clumps.

It's smart to keep two sprayers on hand, one for herbicides and one for insecticides and fungicides. That way, you won't accidentally kill your flowers by using a sprayer that may have herbicide residue in the tank.

5

SOLVING PROBLEMS

2 MIX THE CHEMICALS

After testing for clogs, unscrew the lid slightly and release any built-up pressure. Follow the directions on the container exactly. Put the right amount of water in the sprayer. Measure the amount of pesticide required and pour into the sprayer. Tighten the lid and agitate (shake) the sprayer to mix.

3 PUMP UP THE CANISTER

Pump the sprayer handle up and down several times to pressurize the canister. Push it all the way down and twist it to lock it into position so you can use it as a handle.

4 SPRAY

Spray on a calm day, so the wind doesn't carry the spray away. Just in case of an unexpected gust, adjust the nozzle so that it sprays coarse droplets; they're harder to blow off course. Spray only the problem areas. Avoid walking on the pesticide you just sprayed. Spray until the sprayer is empty.

5 CLEAN THE SPRAYER

Once you've used all the liquid, loosen the lid to release the pressure. Refill the tank with water until it's about 10 percent full. Put on the lid, and slosh the water around. Pump up the pressure, then spray to empty the tank a total of three times.

The truth about thatch

▲ A thick layer of thatch is bad for the lawn. A power rake pulls out the thatch, but be prepared to do a lot of hand raking afterwards. Even moderate amounts of thatch quickly result in large piles of debris.

Thatch is a much feared and much misunderstood buildup of organic matter between the grass blades and the soil. When layers are more than ½ inch thick, thatch lives up to its reputation of being bad for the lawn. In thinner layers, however, thatch is actually good news.

Thatch is the layer of organic matter that collects on top of the soil. It's made of old stolons and rhizomes that are building up faster than they decay. (Grass clippings, which are mostly water, don't contribute to thatch.) In small amounts, thatch helps prevent soil compaction and protects the crown of the plants. In larger amounts, however, thatch can keep rain and irrigation water from filtering into the soil. The lawn will have shorter roots, and sometimes the roots don't even reach the soil. At its worse, thatchy lawns are at the mercy of the climate.

You can begin to suspect a thatch problem if the lawn feels spongy when you walk on it. You may also see localized dry spots. To verify your suspicions, cut a wedge out of the lawn, look at it, and measure the thickness of the stemmy layer at the base of the leaves.

The threshold between good thatch and bad thatch is at about ½ inch. A layer of thatch less than ½ inch thick is good. If it's around ½ inch thick, start thinking about how to keep it from getting any deeper. More than ½ inch, and it's time to remove it.

There are two ways to get rid of thatch: power raking and aerating. A power rake has long, slender tines that comb through the grass and pull up the thatch. This method is immediately effective, but it stresses the lawn and doesn't remove all of the thatch.

An aerator pulls up cylinders of soil that are about 3 inches long and ¾ inch in diameter and deposits them on the lawn. The openings that the cylinders leave behind let water and air filter into the soil. With more air and water in the soil, soil microbes are more active, and they begin to digest the thatch. Aerating provides no immediate effects, but it is easier on the lawn and provides longer-lasting benefits. In addition, it helps to solve compaction problems (see page 154). Both power rakes and aerators are widely available at rental stores.

Although a power rake excels at removing thatch, it doesn't collect it. All the thatch that gets pulled from the base of your lawn is left where it falls, and all of it must be raked up, removed, and disposed of. The raking and removing are the hard part of the job. A large lawn can generate as much as 80 bushels of thatch. Disposing of this much thatch can present a problem.

▲ A power rake has tines that reach down into the lawn to pull up thatch. Power raking followed by aerating can virtually eliminate thatch problems.

▲ To judge thatch build-up, cut and remove a small section of lawn. Turn it on its side and measure. This wedge has a ¾-inch-thick layer of thatch. Anything more than ½ inch is too much and needs treatment.

Many states no longer allow yard waste in landfills, although some municipalities collect yard waste separately and compost it. You can compost it yourself for use as a mulch, as a soil amendment, or as topdressing for your lawn. Put as much of the debris as you can in an out-of-the-way part of the yard, turning it from time to time with a pitchfork. Nature does the rest, changing the thatch into a rich organic compost for your garden.

What causes thatch?

Thatch occurs naturally and is a normal part of the environment in which grass grows. Excessive thatch, however, is caused when organic matter is created at a rate greater than the rate at which it can decay. The single biggest cause of excessive thatch buildup is overuse of fertilizers. The nitrogen in fertilizers may give you a deep green lawn, but more is not better. Overfertilizing increases growth of the stolons and rhizomes that contribute to thatch. Conduct a soil test and apply fertilizer at the rate recommended.

Cutting the grass improperly also contributes to thatch. When you mow, cut off no more than the top third of the leaf. If the desired height of your grass is 2 inches, cut it when it reaches 3 inches. Leave the clippings on the lawn

as a natural fertilizer. Unless you're cutting off more than you should, the grass won't contribute to thatch.

If you have a thatch problem, you can expect to power rake or aerate once a year for a couple of years until you get it under control. Once you have, however, proper watering, fertilizing, and mowing will control the problem without power raking.

When to remove thatch

Though beneficial in the long run, power raking is hard on the grass in the short run. Plan to dethatch during the lawn's most active period of growth, leaving enough time to recover before hot, cold, or dry spells. The grass will need about 30 days of active growth afterward so it recovers quickly without developing disease. Because the growth cycle of cool-season (northern) grasses is different from that of warm-season (southern) grasses, the time to dethatch varies depending on the type of grass in your lawn.

Power rake cool-season grasses in spring before the grass turns green or in early fall. Dethatch no later than 30 days before the first frost is expected. Because power raking results in a thin lawn for a few weeks, doing it in fall minimizes weed growth because weed seeds don't germinate in cool weather. Do not power rake cool season grasses in summer when grass is stressed by heat or drought.

Dethatch warm-season grasses in early or midsummer. Wait until warm-season grasses have been green for at least two to three weeks before power raking. Do not power rake warm-season grasses in the fall because it leaves them weak for the winter.

Power raking thatch

PROJECT DETAILS

SKILLS: Examining grass for thatch, operating a power rake
PROJECT: Removing thatch with a power rake

TIME TO COMPLETE

The time involved will depend on the size of the lawn.

STUFF YOU'LL NEED

TOOLS: Shovel, power rake, wheelbarrow, leaf rake
MATERIALS: Fertilizer

▶ Because it's a labor-intensive job that's hard on the lawn, resolve to mow, water, and fertilize correctly to avoid having to power rake again.

Make sure your lawn needs to be dethatched before you start work. Power raking is labor intensive and hard on the lawn. Power raking unnecessarily or doing it on an automatic, yearly schedule can actually do more harm than good.

To evaluate whether thatch is a problem in your lawn, cut out a section of turf and look at it edgewise to see how much thatch you have. Dethatch only if there's more than a ½-inch buildup.

If your lawn has a thatch problem, you'll probably have to power rake for a couple of years in order to bring it under control. Once you start mowing and fertilizing properly, however, the buildup usually stops, and the need for power raking soon stops as well.

When you go to the rental store for a dethatcher, you might be given a choice between a power rake and a vertical mower. A power rake has flexible or spring-loaded tines that comb through the thatch and flex around rocks. The blades of a vertical mower are rigid, which means

rocks can break, jam, or dull the tines. Since the average yard is likely to have a few rocks in it, a power rake is your best choice.

There is also a third option. Long before the advent of power rakes, there were dethatching rakes that operated on muscle power. They still make them, and most stores carry them. Unlike the power rake, which resembles a lawn mower, hand-operated dethatching rakes—or cavex rakes—look pretty much like what they are—rakes. They're the same size and shape, with the difference being that instead of teeth, these rakes have thin crescent-shaped tines. The point of the crescent cuts through the thatch, and the rest of the tine pulls it up as you rake.

Since even a regular-sized yard generates a lot of thatch, be prepared for what you're getting into if you opt to dethatch by hand. You *may* be able to dethatch it without resorting to a power mower. Know how thick the thatch is, measure your yard, and talk to a garden store associate before you make your final decision.

1

CHECK FOR THATCH

Cut a wedge from an inconspicuous area of the lawn and look at its edge. Measure the organic debris that has built up between the green part of the leaf and the soil. Test several areas to get an overall picture of the problem.

2

POWER RAKE

Before power raking, mow the lawn, cutting the grass 1 to 1½ inches tall. Run the power rake over the lawn immediately afterward, travelling back and forth in adjacent rows. The tines on the rake will pull up the thatch and leave it on the lawn. Power rake the entire lawn in one direction, then do it again, traveling perpendicular to the first pass.

3

RAKE UP THE DEBRIS

Power raking pulls up a tremendous amount of thatch. Immediately rake it off the lawn so that it doesn't smother the grass. Pile it up somewhere out of the way and let it break down into compost that you can use to fertilize your garden or to topdress the lawn. Water the lawn after dethatching to keep it from dehydrating.

4

FERTILIZER

About a week after power raking, fertilize lightly to help the lawn recover. For warm-season grasses and cool-season grasses power raked in fall, apply the fertilizer at a rate of ¾ to 1 pound of nitrogen per 1,000 square feet. For cool-season grasses that you power rake in spring, apply ½ pound of nitrogen per 1,000 square feet along with a preemergence herbicide to control crabgrass.

Weeds

Weeds are simply plants out of place, according to conventional wisdom. In the case of lawns, this means they are a different species. They look different from the lawn, even if the weed itself is a grass. Not only are weeds unsightly, but they compete with lawns for nutrients and space, crowding out spotty, unhealthy, or drought-stressed lawns.

Weeds continually find their way into lawns; their seeds are dropped on your lawn by birds, blown in on the breeze, or tracked in on the shoes of your visitors. Or their rhizomes and stolons creep into your lawn from neighboring areas. Because of nature's abundance, you may never completely rid your lawn of weeds, but the good news is that by keeping your lawn healthy, it will vigorously crowd out weeds with little help from you.

Chapter 6 highlights

Controlling weeds

▶ Spraying an herbicide is sometimes the easiest way to get weeds under control, especially when they have taken over your lawn or are perennial grasses. However, the best way to control weeds is to keep your lawn healthy so it has no thin spots in which the weeds can grow.

🅢 BUYER'S GUIDE

REMOVING TAPROOTS

Deep-rooted weeds like dandelions are tough to pull. A couple of simple hand tools, available at garden centers and home centers, are designed to pry out stubborn taproots. An asparagus knife has a sturdy, 14-inch shank with a forked blade on the business end. To use it, push it deep into the soil and lever out the root. A dandelion digger is a 3-foot-long tool similar to the asparagus knife, but its long, tang-and-ferule handle allows weeding while standing or sitting. Even these tools may leave root fragments behind to resprout so plan to weed frequently.

S o how do you grow a weed-free lawn? It's as simple as keeping your lawn healthy. Healthy lawns have few holes—or thin spots—where weeds find an opportunity to move in. Set up a regular routine for watering, fertilizing, and mowing tailored to the grass in your lawn. Avoid compacting the soil and prevent thatch from accumulating.

Time your fertilizer applications so that you feed only your lawn and not the weeds. Cool-season grasses, which grow vigorously in spring and fall and go dormant in the heat of summer, are often plagued with warm-season weeds such as crabgrass and foxtail. By fertilizing in spring and fall, you feed the grass, not the weeds.

Water deeply and infrequently. Not only does this encourage the grass roots to grow deeply, but it also allows the soil surface to dry out. The dry conditions mean that weed seeds on the soil's surface are less likely to sprout.

By keeping your lawn thick and healthy, you'll see few weeds in your lawn. With such small numbers, you can pull or dig them up while they are small. (Those that don't regenerate from root fragments or from runners can be pulled even when mature.)

If you attempt to pull weeds with taproots, such as dandelion, or those that reproduce from runners, such as quackgrass, be patient and watchful. Look for the weeds to resprout and grub out the sprouts as many times as it takes to get them all.

⊘ SAFETY ALERT

HANDLING HERBICIDES

Take time to read herbicide label instructions carefully and follow them to the letter. The following safety guidelines are universal:

■ Spray herbicides on a calm day to avoid drifting spray, which can kill desirable plants.

■ Apply in dry weather when the temperature is between 65°F (18°C) and 85°F (29°C).

■ Keep children and pets away from treated areas for as long as labels recommend.

■ Wear protective clothing as recommended on the label: rubber gloves and shoes, hat, a mask or respirator, safety glasses, long sleeves, and trousers.

■ Use a dedicated set of clothes for applying herbicides; wash them separately.

■ Do not eat, drink, or touch your face while applying herbicides or other pesticides; shower and shampoo afterward, and wash your clothing before wearing it again.

Clues from weeds

Because many weeds are particular about their growing conditions, identifying a weed can help you identify what's going on in your lawn. Here are some common weeds and the problems they reveal.

WEED	INDICATES
Bentgrass, dandelion, plantain	Acid soil
Chickweed, goosegrass, knotweed, prostrate spurge	Compacted soil
Black medic, plantain	Dry and infertile soil
Dandelion	Heavy clay
Annual bluegrass, bentgrass, crabgrass, purslane	Excessively fertile soil
White clover	Moist, infertile soil
Annual bluegrass, nimblewill	Moist shade
Annual bluegrass, bentgrass, chickweed, crabgrass, goosegrass, ground ivy, yellow nutsedge, plantain	Poorly drained soil
Annual bluegrass, chickweed, ground ivy, nimblewill	Shade

SAFETY ALERT

PESTICIDE HOTLINE

The National Pesticide Information Center (NPIC) is a pesticide information service funded by the Environmental Protection Agency (EPA) for consumers. The toll-free telephone help line is 800/858-7378. You can call daily from 8:30 a.m. to 6:30 p.m. (Central Time), or go to the center's website at npic.orst.edu to obtain comprehensive information on specific herbicides, insecticides, and fungicides; their lasting effects and environmental impact; toxicological and medical information; as well as proper application and disposal procedures.

▶ The prongs of an asparagus knife easily slip under the crown of weeds such as broadleaf plantain. Once in place, pull down on the handle and the weed pops out. Broadleaf plantain has a dense fibrous root system that is hard to pull without the help of the knife.

GOOD IDEA

CONTROL WEEDS BY MOWING

Here are three mowing tricks to help keep your lawn weed free.

■ Aim your mower's chute away from newly seeded lawn areas to keep from peppering them with weed seeds.

■ Bag and dispose of clippings when weeds are in flower and for a few weeks afterward to avoid spreading weed seeds across the lawn.

■ Take a few minutes to clean the underside of your mower after mowing the lawn to ensure that weed seeds haven't become caught in the debris. This will avoid spreading them across the lawn the next time you mow.

■ Set your mower ½ inch higher than the recommended height for your grass to maintain a thick, tall lawn that will shade out weeds.

6

WEEDS

BUYER'S GUIDE

HITCHHIKER WEEDS

Many weeds sneak into your yard in container plants from the garden center. Once in your garden or shrub bed, they quickly move into the lawn. Keep a sharp eye out for weeds when you go plant shopping. When you are ready to put your new plants in the ground, carefully separate the weeds from the plant's roots. If a weed has started going to seed, you want to do this before carrying the plant over to its new bed.

Using herbicides

▲ The first step in identifying weeds is to look at their leaves. Wide-leafed plants such as this plantain are broadleaf weeds.

When weeds get out of hand, the easiest way to regain control is with herbicides. Preemergents prevent weed seeds from germinating or growing. Postemergents kill weeds that have already sprouted. To know which to use, it helps to know a little about how weeds grow.

Grassy vs. broadleaf weeds

Weeds fall into two large categories: grassy (or narrowleaf) and broadleaf. As their name suggests, grassy weeds such as wild onions and crabgrass have narrow leaves with veins parallel to the edges of the leaf. Annual grassy weeds live, go to seed, and die in a single season. Perennial grassy weeds survive for more than a year and may reproduce by roots, runners, or crown division, as well as by seeds.

Broadleaf weeds have variously shaped leaves with veins in netlike patterns. Like grassy weeds, broadleaf weeds can be annual or perennial. They may have fibrous roots or deep taproots. Grassy weeds generally only have fibrous roots.

Both broadleaf and grassy weeds can be further classified as cool-season and warm-season weeds. Cool-season weeds grow actively during spring and fall and have a dormant period during summer's heat. Some of these are called winter annuals because their seeds germinate in late summer or early fall. The plants then

▲ Narrow leaf weeds, such as foxtail, are called grassy weeds. The width of the leaf also indicates which herbicides will control it.

overwinter, grow for a month or more in spring, then set seed and die.

Warm-season weeds grow vigorously in the heat of summer, and rest during spring and fall. Seeds of annual warm-season weeds may start to germinate in spring and continue to germinate through summer.

When to control weeds

Treating weeds at the right time is crucial—some should be treated when they are actively growing, others when they are dormant, still others before they germinate. Applications may take place as late as May in cool climates and as early as January in warm ones. Check the "chemical control" entries in the pages that follow for advice on the best times to apply herbicide.

These days the odds are in your favor when it comes to fighting weeds. You not only have an arsenal of effective herbicide options from which to choose, but also have inherited a legacy of organic lawn-care techniques that are proven successful and environmentally friendly.

Preemergence herbicides

Herbicides provide convenient and effective weed control, and certain herbicides are designed to kill weeds at their most vulnerable growth stages. Preemergence herbicides prevent seeds from sprouting or kill them as they sprout. They're best applied before weed seeds germinate. In the case of crabgrass, you want to apply them when soil temperatures are around 55°F (13°C), which is often around the time that forsythia finishes blooming. In the case of winter annual weeds, you need to apply the herbicide in late summer to early fall to prevent germination.

Water the lawn after applying preemergence herbicides. This carries the herbicide down into the soil and creates a layer that stops the weed seedlings from growing. Most preemergents are derived from chemicals, but there is a relatively new one available to home gardeners that is derived from corn gluten, which is a by-product of milling, once considered a waste material.

Only one preemergent—siduron—allows you to seed a lawn after application. If applying any other preemergence herbicide, wait at least two months—four is even better—to seed or sod a new lawn. Because preemergence herbicides linger in the soil, they can keep grass seed from

▲ Some weed killers, such as Roundup, are nonselective, killing any plant you apply them to. Others are selective, targeting specific types of plants. Weed-B-Gon, for example, targets broadleaf weeds. You can spray it on the lawn to kill broadleaf weeds without fear of killing the grass.

sprouting and inhibit sod rooting. Also do not power rake to remove thatch or aerate after applying a preemergent. Doing so disrupts the herbicide layer, reducing its effectiveness.

Postemergence herbicides

Postemergence herbicides target weeds while they are actively growing. There are two types: nonselective and selective.

Nonselective herbicides, such as those containing the active ingredient glyphosate, kill any plant they're applied to. If you're getting ready to replace your lawn and need to kill all the grass and weeds beforehand, apply a nonselective herbicide. Otherwise, use nonselective herbicides sparingly. They'll kill your lawn as well as the weed. Apply nonselective herbicides precisely to avoid creating larger-than-necessary bare spots in the lawn, which will be susceptible to invasion by even more weeds.

Selective herbicides target specific types of plants. For example, they'll kill broadleaf weeds without damaging surrounding grass. When using this type of herbicide, take care to protect shrubs and garden areas. Spray on a calm day and adjust the nozzle to spray coarse droplets. Spread granules on a cool day when herbicides such as 2,4-D are unlikely to vaporize. Even a little bit of drift or vapor can damage desirable broadleaf plants as well as the undesirable ones. It may not kill the plants but they will exhibit symptoms ranging from twisted and distorted growth to brown spots.

Spot-treating weeds

Perennial grassy weeds in the middle of healthy turf can be hard to treat without killing the surrounding lawn. You have a couple of options. One is to spray nonselective herbicide and plan on reseeding or patching the spots.

You could also "paint" the weed with the herbicide, using a paint brush or a foam applicator made for the purpose.

Some ready-to-use herbicides have spot applicators that look much like the nozzles on other spray bottles, but have a narrower, more focused pattern. Read the label carefully to make sure the gun is a spot sprayer, not a regular broadcast sprayer.

When spot-treating broadleaf weeds in the lawn, you'll want to protect your garden plants from the spray. Some ready-to-use products spray a foam that keeps the chemical from drifting and makes it easy to see where you've been.

No matter what you use, spray on a calm day, so that the wind doesn't scatter the spray. If necessary, shield nearby plants with a plastic tarp or a large sheet of cardboard. Always identify the weed you're trying to control and make sure the herbicide is effective against it.

Apply postemergents during dry weather and do not irrigate for 48 hours afterward to prevent the herbicide from washing off the weeds.

Other classifications

Systemic herbicides move into and travel throughout a plant, killing all of its parts. As a result, they may be somewhat slow acting. Because systemics affect the entire plant, they are often used to control perennial weeds.

Contact herbicides kill only the part of the plant they touch. While they work more quickly, the entire plant must be sprayed for maximum effectiveness. Even so, because they don't kill the roots, it's possible for a weed to regenerate new stems and leaves. Contact herbicides are often used on annual weeds, because they kill quickly,

and because annual plants won't come back the next year.

Finally, herbicides are available in liquid or granular formulations. Neither formulation has an advantage over the other. Some materials are available only in liquid form; some can be bought in either form. The formulation does affect the type of application equipment you'll need.

Choosing and applying herbicides

Before buying an herbicide, read the label. Make sure that the weed you are trying to eliminate is listed. Otherwise, you could be wasting your time using a product that may not work. Make sure the type of grass in your lawn is on the label as well. Some herbicides can damage certain grasses. For example, 2,4-D will damage St. Augustinegrass.

CLOSER LOOK

WHAT TO DO WHEN THE WEEDS ARE FINALLY GONE?

■ Patch the empty holes they left behind, if there are only a few bare spots (see pages 179–180).

■ Overseed if you have little lawn left (see pages 181–183).

A guide to lawn herbicides

	WHAT IT DOES	WHEN TO APPLY
Broadleaf herbicide	Kills most weeds with larger (not grassy) leaves, including dandelions.	Apply any time weeds are actively growing. Materials are most effective in spring and early summer when newly emerging broadleaf weeds are still small and growing rapidly.
Grass herbicide	Kills grassy plants such as johnsongrass and turfgrass. It doesn't affect most broadleaf plants. It may, however, kill bamboo, iris, flax and lilies. When used in lawns, the treated areas will need to be reseeded or patched.	Apply any time of year that weedy grasses are actively growing.
Nonselective herbicide	Kills all plants it touches. Avoid spraying desirable plants. In lawns, it is best used to kill patches of problem grass.	Apply any time of year that the target plant is actively growing.
Preemergence herbicide	Prevents weed seedlings from emerging from the ground; some prevent germination.	Apply before the weed seeds germinate (for crabgrass and other cool-season annual weeds, that time is in spring about when spent forsythia blossoms start to drop).
Postemergence herbicide	Kills actively growing weeds, mainly broadleaf weeds.	Apply while the weed is young, succulent, and actively growing. Weeds become harder to kill as they mature.
Systemic herbicide	A postemergence herbicide that travels through the plant and kills the weed entirely.	Apply while the weed is young, succulent, and actively growing.
Contact herbicide	A postemergence herbicide that kills the parts of the plant it touches. To kill the plant, make sure you spray the entire plant.	Apply while the weed is young, succulent, and actively growing.

6

WEEDS

Spreading herbicides

When your lawn is peppered with weeds, reach for a piece of equipment that's big enough to let you treat the whole yard in a short time. You probably already have the tool you need in your garage—the humble fertilizer spreader.

You'll need the right kind of herbicide for the job. Fertilizer spreaders take granular herbicides, which may be mixed with fertilizer in all-in-one or weed-and-feed formulas timed to the season. Some are to be spread over the lawn in early spring to prevent weed seeds from germinating while feeding the lawn; others are designed to be spread during the growing season to kill broadleaf weeds and strengthen the lawn to help crowd out future weeds.

Once you've applied the herbicide, wait at least six weeks to overseed an existing lawn or start a new one—otherwise lingering herbicide will undo your hard work. Whichever formulation of granular herbicide you use, the method of application follows the steps below.

Applying herbicide is much like applying fertilizer. See How to Fertilize, page 84 to 85, for more information.

1

WATER THE LAWN
Most preemergent herbicides need to be applied to a wet lawn. Read the label, and if you're using one of them, apply the water called for with a hose, sprinkler system, or lawn sprinkler.

2

TUNE UP THE DROP SPREADER
Put a shallow layer of herbicide into the hopper (about 2 inches deep); roll the spreader over pavement to check its distribution. If any hopper holes are clogged, pour out the granules, pick the debris out of the hole, refill, and test again. When it is working properly, sweep or vacuum up the spilled granules and return them to the bag, then fill the hopper according to label directions.

3

TREAT THE LAWN
Adjust the setting on the spreader to the level called for on the herbicide bag. Push the spreader back and forth across the lawn, overlapping each pass slightly. Refill and repeat as necessary until the entire lawn is treated. If the herbicide you're using calls for watering the lawn after application, water as directed.

Weed encyclopedia

BUYER'S GUIDE

GET BETTER RESULTS WITH STICKING AGENTS

Spreader-stickers, sometimes called sticking agents, are oil- or soap-based additives that make herbicides adhere to plant surfaces better and longer. They're especially useful in controlling weeds with waxy leaves that repel herbicides. Spreader-stickers are included in some herbicides. Check the label. If there's no spreader-sticker, you can buy one separately and add it according to package directions. Or you can make your own: Add 2 tablespoons of liquid dishwashing detergent to 1 gallon of prepared liquid herbicide and spray weeds according to herbicide directions.

The first step in controlling weeds is to identify the enemy. To help you get to know your weeds, this encyclopedia is divided into two sections, Grassy Weeds and Broadleaf Weeds, for quick identification.

The weeds in each section are listed alphabetically by the common names most widely used for the plants, followed by their botanical names for a more precise identification. Each weed is accompanied by a color photograph and description of key features, which will help you identify your lawn weeds.

Once you identify a weed, you can scan the cultural and chemical controls in that entry to quickly learn how to keep it in check. And you'll also learn to grow a healthier lawn, which creates an inhospitable environment for these and many other weeds.

▲ Entries are organized by broadleaf weeds such as dandelion (top), and grassy weeds such as wild garlic (above). Not all grassy weeds are grasses. Wild garlic, for example, belongs to the lily family. The same can be said for broadleaf weeds. Plantain, for example, also belongs to the lily family.

Grassy weeds

Annual bluegrass

(Poa annua)

Annual

Description:
A cool-season annual grass. This weed's prolific seed heads give a lawn an unsightly white cast; the seeds germinate eight days after pollination. Plants die during hot, dry weather, leaving unsightly brown spots in the lawn. Seeds sprout in fall, and the new plants continue growth in spring.

Conditions that promote:
Full sun or partial shade, moist soil, and cool, wet weather. Mowing low encourages its growth. Seeds spread by foot traffic, birds, and cultivation.

When to control:
Early spring through early winter.

Cultural controls:
Hand-pull plants before they go to seed. Overseed bare spots in lawns. Remove grass clippings and hose off mowers and tools to avoid spreading seeds. Mow at 2½ inches or higher, improve drainage in wet areas, and avoid soil compaction.

Chemical controls:
Apply preemergence herbicide in late summer or early fall.

Bahiagrass

(Paspalum notatum)

Perennial
Present year round. May go dormant in winter.

Description:
A turfgrass in some areas, bahiagrass can be an invasive weed. It is characterized by woody-looking rhizomes and stolons. Leaves are difficult to mow because of their high-fiber content.

Conditions that promote:
Acid soil.

When to control:
Apply postemergence herbicides when grass is actively growing. Make a second application six weeks later.

Cultural controls:
None.

Chemical controls:
No herbicides are available to homeowners. Contact a landscape contractor to apply herbicides available to pros.

Barnyardgrass

(Echinochloa crus-galli)

Annual, summer

Description:
A shallow-rooted, warm-season annual grass. Barnyardgrass stems creep along the ground before rising up and becoming an upright grass. In mowed lawns, it remains in a low rosette. The plant has drooping flowerheads. Its seeds begin germinating in late winter and continue throughout summer.

Conditions that promote:
Moist soil and infertile soil.

When to control:
Spring and summer.

Cultural controls:
Pull plants before autumn when they go to seed. Mow high; improve soil fertility and drainage.

Chemical controls:
Apply preemergence herbicide two weeks before the last expected spring frost. Spot-treat during the growing season with nonselective herbicide; repeat at seven-day intervals until weeds die.

Common bermudagrass

(Cynodon dactylon)

Perennial
Present year round. May go dormant in winter.

Description:
Although common bermudagrass is a desirable turf, it is invasive, readily moving into gardens and overtaking other grasses in a lawn. Bermudagrass has smooth leaves with a ring of white hairs where the blade and sheath meet.

Conditions that promote:
Well-watered lawns and full sun.

When to control:
Early to late spring or summer.

Cultural controls:
None.

Chemical controls:
Apply nonselective herbicides in spring when bermudagrass rhizome growth is less than 6 inches long. Reapply before the regrowth reaches 6 inches. Additional applications may be required. Read the herbicide label to make sure you aren't applying it more often than you should.

Make spot applications of nonselective herbicides in late spring or during summer when bermudagrass is rapidly growing. Don't withhold water before applying, but withhold it for two to three days after application. Do not mow for two to three weeks before application.

Crabgrass

(Digitaria spp.)

Smooth crabgrass *(D. sanguinalis)*
Large hairy crabgrass *(D. ischaemum)*

Annual

Description:
A spreading, warm-season annual grass with light green leaves. Seed heads are shaped like a crow's foot. Although nodes on the stems of plants can take root, crabgrass spreads only by seed.

Conditions that promote:
Any bare or thin spot in a lawn; lawns stressed by drought, insects, or disease are especially susceptible.

When to control:
Spring and summer

Cultural controls:
In spring, pull plants before they go to seed. Bag clippings to avoid spreading seeds. Prevent crabgrass by keeping your lawn thick and healthy; water, mow, and fertilize appropriately.

Chemical controls:
In climates with a warm winter, use a preemergence herbicide labeled for crabgrass in mid-January; in cool climates, apply it in March. In summer, use a postemergence herbicide labeled for crabgrass. Apply when plants are still small; the larger plants become, the harder they are to control.

Creeping bentgrass

(Agrostis palustris)

Perennial
Present year round. Grows best in cool temperatures.

Description:
Narrow-bladed grass that forms pale green patches that choke out turf. Spreads by seeds and creeping stolons, which root and form thick thatch. During droughts, it browns and dies. In cool, wet weather, it can develop mold and turn gray.

Conditions that promote:
Open spots in a lawn. Seeds may be present in some lawn seed mixes.

When to control:
Spring to fall.

Cultural controls:
Dig up patches and overseed bare spots. Repeat if clumps grow back. Withhold water to discourage seeding and spreading by runners. Remove clippings to prevent spreading seed. In a severely infested lawn, use a sod cutter to strip the lawn and reseed or sod in August or September. Do not buy lawn seed mixes that contain bentgrass.

Chemical controls:
Spot-treat clumps with postemergence weed killer containing glyphosate. Repeat as needed to kill the clump and then overseed the bare spot. Selective herbicides that kill bentgrass will also kill Kentucky bluegrass, so take care when choosing an herbicide.

Foxtail

(Setaria spp.)

Annual, summer

Description:
A warm-season annual. Foxtails have foliage that looks like crabgrass, but they grow more upright. Their name arises from the long, fluffy flower heads, which produce as many as 34,000 seeds per plant. Seeds sprout from July to late fall, when plants die.

Conditions that promote:
Fertile soil, spotty lawns.

When to control:
Spring to fall.

Cultural controls:
Hand-pull, mow frequently, and dispose of clippings when seeds set. This weed is not usually a problem in healthy lawns because it doesn't stand up to mowing.

Chemical controls:
Spot-treat with a selective or nonselective postemergence herbicide, remove dead foliage, and overseed bare spots. For broad control, apply a preemergence herbicide two weeks before the last expected spring frost.

Goosegrass

(Eleusine indica)

Annual, summer

Description:
Coarse-leaved, annual warm-season grass. Goosegrass forms a silvery mat that radiates outward from a central point. Its flower and seed heads are shaped like a bird's foot. This seed-sown weed germinates in April and May, sets seed from June to September, and dies in late fall.

Conditions that promote:
Compacted soil; sparse, spotty lawns.

When to control:
Spring through summer.

Cultural controls:
Pull or dig up clumps. Overseed to eliminate spots where it can move in. Core aerate to reduce compaction. Prevent goosegrass by mowing, fertilizing, and watering properly to keep your lawn healthy.

Chemical controls:
Apply a preemergence herbicide in spring or early summer. Spot-treat existing clumps with a nonselective herbicide. After 10 days, remove top growth (the roots will be dead) and seed over the spot.

Green kyllinga

(Kyllinga brevifolia)

Perennial
Present spring through fall.

Description:
Long narrow leaves. Flowers, forming from May to October, are globe-like and sit on triangular stems. Spreads rapidly via rhizomes.

Conditions that promote:
Overwatering or poorly drained turf.

When to control:
Apply cultural controls year round. Apply preemergence herbicides in spring and postemergents when kyllinga begins actively growing.

Cultural controls:
Water correctly and solve drainage problems. When kyllinga appears, remove the entire plant, leaves, stems, roots, and rhizomes. Repeat often. Wash plant debris from lawn equipment after using.

Chemical controls:
Apply preemergence herbicides before soil temperatures reach 60°F (16°C) to keep seeds from sprouting. Apply selective postemergents every two weeks as directed.

6

WEEDS

Kikuyugrass

(Pennisetum clandestinum)

Perennial
Present year round. May go dormant in winter.

Description:
A low-growing perennial grass, sometimes used in lawns in the Southwest, but an invasive grass elsewhere, especially in California. Leaves are light green. Stolons form a heavy mat of thatch.

Conditions that promote:
Mowing too short. Seed is spread by lawn mowers and other lawn equipment.

When to control:
Cultural controls year round; preemergents in spring; postemergents when grass is actively growing.

Cultural controls:
Let the lawn grow to the upper edge of its height range to shade out the kikuyugrass. Wash lawn equipment to remove any remnant of the plant that might sprout vegetatively.

Chemical controls:
Apply preemergence herbicides in March to limit seed sprouting. Apply selective postemergents later in the year, to control spreading via stolons. Multiple applications may be necessary.

Nimblewill

(Muhlenbergia schreberi)

Perennial
Goes dormant in cool weather.

Description:
Grassy, mat-forming perennial grass with gray-green leaves that root where they touch soil. Nimblewill sets seed from August to October; seeds sprout the following spring. Plants go dormant early in fall and resume growth in spring.

Conditions that promote:
Moist, fertile, well-drained soil and shade.

When to control:
Early spring to midsummer.

Cultural controls:
Fibrous roots make it easy to pull or dig nimblewill. Remove large patches with a sod cutter and patch with sod. If replacing a lawn, lay sod to smother the seeds. Prevent nimblewill by keeping your lawn thick and healthy.

Chemical controls:
Spot-treat with a postemergence herbicide containing the active ingredient glyphosate or glufosinate. Start when the plants are small and, if necessary, make two treatments 10 days apart. Remove dead growth and sod the empty spot.

Nutsedge

(Cyperus spp.)

Purple nutsedge *(C. rotundus)*
Yellow nutsedge *(C. esculentus)*

Perennial

Description:
A perennial, warm-season sedge. Nutsedge has stiff, upright leaves that are grasslike but triangular in cross section. It produces hundreds of thousands of seeds and sprouts from tubers that develop on the shallow roots and on underground rhizomes. The tubers make nutsedge particularly insidious because they remain in the soil when you pull or dig up the clumps.

Conditions that promote:
Wet soil.

When to control:
Late spring or early summer.

Cultural controls:
Core aerate to improve drainage. Withhold water when nutsedge is actively growing in early spring and summer. Shade or smother patches with black plastic sheeting for six weeks or until nutsedge dies, then remove dead growth and overseed. Or dig out patches to a depth of 1 foot. Repeat every two weeks until nutsedge is dead, fill holes, and overseed. Prevent by proper mowing, fertilizing, and watering to keep your lawn healthy.

Chemical controls:
For large areas, apply a nonselective herbicide. It is important to follow product instructions and apply at 10- to 14-day intervals to kill this tenacious weed; then remove dead growth and overseed or sod spots.

6

WEEDS

Orchardgrass
(Dactylis glomerata)

Perennial
Present year round. Prefers cool temperatures.

Description:
A cool-season perennial bunchgrass. Because it grows faster than the turf, the wide, pale green leaves of orchardgrass are especially unsightly.

Conditions that promote:
Moist, fertile soil and shade, but it also tolerates full sun. It is sometimes brought into a lawn through cheap lawn seed, especially fescue and Kentucky bluegrass mixes.

When to control:
Spring through fall.

Cultural controls:
Dig up clumps, making sure to remove the deep roots, and replace the soil. Overseed the area or patch it with sod. Prevent orchardgrass by keeping your lawn thick and healthy. When starting a lawn, check the seed label and make sure the package contains no (0 percent) "other crop seed."

Chemical controls:
Orchardgrass does not spread, making it easy to isolate. Spot-treat with a nonselective herbicide containing glyphosate. Remove the dead weed and overseed or patch with sod.

Quackgrass
(Agropyron repens)

Perennial
Present year round. Prefers cool temperatures.

Description:
Fast-growing, grassy weed that spreads by seeds and rhizomes. Quackgrass goes dormant in fall and resprouts in spring. Plants have blue-green leaves that are rough on the upper surface and flower heads resembling those of wheat.

Conditions that promote:
All types of soil; spreads rapidly in fertile soil.

When to control:
Spring through fall.

Cultural controls:
Dig up clumps, removing all rhizomes; even the smallest piece of quackgrass left in the ground can grow into a new plant. Patch bare areas with sod; this aggressive weed will overtake seedling grass. If large areas of your lawn are infested with quackgrass, set your mower at the lowest setting and mow routinely until the scalped quackgrass finally dies. Prevent by proper mowing, fertilizing, and watering to keep your lawn healthy.

Chemical controls:
Kill large infested areas with a postemergence herbicide containing the active ingredient glyphosate. For small areas, spot-treat with glyphosate. Remove the dead grass and patch the area with sod.

Tall Fescue
(Festuca arundinacea)

Perennial
Present year round. May go dormant in winter.

Description:
Tall fescue makes an excellent turf, but it stands out when it grows among fine-textured turfgrasses. Pasture-type tall fescues are bunchgrasses and are unsightly in lawns.

Conditions that promote:
Tall fescue is often found in cheap seed mixtures.

When to control:
Spring.

Cultural controls:
Dig 3 to 4 inches into soil around the edge of the grass clump and remove. Fill the hole and reseed immediately.

Chemical controls:
Spray with nonselective herbicide in spring, before the surrounding grass begins to grow. Professionals have access to a selective postemergent herbicide designed for tall fescue.

6

WEEDS

Broadleaf weeds

Torpedo grass
(Panicum repens)

Perennial

Description:
A spreading, gray-green grass named for its pointed rhizome tips. Torpedo grass has spiky yellow flowers. It forms dense colonies with roots extending 2 feet deep into the soil, making this weed very hard to remove by digging.

Conditions that promote:
Damp areas and sandy soil.

When to control:
Spring.

Cultural controls:
To remove individual plants, dig deeply to remove the entire root; overseed the empty spot. Cover large patches with black plastic sheeting for one year, then seed or lay sod for a new lawn. Reduce regular lawn irrigation; improve drainage in wet areas. Prevent by proper mowing, fertilizing, and watering to keep your lawn healthy.

Chemical controls:
Spot-treat with a nonselective postemergence herbicide containing either glyphosate or diquat as the active ingredient. Repeat as needed until the clump dies, then overseed or lay sod to fill the spot. If your lawn is overtaken with torpedo grass, kill the entire lawn and seed or sod a new lawn.

Wild garlic *(Allium vineale)*
Wild onion *(A. canadense)*

Perennial
Present spring through fall.

Description:
Although they look similar, the narrow leaves of wild garlic are hollow and smell garlicky, while those of wild onion are solid and smell like onion. These persistent weeds sprout from underground bulbs, bulblets on leaf tips that drop to the ground, and from seeds.

Conditions that promote:
Thin, poorly managed lawns.

When to control:
Spring to fall.

Cultural controls:
Dig clumps repeatedly until you remove all bulbs. Mow often to keep them from going to seed. Prevent by proper mowing, fertilizing, and watering to keep your lawn healthy.

Chemical controls:
A spreader-sticker will help the herbicide adhere to the waxy leaves. Add a spreader-sticker to your tank or buy a premixed product. Bruise leaves before spraying to increase absorption. Spot-treat in November and again in March with a postemergence broadleaf herbicide. Spot-treat in winter with a nonselective herbicide containing the active ingredient glyphosate and overseed when weeds are dead.

Black medic
(Medicago lupulina)

Annual, summer

Description:
A yellow-flowered, creeping plant with a shallow taproot and leaves similar to those of clover. Black medic spreads by seed in July and August. It sometimes survives winter and grows as a biennial or perennial.

Conditions that promote:
Infertile or compacted soil.

When to control:
Summer and fall.

Cultural controls:
Hand-pull or dig individual plants. Mow high and water regularly. In fall, aerate the soil (use a garden fork in small areas, a core aerator when aerating an entire lawn). Overseed to fill thin spots and fertilize.

Chemical controls:
Spot-treat with a postemergence herbicide containing the active ingredient glyphosate, remove dead foliage, and overseed the empty spots. Or in late May or early June, treat your entire lawn with a postemergence broadleaf herbicide. Reapply, according to product label, to kill all black medic.

Buttonweed

(Diodia spp.)

Common buttonweed *(D. teres)*
Virginia buttonweed *(D. virginiana)*

Annual, perennial, warm season

Description:
Creeping plants with wiry stems, narrow leaves, and small, white, four-petaled flowers. Common buttonweed, which has more upright stems, is an annual; Virginia buttonweed is a perennial, rooting where stem nodes touch the ground.

Conditions that promote:
Moist and wet areas.

When to control:
Spring and summer.

Cultural controls:
Dig up all underground roots and stem pieces. Reduce irrigation to discourage this moisture-lover. Prevent by proper mowing, fertilizing, and watering to keep your lawn healthy.

Chemical controls:
Apply a postemergence, broadleaf herbicide labeled for buttonweed in spring and again in summer. Follow label directions—it will take several applications to kill this weed.

Chickweed

(Stellaria spp.)

Common chickweed *(S. media)*
Mouse-ear chickweed *(Cerastium fontanum vulgare)*

Annual, perennial, cool season

Description:
Cool-season broadleaf weeds. Common chickweed is a winter annual; mouse-ear chickweed is a perennial. Both are ground-hugging plants with small leaves and tiny, star-shape white flowers. Mouse-ear chickweed has hairy leaves. The hairs prevent herbicide from touching the leaf and make this weed hard to control. Both chickweeds have succulent, threadlike stems that root where they touch soil. Plants reproduce from seed. Chickweeds grows rapidly in spring and fall and go dormant in hot weather.

Conditions that promote:
Open spots in lawns; both thrive in shady, cool, and moist conditions.

When to control:
Spring through fall.

Cultural controls:
Hand-pull before seeds set. Prevent by mowing, fertilizing, and watering properly.

Chemical controls:
Spot-treat with a postemergent containing glyphosate while weeds are growing. Apply a preemergent in early spring or early fall for common chickweed. Use a selective postemergence broadleaf herbicide labeled for mouse-ear chickweed and add a spreader-sticker to help it adhere to the hairy leaves.

Cinquefoil

(Potentilla spp.)

Annual or perennial

Description:
Creeping broadleaf plants. Cinquefoils have leaves similar to those of strawberry plants, but their flowers are yellow instead of white. There are several species; they may be annuals, biennials, or short-lived perennials. Most species spread by seed, but oldfield cinquefoil *(P. simplex)* roots where the nodes on its stems touch soil.

Conditions that promote:
Prospers in poor soil and is drought tolerant. Cinquefoil hitchhikes into lawns in potted nursery plants and contaminated grass seed mixes.

When to control:
Spring through fall.

Cultural controls:
Hand-pull before plants go to seed. Patch empty spots in the lawn to prevent cinquefoil from moving into them. Dispose of lawn clippings when the plants are in bloom or are setting seed to avoid spreading the seeds. Prevent by proper mowing, fertilizing, and watering to keep your lawn healthy.

Chemical controls:
Spot-treat with a nonselective postemergence herbicide containing glyphosate. Wait until the plant is dead before removing it, then seed or sod the empty spot. Apply a selective broadleaf herbicide in fall to treat large areas.

6

WEEDS

Common mallow

(Malva neglecta)

Annual, winter

Description:
Cool-season broadleaf weed. Common mallow has creeping stems with small, round, scalloped leaves and a deep taproot. Plants bloom from May to October. Their white to lavender flowers are followed by seeds carried in pods that look like tiny wheels of cheese. This weed only reproduces by seed.

Conditions that promote:
Bare ground in newly seeded areas and bare patches in established lawns, where its deep taproot makes it tenacious and drought tolerant.

When to control:
Spring to fall.

Cultural controls:
Uproot taproots. Mow to prevent seed set. Prevent by proper mowing, fertilizing, and watering to keep your lawn healthy.

Chemical controls:
Spot-treat with a nonselective postemergence herbicide containing the active ingredient glyphosate; remove dead foliage and overseed or sod patches. For large areas, apply a selective postemergence broadleaf herbicide labeled for mallow, such as 2,4-D, while plants are seedlings or when they are flowering.

Common purslane

(Portulaca oleracea)

Annual, summer

Description:
A ground-hugging, spreading plant with small, succulent leaves and a taproot with fibrous secondary roots. Small yellow flowers open on sunny days. The plant reproduces from seed dropped in spring.

Conditions that promote:
Full sun. Seeds can live for several years and sprout when soil is cultivated.

When to control:
Spring through fall.

Cultural controls:
Hand-pull and dispose of the weeds to keep them from rooting in the compost pile. Prevent by proper mowing, fertilizing, and watering to keep your lawn healthy.

Chemical controls:
Spot-treat with a selective broadleaf herbicide. Wait a minimum of two weeks to overseed the resulting bare areas.

Corn speedwell

(Veronica arvensis)

Annual, winter

Description:
A ground-hugging, creeping plant with stems that root at the nodes. It has rounded, hairy, toothed leaves, blue flowers, and heart-shape seed capsules.

Conditions that promote:
Shady, cool, moist areas; thin, spotty, and newly seeded lawns.

When to control:
Spring through fall.

Cultural controls:
Thin trees to increase sunlight in shady areas and improve soil drainage in wet spots. Prevent by proper mowing, fertilizing, and watering to keep your lawn healthy.

Chemical controls:
Apply a selective postemergence herbicide while the weed is blooming.

6

WEEDS

Dandelion
(Taraxacum officinale)

Perennial

Description:
Ground-hugging rosettes of jagged leaves, topped with yellow multipetaled flowers followed by fluffy seed heads, which disperse in the breeze. A long taproot that sprouts from broken root fragments makes dandelions difficult to remove.

Conditions that promote:
Full sun, open areas, and spotty lawns.

When to control:
Spring through fall.

Cultural controls:
Dig individual plants using a tool designed to pull the taproot; repeat frequently when the plant returns. Pick flowers to prevent seeds from forming. Responds to mowing by flowering on short stalks that are too low to cut. Instead of mowing low, mow high to shade out the plant. Prevent by proper mowing, fertilizing, and watering to keep your lawn healthy.

Chemical controls:
Spot-treat or treat entire lawns with a selective postemergence broadleaf herbicide in late spring or fall, or both if needed.

Dog fennel
(Eupatorium capillofolium)

Perennial

Description:
A plant with red stems bearing ferny leaves that emit an acrid odor when crushed. Many-branched flower heads sport small, white blooms. Dog fennel spreads by seed; it resprouts from its woody base each spring.

Conditions that promote:
Poorly drained soil.

When to control:
Spring and summer.

Cultural controls:
Use a low mowing height; fertilize and irrigate as recommended for the lawn species to promote a dense, healthy lawn that can crowd out dog fennel.

Chemical controls:
Spot-treat or spray larger areas with a nonselective postemergence herbicide when plants are actively growing and flowering.

Ground ivy
(Glechoma hederacea)

Perennial

Description:
A vining groundcover with scalloped-edged, rounded leaves that have a strong odor when crushed. Ground ivy has tiny blue flowers. It spreads by seeds and stems that root where they contact soil.

Conditions that promote:
Damp, shady locations; plant is also sun-tolerant.

When to control:
Fall.

Cultural controls:
Hand-pull plants repeatedly. Spot-treat with a borax solution (10 ounces borax dissolved in 2½ gallons of warm water). Borax contains the plant nutrient boron, which ground ivy has a lower tolerance for than most turfgrasses. Avoid using it on Kentucky bluegrass, which is sensitive to excess boron. Remove dead foliage and overseed or sod bare spots. Prevent by proper mowing, fertilizing, and watering to keep your lawn healthy.

Chemical controls:
Use postemergence broadleaf herbicides with the active ingredient dicamba and apply twice, 10 days apart, in fall. Remove dead plants and seed or sod to fill empty spots in the lawn.

6

WEEDS

Hawkweed

(Hieracium spp.)

Mouse-ear hawkweed *(H. pilosella)*
Orange hawkweed *(H. aurantiacum)*
Yellow hawkweed *(H. caespitosum)*

Perennial

Description:
A rosette-shaped clump with yellow or deep orange dandelion-type flowers. Plants spread by rooting stolons and seed.

Conditions that promote:
Slightly acid soil; full sun to part shade; and shallow, sandy and rocky soil.

When to control:
Spring through fall.

Cultural controls:
Hand-pull plants before they go to seed. Collect and dispose of lawn clippings while hawkweed is forming seed (from July to September) to avoid spreading it around. Prevent by proper mowing, fertilizing, and watering to keep your lawn healthy. Increase soil acidity by applying sulfur according to directions.

Chemical controls:
Spot-treat with a nonselective postemergence herbicide containing glyphosate. Treat lawn with a selective broadleaf herbicide in spring and, if needed, again in fall; wait to mow until treated weeds turn brown.

Heal all

(Prunella vulgaris)

Perennial

Description:
A ground-hugging plant with small, oval, puckered leaves on square stems. Heal all can hide in a lawn until it sends stalks of purple flowers above the grass. It spreads by seeds, and stems root where they touch soil.

Conditions that promote:
Moist, heavy soil; shade but tolerates sun.

When to control:
Spring through fall.

Cultural controls:
Hand-pull plants and fill bare spots with seed or sod. Prevent by proper mowing, fertilizing, and watering to keep your lawn healthy.

Chemical controls:
Spot-treat with a nonselective herbicide containing the active ingredient glyphosate. Remove dead growth and overseed or sod bare spots. To treat large areas, apply a postemergence broadleaf herbicide labeled for use on heal all in autumn.

Henbit

(Lamium amplexicaule)

Annual, winter

Description:
A ground-hugging plant with round leaves that are scalloped along the edge. Its square, purple-tinged stems hug the ground and root at their nodes. Purple flowers appear in spring; plants spread by seed.

Conditions that promote:
Cool, moist, shady conditions; invades newly seeded lawns or bare spots and thin turf in established ones.

When to control:
Spring through fall.

Cultural controls:
Hand-pull individual plants and overseed resulting bare spots. Improve drainage in wet areas, thin trees to let in light, and sow shade-tolerant grass seed under trees. Prevent by proper mowing, fertilizing, and watering to keep your lawn healthy.

Chemical controls:
Apply a selective postemergence broadleaf herbicide in spring when plants are flowering or in fall. Follow label directions carefully when applying to newly seeded areas to avoid harming new grass.

Mock Strawberry
(Duchesnea indica)

Perennial
Present spring through fall.

Description:
A three-leafed plant with yellow flowers that produce small strawberries.

Conditions that promote:
Poorly maintained but well-drained soil.

When to control:
During active growth.

Cultural controls:
Dig up to remove. Hard to control once established, but proper mowing, fertilizing, and watering help prevent.

Chemical controls:
Apply a postemergent broadleaf herbicide anytime plants are actively growing.

Plantain
(Plantago spp.)

Blackseed plantain *(P. rugelii)*
Buckthorn plantain *(P. aristata)*
Common plantain *(P. major)*
Narrowleaf plantain *(P. lanceolata)*

Perennial

Description:
Low rosettes of leaves from which flower spikes emerge on 4- to 10-inch-long wiry stalks. The leaves may be long and narrow or short and wide. Raised veins run parallel to the edges of the leaves. Plantain reproduces by seed from spring through fall.

Conditions that promote:
Bare spots, but is widely adapted.

When to control:
Spring through fall.

Cultural controls:
With its shallow, fibrous roots, plantain is easy to pull. Mow often to keep it from going to seed. Prevent plantain by proper mowing, fertilizing, and watering to keep your lawn healthy.

Chemical controls:
Spot-treat with a postemergence broadleaf herbicide. Treat large stands in spring or fall with a weed-and-feed formula labeled for plantain. Remove dead foliage and overseed bare spots.

Prostrate knotweed
(Polygonum aviculare)

Annual, summer

Description:
A creeping broadleaf weed. This ground-hugging plant can grow to 3 feet in diameter and spreads by seed throughout the growing season. It has a thin taproot.

Conditions that promote:
Full sun and compacted soil; thrives in high-traffic areas and newly seeded lawns.

When to control:
Fall.

Cultural controls:
Pull by hand. In August or September, aerate small areas of soil with a garden fork; use a core aerator for larger lawn areas, and overseed.

Chemical controls:
Apply a postemergence broadleaf herbicide in spring. Follow label directions carefully; repeat applications may be necessary.

6

WEEDS

Spurges
(Chamaesyce spp.)

Prostrate spurge *(Chamaesyce maculata)*
Spotted spurge *(C. nutans)*

Annual, summer

Description:
Spotted spurge, a lawn threat in the West, is a low, mat-forming weed with tiny pink flowers and a red spot on each leaf. Its taproot extends 2 feet deep. Prostrate spurge is similar but lacks the red spot. These weeds spread by seed and can choke out lawns, but seed that's buried more than ½ inch will not germinate. Prevention is key.

Conditions that promote:
Spotty, unhealthy lawns with open areas and full sun.

When to control:
Spring through fall.

Cultural controls:
Uproot plants before they go to seed. Renovate the area by covering infested areas with 1 inch of soil and then reseeding. Or cover it with black plastic for one year, then reseed. Prevent by proper mowing, fertilizing, and watering to keep your lawn healthy.

Chemical controls:
Apply preemergence herbicide in late winter. During the growing season, apply a postemergence contact herbicide containing glufosinate or glyphosate according to label directions; follow label instructions, as multiple treatments may be needed. Remove dead foliage and overseed or sod spots.

White clover
(Trifolium repens)

Perennial

Description:
An aggressive weed with characteristic three-part, shamrock-shaped leaves. Tight balls of white flowers bloom all summer and attract bees. Plants spread by underground stolons, rooting stems, and seed. White clover goes dormant during drought, leaving unsightly bare spots, but it emerges from dormancy when watering resumes or in spring.

Conditions that promote:
Poorly managed, infertile lawns.

When to control:
Fall.

Cultural controls:
Mow, fertilize, and water as recommended for the grass species to promote a dense, healthy lawn that can crowd out white clover.

Chemical controls:
Apply a postemergence broadleaf herbicide labeled for white clover in fall.

Yellow rocket
(Barbarea vulgaris)

Annual, winter

Description:
A plant with shiny green leaves that grow in a ground-hugging rosette until it blooms. If left unmowed, plants will send up 3-foot-tall flower stalks. The four-petaled yellow blooms appear from May to August. Yellow rocket has a taproot that is surrounded by fibrous roots. It sometimes grows as a biennial.

Conditions that promote:
Fertile, friable soil.

When to control:
Spring, fall.

Cultural controls:
Dig out taproots. Mow low and often in late spring when yellow rocket is in bloom to prevent seeding.

Chemical controls:
Use a selective postemergence herbicide in fall when plants are actively growing.

6

WEEDS

Yellow woodsorrel

(Oxalis stricta)

Perennial

Description:
A weed whose leaves, like those of white clover, have three parts; however, its leaves often fold downward. Small, bright yellow flowers bloom from midsummer to fall. Plants spread by seed.

Conditions that promote:
Fertile soil, shade.

When to control:
Spring to fall.

Cultural controls:
Hand-pull plants before they go to seed. Prevent by proper mowing, fertilizing, and watering to keep your lawn healthy.

Chemical controls:
Apply a postemergence herbicide containing the active ingredient 2,4-D when plants go dormant in fall.

Violets

(Viola papilionacea)

Perennial
Present in spring and summer

Description:
Small blue to white flowers, heart-shaped leaves.

Conditions that promote:
Wild violets will grow almost anywhere. They do especially well in shade, moist soil, and cool temperatures.

When to control:
In fall, when roots are storing energy for the winter.

Cultural controls:
Dig to remove.

Chemical controls:
Apply broadleaf herbicide in fall. An additional application in spring is helpful, but you are unlikely to eliminate violets completely.

GOOD IDEA

ATTACK TAPROOTS IN THE SPRING

Pull taprooted weeds, such as dandelions, and perennial grassy weeds as soon as they green up in early spring. The ground is soft and moist at this time, and the growth is weak, giving you a better shot at getting all of the roots out of the soil. By late spring weeds will have an extensive root system, which will give you a much harder time.

WORK SMARTER

DRY OUT WEEDS BEFORE COMPOSTING

Weeds can actually survive being uprooted long enough to take root or sow seed wherever you dispose of them. To keep from pulling the same weeds twice, spread your weeds on hot pavement or a sheet of black plastic until they are dried and brown before composting. If you pull weeds that are flowering or have seed pods, skip composting altogether and trash them to keep from spreading the seeds.

6

WEEDS

Soil basics

The health of your lawn depends on the soil in which it is growing. Topsoil is a mixture of clay, sand, and silt, laced with a brew of organic matter, bacteria, and fungi, most of which are beneficial to plant life and not harmful. How rich in organic matter, how airy, and how well drained the topsoil is determine how well your grass roots can grow and absorb nutrients. Ideally the layer of topsoil should be as deep as the roots can grow, which is about 8 inches in most cases.

Starting a new lawn gives you the opportunity to remake the topsoil. But even if you have an existing lawn and no plans to start anew, you can improve the growing conditions for your lawn's roots.

Chapter 7 highlights

Soil basics

Soil is actually a blend of minerals, air, water, and organic matter. Most soils are about 45 percent mineral, 25 percent air, 25 percent water, and 5 percent organic matter. The minerals may be clay (tiny particles), sand (large particles), or silt (intermediate size particles).

Loam, the ideal topsoil, is a mix of large and small mineral particles, with about 40 percent of the particles sand, 40 percent silt, and 20 percent clay. Loam is relatively dark colored, damp, and loose. The dark color indicates that organic matter is plentiful in the soil, although still only around 5 percent of the total. Dampness indicates that the soil can hold moisture, a result of the clay and organic matter.

Because loam soil is loose, it has plentiful pore space for water and air to pass through to nourish roots and for roots to grow in. Large particles, such as sand, help loosen the soil. Organic matter helps bind soil particles into larger granules, which also creates porosity.

The sand, silt, and clay content of your yard may not be ideal, but you can help it become more airy and moist, and you can add organic matter to it. First, however, you need to learn the type of soil making up your ground.

▲ Turn the soil over with a shovel to see what it's made of. This soil is a good loamy mixture. Its rich black color indicates that it is high in organic content.

Take a good look at your soil

A laboratory soil test is the best way to find out the exact makeup of your soil, but you can get a quick idea of its composition before sending off a sample. Dig a hole about 12 inches deep. Pay attention when you put the shovel in the ground. If it meets resistance, the soil may be compacted. (Compacted topsoil is an indication that the organic matter content of the soil may be low.) Finish digging the hole, and then look at the layers in the soil from the top down.

■ There should be a layer of decomposing leaves and grass and other organic matter on the top. If not, your soil may not have the organic content it needs.

■ Look below the layer of humus to see how deep the topsoil is. At a minimum, you'll need a 4-inch-thick layer of topsoil. Deeper is better, but the most you'll need is around 8 inches.

■ Also check to see how dark the topsoil is. The darker it is, the richer in organic matter and the more fertile it is. If it is light colored, it is sandy and less fertile.

■ Subsoil, the layer below the topsoil, is pretty much just dirt. The same mixture of clay, sand, and silt is there, but the brew of organic matter and simple life forms is missing. Quite simply, there isn't enough there to support a healthy lawn.

▲ Loamy soil with good organic matter

▲ Shallow layer of clay topsoil with little organic matter

▲ Light-colored sandy soil containing little organic matter

7

SOIL BASICS

Sand, silt, and clay

The composition of your soil has a lot to do with the way the grass in your yard grows. As the components vary, so does the grass. No soil is 100 percent sand, silt, or clay. Instead soil is a mix of all of these particles in varying proportions. You could have a sandy loam or a loamy sand, a sandy clay loam, or a sandy clay. Each individual component influences how water and air move through the soil and the soil's fertility.

■ Clay is fertile but compact.
It is made up of microscopic particles that pack together tightly. For that reason, clay soil is dense, so dense it may stunt the roots of plants growing in it. Clay absorbs water slowly, so rain and irrigation water don't move very deeply into it. If water is applied more quickly than the clay can absorb it, it runs off before it can soak in. What does soak in, the clay holds onto and very often doesn't share with the grass or other plants. If clay soil becomes saturated, it drains slowly. If it dries out, it becomes rock hard.

If your soil is very high in clay, work organic matter into it as explained in "Improving Your Soil," page 152. Organic matter has a larger particle size that helps to break up the soil's tight structure. As it decomposes, organic matter creates a substance that glues clay particles into larger clumps. This, in turn, creates larger pores in the soil that allow water and air to move freely.

■ Sand is infertile but loose and granular.
Sandy soil is almost the exact opposite of clay. It is comprised of large mineral particles, which means it has large pores so water moves in and out of it quickly.

If your soil has a high sand content, the solution is the same as if it were high in clay: Work organic matter into it. Organic matter holds water, and as it breaks down it releases nutrients. Sandy soil that has an organic content up to about 5 percent is excellent for growing plants.

■ Silt is relatively inert.
It consists of small mineral particles that either settled out of water during flooding or blew into an area as the result of wind erosion. It adds relatively little to the characteristics of your soil. However, a soil that is high in silt can have drainage problems.

Test for sand, silt, and clay

The following three tests are neither very scientific nor very hard, but together they can tell you quite a bit about the makeup of your soil. After doing the tests, check the chart on page 145. Find the row in the chart that matches the results of all three tests. The box at the end of the row will give you a rough idea of whether your soil is mostly clay, silt, or sand. Remember, the ideal soil is a mixture of the three—40 percent sand, 40 percent silt, and 20 percent clay.

Ribbon test

Pick up a handful of topsoil. Knead it in your hands to work out the lumps. Gradually add water until the soil feels elastic. If the soil won't cling together, it's still too dry or it contains lots of sand. If you add too much water, mix in some more dirt. Now roll the soil between your hands to form a cylinder roughly the diameter of a pencil. Holding the soil in one closed hand, flatten an end with your free thumb and forefinger to form a ribbon. Keep feeding a little more of the cylinder between your thumb and finger and flattening it to form a ribbon. If the soil is silty or sandy, the ribbon will flake and fall apart. Clay helps hold the ribbon together—the longer the ribbon you can make, the higher the clay content of your soil.

Ball test

Now roll the soil into a ball, squeeze it, and pass it back and forth between your hands. The longer it retains its shape, the higher the clay content. Soil high in sand will break with a bit of pressure. Soil high in silt will stick together but be easy to reshape.

Texture test

Rub your fingers over the handful of soil. The grainer it feels, the more sand it contains. The more silt the soil contains, the more floury it will feel. The stickier it is, the more clay in the soil.

RIBBON TEST

▲ Moisten a tablespoon or so of soil. Knead it to work out the lumps, then roll the soil into a snake. Begin squeezing the end into a ribbon. The length of the ribbon will help determine whether your soil is predominantly sand or clay, as here.

BALL TEST

▲ Roll the moistened soil into a ball, then bounce it between your hands. How long does it stay together?

TEXTURE TEST

◄ Rub the soil between your fingers to see how it feels.

Check your results

RIBBON TEST	BALL TEST	TEXTURE TEST	SOIL MAKEUP
No ribbon forms	Ball won't form	Grainy	Sand
No ribbon forms	Ball falls apart when handled	Grainy, slightly floury in texture	Loamy sand
No ribbon forms	Ball falls apart when handled	Grainy, floury in texture	Silty sand
Ribbon ½ to 1 inch long	Ball can be handled gently without breaking	Grainy, moderately floury in texture	Sandy loam
Thick ribbon, up to 1 inch long	Ball handles easily	Soft and smooth, but with obvious grain	Loam
Flakes, no ribbon forms	Ball can be handled gently without breaking	Floury, some grain	Silt loam
Flakes, no ribbon forms	Ball can be handled gently without breaking	Very floury	Silt
Thick ribbon, 1 to 2 inches long	Forms ball moderately well	Very grainy	Sandy clay loam
Thin ribbon, breaks under own weight	Forms ball easily	Moderately grainy	Clay loam
Thin ribbon, breaks under own weight	Forms ball extremely easily	Smooth and floury	Silty clay loam
Thin ribbon, 2 to 3 inches long, able to support its weight	Forms ball extremely easily	Extremely grainy	Sandy clay
Thin ribbon, 2 to 3 inches long, able to support its weight	Forms ball extremely easily	Smooth	Silty clay
Very thin ribbon, 3 inches or longer	Forms ball extremely easily	Smooth	Silty clay

7

SOIL BASICS

Looking at the soil makeup

A more accurate way to determine the mineral composition of your soil is to do a jar test. It's a simple test that takes several days to complete.

1 GATHER A SOIL SAMPLE
You will need only about 1 cup of soil, but it's best to gather it the same way you would for a soil test. Dig a hole the size of your hand. Slice some soil off the side of the hole and put it in a bag. Gather 10 samples randomly from different areas of your yard.

2 MIX THE SOIL
Mix the samples together well, then spread the soil on a newspaper to dry. Remove roots, stones, and other debris. Break up any clumps of soil.

3 PUT THE SOIL IN A JAR
Put 1 cup of soil in a quart jar. Add 2 cups of water and 1 teaspoon of powdered, nonfoaming dishwasher detergent to it.

4 SHAKE THE JAR
With the lid on, shake the jar for 10 minutes to break the soil down into its components—sand, silt, and clay.

5 MARK THE SAND LEVEL

Put the jar somewhere where it won't be disturbed. After one minute, sand will have settled to the bottom. Mark its level on the side of the jar.

6 MARK THE SILT LEVEL

Let the jar sit for two hours, then mark the depth of the silt that has accumulated on top of the sand.

7 MARK THE CLAY LEVEL

Leave the jar undisturbed until the water clears. This may take several days to a month or more. When the water is clear, mark the level of the clay on the side of the jar.

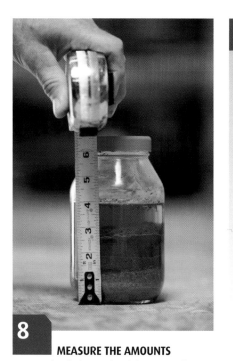

8 MEASURE THE AMOUNTS

Measure the thickness of each layer, as well as the total depth of soil in the jar. In this case, the sand layer was 1¼ inches deep, the silt layer was about 1½ inches deep, and the clay was ¼ inch deep. The total accumulation measured 2¾ inches.

And the results are...

To figure out the composition of your soil, get out your calculator. If there are fractions in your measurements, convert them to decimals by dividing. For example, if one of the measurements is 1⅜ inches, you would first convert the fraction to decimals, then add in the 1.

⅜ inch = 3 ÷ 8 = 0.375;
1⅜ inches = 0.375 inch + 1 = 1.375 inches

To find the percentage of sand, silt, and clay in your soil, divide the thickness of each layer by the total depth of the soil in the jar, then multiply the result by 100. For example, say the sand is 2½ inches deep and the total soil depth is 6 inches.

2.5 ÷ 6 = 0.416 × 100 = 41.6 percent sand

Your calculations:

$\dfrac{\text{Sand thickness}}{\text{Total depth}} = $ _____ percent sand

$\dfrac{\text{Silt thickness}}{\text{Total depth}} = $ _____ percent silt

$\dfrac{\text{Clay thickness}}{\text{Total depth}} = $ _____ percent clay

Chemical makeup

As good as the ribbon, ball, texture, and jar tests are, an important part of the soil's makeup is completely invisible to you. Without lab analysis, there is no way to know the chemical makeup of the soil. Among other things, a soil test will tell you the potassium and phosphorus content of the soil and make recommendations on the type and amount of fertilizer you should use. If you're starting a new lawn, it will also tell you how much organic matter to mix into the soil.

To perform the test, you take a few soil samples from your yard, mix them thoroughly, and put them in a bag supplied by your county extension agent. For a few dollars, the state university will analyze the samples and mail you the results.

You can test the soil at any time, but the best time to do so is before you apply fertilizer for the first time, and then every three to five years after that. (For step-by-step directions on doing a soil test, see pages 150–151.)

The way the results are listed varies from state to state, but the form shown on the facing page is typical. After listing your name and address, the date and lab number, the form gets down to business.

Soil nutrient levels
Here's where you learn soil pH and phosphorus and potassium levels. In this example, the soil pH is 6.1, the phosphorus level is 22 parts per million, and the potassium level is 50 parts per million.

Graph
The bar graph to the right of the entries tells you what the numbers mean. In this case, soil pH is just barely optimum, and both the phosphorus and potassium levels are below optimum. (The very bottom of the report gives a more complete breakdown, using chemical symbols—something you probably don't need unless you're running a golf course.)

Limestone
A recommendation for limestone needs follows the soil nutrient levels. Eastern states in particular have a problem with soil acidity because of acid rain. Soils in western states, on the other hand, tend to be alkaline. For more on treating acid and alkaline soils, see pages 158–159.

Nitrogen
Notice that there is no mention of nitrogen. As important as nitrogen is, testing for nitrogen is difficult. Nitrogen appears in several forms. It is in one form in the atmosphere. In the soil it may start out as one form, then change to another form as microbes use it. And it can be washed from the soil by rain. Even if you could get a reading, it might change after every rainfall. Because most grasses use nitrogen at about the same rate, however, it's a fairly easy matter for the extension service to develop a recommendation for nitrogen that is in the proper ratio to

▲ **For a precise report on the makeup of your soil, take soil samples and have your local extension service or state university analyze them. The analysis will recommend the proper fertilizer formula and when to apply it, as well as point out other problems, such as low levels of iron.**

the phosphorus and potassium the plants need and come up with a recommended grade of fertilizer.

Fertilizer needs
This column lists several fertilizer recommendations. Choose one, and, if you can't find the formulation exactly, come as close as you can. Apply it at the rate given in the second column, which lists pounds of fertilizer required per 1,000 square feet. Fertilizer bags usually provide spreader settings for fertilizing at that rate.

When to fertilize
The longer entry to the right of the list of fertilizers completes the picture: It tells you when to apply the fertilizer for the results you desire. For a thick, luxuriant lawn, it says to apply any one of the listed grades three times a year—May, September, and November in this case. For a less luxurious lawn, you can apply the fertilizer less frequently.

7

SOIL BASICS

SOIL TEST FORM

SOIL TEST REPORT FOR:	ADDITIONAL COPY TO:
JOHN JONES HARMONY LANE SMITHVILLE PA 11111	SAM COOK GREEN LAWN ENTERPRISE 111 HILLTOP LANE SMITHVILLE PA 11111

DATE	LAB #	SERIAL #	COUNTY	ACRES	FIELD ID	SOIL
02/20/2001	S00-00003	0044599				

SOIL NUTRIENT LEVELS

			Below Optimum	Optimum	Above Optimum
Soil pH	6.1				
Phosphorus	22	ppm			
Potassium	50	ppm			

RECOMMENDATIONS FOR: *Maintain Home Lawn*   *Annual Bluegrass*

Limestone Needs:

Limestone: 20 lb/1000 square feet

Apply the quantity of limestone recommended above to your soil in a single application.
See back of form for maximum recommended application rate.

Fertilizer Needs:

Fertilizer*	Rate: lb per 1000 square feet**
24-5-10	4.0
18-6-6	5.5
13-13-13	7.5
10-10-10	10.0
10-6-4	10.0
10-5-5	10.0
9-4-4	11.0
8-4-4	12.5
7-5-5	14.0

For a simple fertilizer program that will provide adquate quantities of nitrogen, phosphate and potash to turf based on your soil test results, apply <u>one</u> of the fertilizers listed on the left at the rates specified three times during the growing season for a three-year period. Apply once in mid-spring (May), once in late summer (September), and once in the late fall (November) each year. If you can not find any of the fertilizers listed below, select a fertilizer with an analysis close to one of those listed.

*Select only one
**Apply three times during the growing season.

Nutrient Needs (lb/1000 sq ft):

2.5	4	3-4	The individual nutrient needs for optimum turf growth are listed to the left. These needs will be met by applying the fertilizer materials listed in the above table three times per year for a three-year period.
P₂O₅	K₂O	N	

LABORATORY RESULTS:

[1]pH	[2]P lb/A	Exchangeable Cations (meq/100g)					% Saturation of the CEC			Organic Matter %	Nitrate-N ppm	Soluble salts mmhos/cm
		[3]Acidity	[2]K	[2]Mg	[2]Ca	[4]CEC	K	Mg	Ca			
6.1	44	2.5	0.1	0.5	13.3	16.3	0.8	2.8	81.4			

Optional Tests:

Test Methods: [1]1:1 soil:water pH, [2]Mehlich 3 Extractant, [3]SMP Buffer pH, [4]Summation of Cations

3394

Home Lawn Maintain

7

SOIL BASICS

Taking samples for a soil test

7

SOIL BASICS

PROJECT DETAILS

SKILLS: Digging, measuring
PROJECT: Measuring the fertility of your soil

TIME TO COMPLETE

EXPERIENCED: 10 min.
HANDY: 10 min.
NOVICE: 10 min.

STUFF YOU'LL NEED

TOOLS: Trowel, quart jar with lid, measuring cup, teaspoon, marker, ruler or tape measure, calculator
MATERIALS: Water, powdered dishwasher soap

Taking a soil sample is the first step in having a soil test done. In most areas, a state university does the testing, and the local extension office of the university will have directions and a kit containing sample bags. Check with your extension agent before doing a test and follow the directions provided, which may be slightly different from those given here.

The quality of the soil in your yard may vary from spot to spot. Collecting a good sample involves getting soil from several places in the yard and mixing them together. As for any study, the subsamples, as they're called, should be collected randomly. Walk in a zigzag pattern across the yard, stopping occasionally to dig up a bag of dirt.

To collect each subsample, you'll have to dig up a small spot in the yard. If you start by working the trowel around the perimeter of the hole, you'll be able to lift out a plug of soil in one piece. Put it back carefully and the bare spot will quickly sprout new grass growth.

WORK SMARTER

USE A CLEAN BUCKET

Don't gather your soil samples in the same container you use to wash the floors, dishes, windows, or the dog. Most soap has phosphate in it—one of the things the lab tests for. Although the residual soap on the walls of the bucket may not be much, it's enough to throw off the soil test, which measures for phosphates in parts per million.

TAKE YOUR FIRST SAMPLE

1 Scrape away grass and any organic debris on top of the soil from an area roughly the size of your hand. Dig a hole with your trowel. To get a sample, slice away a piece of soil from the side of the hole, making sure you don't dig up any subsoil in the process. Put the sample in your bucket.

2 WALK ACROSS THE YARD AND TAKE MORE SAMPLES

Walk in a zigzag pattern across your lawn, stopping randomly to dig up some soil. Continue until you have a total of 10 samples. Don't mix soil from garden areas with soil from the lawn or lawn-to-be area. Do a separate soil test for front yards and backyards.

3 MIX YOUR SAMPLES THOROUGHLY

Mix all 10 samples in the bucket with your trowel.

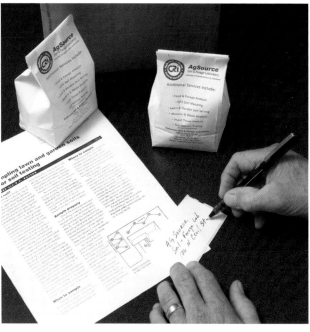

4 SEND THE SAMPLE

The soil test kit from the extension service most likely contains a bag for the samples, though some testing labs accept soil samples in regular bags. Measure out 2 cups—or as directed—from the bucket and dump them in the sample bag. Fill out the required paperwork, answering all questions thoroughly. (There are often questions about whether the lawn is newly seeded, how often you water, and so on.) Pack the sample bag in its mailer and drop it in the mail.

Improving your soil

Once you have a profile of your soil, you can address any weaknesses. If you will be installing a new lawn, you will strip any existing vegetation and rototill organic matter, fertilizer, and the other amendments recommended by the soil test into it. Turn to page 164, "Preparing the Yard for Sod or Seed," for the details on how to do this.

If you have no plans to start all over, you can improve the soil in three ways. You can fertilize the lawn, aerate it with an aerator (a special machine that cuts holes in the ground), or topdress by spreading a thin layer of organic matter over the lawn. Or you can do all three.

Aerating creates holes in the soil, making it more porous. This is something that you do when the soil is compacted or when you have a layer of thatch building up on the lawn. By making the soil more porous, aerating gives the roots room to grow, with their length increasing by as much as one-third. Topdressing makes the soil more fertile. When combined with aerating it further helps to break up compaction. Over time, topdressing can help to change the composition of the soil. For step-by-step directions on aerating and topdressing, see "Treating Soil Compaction," page 154, and "Topdressing Your Lawn," page 156–157.

■ Treat compacted soils with a soil aerator (right). The plugs that it pulls out (below) eventually break down and filter into the soil. The organic matter and microbes in the plugs help break up compaction and thatch.

Aerating

Soil compaction is easy to spot. The classic case is the path that you, your kids, or your pets wear through the yard from day-to-day use. The surface of compacted soil is hard and impenetrable. The ground is bare, except for weeds that flourish in hardpan, such as goosegrass and knotweed. Digging will confirm compaction. Compacted soil is hard to get through—for shovels, for air, for water, and for nutrients.

Compacted soil obviously begins with usage. The more you walk, drive, or play on a spot of lawn, the more the soil will compact. But there are other causes too. Lawns in new developments may have only a thin layer of topsoil over soil that was compacted by heavy construction equipment. Wet soils compact easily, as do soils high in clay or silt. Soils containing lots of sodium also compact easily. Sandy soils rarely become compacted.

If your soil is compacted, you need to fix the problem. Compaction forces soil particles together, eliminating the spaces between them and leaving little room for water or air to move through. A compacted layer as thin as ½ inch can slow absorption of water and nutrients and interfere with the exchange of oxygen between the soil and the atmosphere. In short, compacted soil

works against everything your grass needs and can stunt its growth by as much as one-third.

Whatever the cause of the compaction, the solution is the same: treating the lawn with a machine called a core aerator. A core aerator pulls small cylinders of soil and grass out of the lawn, dumping them on top. Core aerators have a cylinder studded with hollow spikes. The spikes, usually about 3 inches long and ½ to ¾ inch in diameter, cut small holes in the lawn as you push or pull the aerator across it. Tine aerators with solid spikes are also available, however, these do not open the soil like core aerators. The holes created by core aerators help loosen the soil, oxygenate it, and improve water filtration and drainage. Aerators with tines up to 6 inches long are available, but 2- to 4-inch-long tines are adequate and most common.

The cores pulled out of the soil are dumped on the lawn as cylindrical plugs. Rain, watering, and people walking across the lawn break up the cores so that the particles filter through the grass, working their way back into the soil. After aerating, you can topdress to fill the holes with organic matter to further improve the lawn or let the sides of the holes collapse with time.

A core aerator isn't the sort of thing you want to go out and buy; luckily, you can rent one at the home center. Make sure you get a core aerator instead of a tine aerator. The tine or "spike" aerator punches holes in the ground without removing cores. This does the exact opposite of what you want. It compresses the soil even more.

Some places sell spikes that strap on to your shoes for use as an aerator. These don't work any better than a spike aerator and neither, unfortunately, does walking across the lawn in golf shoes.

When to aerate

On most lawns, aerating is a once and done operation, providing that you mow, water, fertilize, and otherwise care for your lawn properly. Other lawns, however, may need aeration every few years. Whichever type of lawn you have, aerate when the grass is growing vigorously. Fall is generally the best time to aerate cool-season grasses. Because cool-season grasses are semi-dormant in summer, they aren't able to quickly grow back in after aeration. Weeds, such as crabgrass, then find it easy to move into the yard. Warm-season grasses, on the other hand, should be aerated in late spring and in summer, their periods of active growth.

Moist soil is easier to aerate than dry soil. If the soil sticks to your shoes or the plugs stick to the aerator, however, the soil is too moist and aerating will actually lead to more compaction.

Aerating gets rid of thatch too

In addition to breaking up compaction, aerating helps remove thatch, the layer of stems and rhizomes that accumulate just below the grass blades. While a little bit of thatch protects the lawn, it becomes a problem when the layer gets to be ½ inch thick or more. At this thickness, the thatch keeps water from penetrating the soil and provides a breeding ground for insects and diseases. Aerating pulls soil up from beneath the thatch, and the microbes in the soil intermingle with the thatch and help break it up.

The other way of removing thatch is to use a power rake that lifts the thatch out of the ground. Although the rake removes the thatch immediately, it is harder on the lawn and doesn't provide a long-term solution. For more information on power raking, see page 116.

7

SOIL BASICS

Improving western soils

Soils in the arid southwest are alkaline and often contain large amounts of sodium, which makes soil impermeable to rain and irrigation water. Working gypsum (calcium sulfate) into the soil before planting a lawn can help improve growing conditions. The gypsum reacts with other minerals in the soil so the sodium leaches out.

Although you may have heard that applying gypsum improves clay soil, it works only in regions with large amounts of sodium in the soil. The best way to find out if gypsum could help your soil is to have a soil test done and ask specifically for gypsum recommendations.

Application rates usually range from 40 to 175 pounds per 1,000 square feet. Thoroughly rototill the gypsum into the soil, then water well. If drainage does not improve dramatically, you may need to repeat the process.

CLOSER LOOK

KICKING SAND IN CLAY'S FACE

Loam, the soil considered best for growing grass and other plants, is roughly 40 percent sand, 40 percent silt, and 20 percent clay. If you've got soil that has too much clay in it, it might *seem* reasonable to make it more like loam by topdressing with sand. Don't bother. It would take 7 tons of sand to improve just 1,000 square feet of clay soil. The amount of sand you could add by topdressing would be a drop in the bucket. And when you mix too little sand into clay soil, you actually worsen the problem, turning the soil into a concretelike base.

WORK SMARTER

KEEP IT CLEAN

Garden equipment is notorious for spreading weed seeds, unwanted grasses or rhizomes and stolons from unwanted species. Core aerators can be about the worst offenders, especially if plugs from another yard remain in the tines. Clean your aerator thoroughly before using. Put it in the driveway, and pop out any plugs that are still in it. A kitchen knife may help. Put the cores somewhere they can't do any harm, and then hose the machine down thoroughly while it is on an impervious surface.

Treating soil compaction

1 MOISTEN THE SOIL

Compacted soil is hard to penetrate, even for a machine. Moisten the soil two days before you aerate to make the job easier, applying about 1 inch of water (place a jar near the sprinkler to measure). Overwatering or a heavy rain before aerating will make the cores stick inside the hollow aerator cylinders.

2 MARK THE LOCATION OF SPRINKLER HEADS, SHALLOW WATER LINES, AND UTILITIES

The tines on an aerator can be up to 6 inches long and could cut through anything buried near the soil surface. Mark the location of sprinkler heads and water, electric, gas, and sewer lines with lime, flour, or landscapers paint before you start. Most states have a toll-free number that you can call to learn the location of buried utilities. Mark the areas well and steer clear of them when aerating.

3 MAKE A FIRST PASS WITH THE AERATOR

Push the aerator across the yard, pulling out cores of soil as you go. Turn the machine, then walk back next to the row you just cored. Continue until you have aerated the entire lawn.

4 AERATE PERPENDICULAR TO THE FIRST PASS

Make a second pass perpendicular to the first, to make sure you have removed enough plugs to break up the compaction—about eight or nine plugs per square foot is adequate. Make a third pass diagonal to the first two, if necessary.

5 LET THE PLUGS DISSOLVE OR RAKE THEM UP

The plugs will break up on their own in a week or two. If you'd like to get rid of them sooner, you can rake them to help break them up. However, it is better to leave them in place. The microbes in the soil help to break up any thatch layer. Topdressing, while not necessary, can improve the soil even more at this point.

Topdressing

Topdressing with organic matter such as compost helps make soil crumbly, granular, and more fertile. When combined with aerating, topdressing helps break up compacted soil, encourages microbe activity, and increases the soil's ability to hold nutrients by as much as tenfold.

When you topdress, apply an amount that leaves the grass blades standing up rather than bent over. Most recommendations call for applying a ¼-inch layer of topdressing, but you can put it down as thick as ½ inch. The more organic matter you apply (up to ½ inch) the more good it does, but even a little organic matter goes a long way toward invigorating your lawn.

Commercial topdressing machines are available, but as a homeowner, the best way to topdress is by hand. Fill a wheelbarrow and scatter the organic matter across the lawn with a shovel. When you're through scattering, rake out what you've applied with a leaf rake to create a fairly uniform layer.

How much topdressing material is required depends, of course, on the size of your yard and on how thick a layer you plan to apply. To cover 1,000 square feet of lawn with ¼ inch of compost takes a little more than ¾ cubic yards of topdressing material. To fill aeration holes as well as apply a ¼-inch layer of topdressing requires about 2 cubic yards per 1,000 square feet. To calculate much topdressing you will need for your entire yard, see page 156.

In order to work, the organic matter in the topdressing has to break down and filter into the soil. Once it breaks down, it's time to topdress again. The most you'll want to topdress is once a year in fall.

To see if an application is necessary, dig up a plug of soil and look at it. If you see no evidence of the last topdressing application, it has worked into the soil, and you can make a new application. If you can still see a layer of topdressing material on the soil surface, wait for it to work its way into the topsoil before you topdress again.

Applying too much topdressing can create layers in the soil, which can create problems with drainage. Using a topdressing material comprised of a soil type that is different from the soil in your yard can also lead to layering.

Choosing a topdressing

Compost Many cities compost the yard waste they pick up, making it available for use on lawns and gardens. If you use this compost for topdressing, make sure that it is ready to use. To do this, check the temperature. Compost warms up while it decomposes, and compost that is ready to use is the same temperature as its surroundings. Also, it should have no recognizable organic matter.

Municipal compost may contain weed seeds and herbicides. Trials with composted city yard waste, however, show it is a very effective topdressing. Before using it, screen it through a ¼- or ⅜-inch sieve.

Peat Moss Unlike compost, peat moss is biologically inactive, containing few organisms that help decompose thatch. Because it is acidic it can increase the acidity of soil when used as a topdressing, which makes it good to use on the alkaline soils commonly found in the West.

Composted biosolids Biosolids are the sludge left over from wastewater treatment plants. When composted, they can be used as a topdressing. Federal standards require that the sludge be treated to remove metal contaminants and be pathogen free. Biosolids are rich in plant nutrients, and have a pH around 7, the level that is best for grass.

Manure Well-rotted cow manure is good topdressing. Anything less than well rotted is trouble, because weed and undesirable seeds are likely to remain in it. Manure is considered well rotted after 60 days. Avoid steer manure and horse manure which make poor topdressing. Also, avoid using manure on the West Coast; it can lead to disease problems there.

Soil Soil can be used as a topdressing, provided it is similar to the soil below the lawn. Using a different soil or applying a layer more than ¼ inch thick can create a top layer that slows water and air movement below the soil surface.

Sand Sand, though used extensively on golf courses, doesn't do much on home lawns. Because sand is low in organic matter, it won't improve soil quality or help fight thatch. It is sometimes recommended for filling the holes created by aerating to keep them open.

Mushroom soil Mushroom soil is a spent mixture of straw, corncobs, peat moss, other organics, and manure. It usually contains residual amounts of the mushroom fungi. Because the manure is often steer manure, it is not a suitable topdressing on the West Coast. If mushroom soil is available locally, call your county extension agent and ask about its suitability for use on your lawn.

Topdressing amounts

SQUARE FEET	CU. YDS. TO TOPDRESS ¼" THICK	CU. YDS. TO FILL ⅝" AERATION HOLES 3" DEEP, HOLES ONLY	CU. YDS. TO FILL AERATION HOLES AND TOPDRESS ½" THICK
1,000	0.771	0.45	1.99
1,500	1.15	0.68	2.99
2,000	1.54	0.9	3.99
2,500	1.92	1.1	4.99
3,000	2.31	1.36	5.99
3,500	2.7	1.58	6.99
4,000	3.08	1.81	7.99
5,000	3.85	2.26	9.99
6,000	4.62	2.72	11.99
7,000	5.4	3.17	13.99
8,000	6.17	3.62	15.99
9,000	6.94	4.08	17.99
10,000	7.71	4.53	19.99

Topdressing your lawn

PROJECT DETAILS

SKILLS: Measuring, shoveling, running machinery
PROJECT: Aerating and topdressing a lawn

TIME TO COMPLETE

Time to complete depends on the size of the lawn.

STUFF YOU'LL NEED

TOOLS: Core aerator, tape measure, calculator, wheelbarrow, shovel, leaf rake
MATERIALS: Peat moss, compost, composted manure, or other organic matter

7

SOIL BASICS

▲ Topdressing adds beneficial organisms, which help to increase the soil's fertility. Topdressing can also help to level out the lawn and raise low spots.

Topdressing—the process of spreading organic matter across the lawn—adds the organic matter that helps improve soil. It also helps break down thatch. Aeration and topdressing can be done alone or together. Aerate to reduce thatch and compaction. Aerate and topdress to speed the process and improve the soil. Topdress by itself to add organic matter to the soil.

To learn how much topdressing you need, you must find the volume of the topdressing layer. To do that, multiply the square footage of your lawn by the depth of the topdressing layer. For example, to cover a 9,500-square-foot yard with ¼ inch of topdressing:

9,500 square feet × 0.25 = 2,375 cubic feet of topdressing needed

Divide the result (2,375) by 324, a number that converts the answer to cubic yards, the measure typically used when ordering topdressing:

2,375 ÷ 324 = 7.3 cubic yards of topdressing

Suppliers usually don't sell a fraction of a cubic yard. Round up to the nearest full number, which is 8 cubic yards in this instance. For an estimating chart, see "Topdressing Amounts," on page 155.

1

AERATE THE LAWN

Aeration is the first step in applying topdressing; it's also something you can do to help break up thatch. Start by pushing the aerator back and forth in rows across the lawn until you have covered the entire lawn. Make a second pass perpendicular to the first, covering the whole yard. Continue aerating until you have removed eight or nine cores per square foot.

2

MEASURE YOUR LAWN

Measure the length and width of your yard by breaking it up into areas that are easy to measure. For more on measuring, see page 160.

3

MULTIPLY THE WIDTH TIMES THE LENGTH OF EACH AREA TO GET ITS SQUARE FOOTAGE

Add up the square footage of each area to get the total square footage of your yard. In the example on page 156, both the front yard and backyard measure 4,000 square feet. Each of the side yards measures 25×30 feet, or 750 square feet. The total square footage is 4,000 + 4,000 + 750 + 750 or 9,500 square feet.

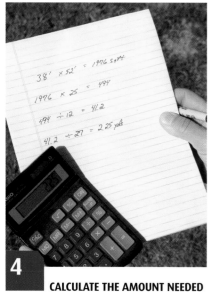

4

CALCULATE THE AMOUNT NEEDED

Multiply the size of your yard by the desired thickness of the topdressing, usually ¼ or ½ inch. (Use a calculator, substituting 0.25 for ¼ inch and 0.5 for ½ inch.) Divide the results by 12, the number that converts your first answer to cubic inches, and then divide by 27, the number of cubic inches in a yard. (You can divide only once if you divide the first answer by 324, the product of 12 times 27.)

5

SPREAD

The topdressing can be composted manure, peat moss, compost, or other decayed organic matter. Load a wheelbarrow with the topdressing and toss it across the lawn with a shovel or spade.

6

RAKE

Use a leaf rake to smooth out the topdressing and, in the process, push it into the holes created by the aerator. When you are done, the topdressing layer should be ¼ to ½ inch thick and the grass blades should still be standing up.

7

SOIL BASICS

How to correct soil pH

7

SOIL BASICS

▲ Grass prefers neutral soil, but soils east of the Mississippi tend to be acidic. Those west of the Mississippi are often alkaline. You can apply soil amendments with a fertilizer spreader to correct the soil pH.

GOOD IDEA

APPLYING LIME

Lime is essentially crushed limestone; it dissolves slowly, moving into the soil about 1 inch every year after it is applied. Because it is so slow moving, experts recommend applying it every three to five years to keep from overloading your lawn. If your soil test shows that your soil is very acidic (requiring more than 150 pounds per 1,000 square feet, or 3 tons per acre), don't apply it all at once; too much at once can retard grass growth. Apply half the amount, wait two years, and retest; then add the other half if it is still required.

Most turfgrasses don't grow well in soil that is acidic. They also grow poorly in alkaline soil. Unfortunately for homeowners, there is no visible difference between the two soils, unless your eyes are sharp enough to see atoms. If they are, you'd see that acids have more hydrogen atoms than alkalis, and the stronger the acid, the more hydrogen atoms there are.

pH is measured on a 14 point scale. Anything with a pH between 0 and 7 is acid, and the lower the number, the more acidic the material. For example, vinegar has a pH of 2.4. Anything with a pH between 7 and 14 is alkaline; the higher the number the more alkaline it is. Household ammonia is alkaline, with a pH of 11.9. Distilled water, with a pH of 7, is considered neutral, which happens to be the perfect pH for soil.

Soil pH influences soil fertility. In alkaline soil, plants have no access to iron and other micronutrients. In acid soil, all of the major plant nutrients become tied up and unavailable to plants. Soil pH—both alkaline and acid—also influences the development of some turfgrass diseases.

Soil falls into the ideal pH 7 range in only a few regions. In the East, soil is acid because frequent rain showers wash calcium and magnesium and other elements from the soil, leaving hydrogen to take their

place. Where acid rains are common in the East, the rain may also dissolve sulfur from the air and transfer it to the soil, thus lowering soil pH even more.

West of the Mississippi, soils tend to be alkaline because little rain falls to leach calcium, magnesium, and other salts out of them. (As minerals build up in soil, the pH goes up.) A desert soil can have a pH as high as 10 or 11. A high pH creates an unhealthy root environment for grass. In alkaline soil, some nutrients become totally unavailable to grass roots, while others become available to the point of toxicity.

Lawn care activities can also affect soil pH. For example, applying ammonium-containing fertilizers and acidic topdressings such as peat moss can increase acidity.

While you can generally assume that soil will be acidic in the East and alkaline in the West, there is no way of knowing whether this is true in your yard or whether you need to treat the problem unless you test the soil. It will not only recommend the right material to use to change the pH, it will tell you how much of the material to apply.

Treating acid soils

Acid soils are treated with lime, which being alkaline, brings the pH closer to neutral. Lime can be applied any

Put a 2-inch layer of pelletized lime, sulfur, gypsum, or gypsite into the hopper and roll the spreader over pavement to check for even distribution. If any hopper holes are clogged, pour out the granules, pick the debris out of the hole, refill, and test again. When the spreader is working properly, sweep or vacuum up the granules you poured out. Return them to the bag and then fill the spreader.

How much, how long?

The speed at which sulfur or lime affects the soil varies. Sulfur reacts quickly, but the effect is short lived. When applying lime, extremely acid soils will react quickly, but in most cases, it takes more than a year for a measurable change to occur. The finer and purer the lime and the more it rains, the faster the soil reacts.

In general it takes about 8 pounds of sulfur per 1,000 square feet to lower the pH by one point. However, the type of soil affects the actual amount needed. A loamy soil requires up to three times more sulfur than a sandy soil.

Calculating the amount of lime needed to raise soil pH is more involved. First you need to know the level of something called the reserve acidity of the soil, or the buffer pH, which can only be determined in a lab. Generally speaking, however, raising the pH of your soil one point, say from 5.0 to 6.0, takes about 25 pounds of lime per 1,000 square feet. Like soil acidifiers, lime is also affected by soil texture. Raising the pH in heavy clay takes about two and a half times more lime as raising it in other types of soil.

Be aware that because you cannot change the conditions that ultimately influence soil pH (climate, rainfall, etc.), any change you make will eventually revert back to the original reading.

---

time of year, but fall, winter, and spring are the best times. If you apply it when the lawn is dormant, the lime will start to dissolve and begin altering the soil pH before the grass resumes growth in spring. Apply lime to a dry lawn so it doesn't stick to leaf blades. Lime is caustic and can burn and brown foliage on contact.

There are two types of lime on the market: dolomitic and calcitic. Dolomitic lime contains magnesium, and is used when the soil lacks magnesium, as noted by the soil test. Otherwise use calcitic lime which is almost pure calcium carbonate. You may also run into hydrated lime and burned lime. These are too caustic for use on a lawn.

The finer ground the lime, the faster it acts. But of your choices on the market—pulverized, granular, and pelletized—most people prefer pelletized and granular materials because they are easy to spread. Pulverized lime is so finely ground that it clogs the spreader.

Alkaline soil
Short of a soil test, water quality provides a bit of a hint that your soil may be alkaline. If you have hard tap water and lime deposits collect on your plumbing fixtures, your soil is most likely alkaline.

Neutralizing alkaline soil is not simple. For example, elemental sulfur lowers pH but must be applied regularly because the effect is temporary. Soil bacteria consume the sulfur, producing sulfuric acid which lowers soil pH. But in as little as two weeks, the bacteria will consume all the sulfur, and the soil begins to revert to its former pH.

The solution is not to double up on applications, which can overdose plants, but to follow the soil test

recommendations carefully, and reapply as needed, either in early spring or fall. Because elemental sulfur acts quickly, break the recommended dosage into smaller increments and apply it as often as every three weeks, not to exceed 5 pounds per 1,000 square feet at one time.

If the soil test indicates that your soil is high in sodium, use gypsum (calcium sulfate) instead of elemental sulfur according to soil test recommendations. A closely related compound known as gypsite is used to treat alkalinity and amend the soil at the same time as you topdress. Gypsite is a mixture of 60 to 90 percent gypsum crystals combined with loam, clay, sand, and humus.

Gypsum can be applied in any season and is not harmful to plants, people, or pets. Gypsum, gypsite and elemental sulfur are all available in either powdered or pelletized form.

Application
By and large, lime, sulfur, gypsum, and gypsite are all applied with a fertilizer spreader to ensure a uniform coating. Use a drop spreader, which controls just where the materials go, to keep lime out of beds containing acid-loving shrubs and perennials and away from evergreens. For small areas, such as around sidewalks and patios, you can broadcast the material by hand.

No matter which material you use, the powdered version is likely to clog the spreader. Stick with pelletized or granular materials.

After application, water in acidifying materials so that they soak into the lawn. Lime does not have to be watered in, though there is no harm to doing so.

Measuring for sod, grass, and topsoil

Planting grass, laying sod, or spreading topsoil will test not only your muscle but also your memory of grade-school math. First, you'll need to know the size of your yard, then you can figure out how much seed, sod, or topsoil to order. The process is the same for any yard, no matter its shape—find the square footage of your lot, subtract the area of your house from the area of the lot, then add 5 percent so that you don't run out in the middle of a job and have to phone in another order.

Here's how to find the area of different shapes: If your yard is square or rectangular—and most yards are—measuring is simple: Multiply the length of one side of your yard by the length of one of the ends. Circles, trapezoids, and triangles are a bit more complex to measure, and irregular shapes are even harder. The best way to find the area of an irregularly shaped yard or house is to break it into a group of easily recognizable shapes.

Find the total square footage of the lawn.
Although most yards are rectangular, many are not. To determine the square footage of an irregularly shaped lawn, measure your yard, then draw it on a sheet of graph paper with one square equaling 1 foot. Also, measure the outside dimensions of your house and locate the house on the drawing. Now, divide your lot into recognizable shapes. Mark out the sections that are square or rectangular. Among the remaining pieces of the lawn, look for circles, triangles, and trapezoids. Figure the square footage of each individual area, then add them all together to find the total size of your yard.

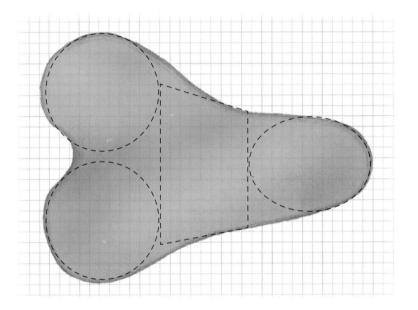

To find the area of squares and rectangles,
measure the length and width of each side by counting the number of squares on the graph paper. Multiply the length by the width to get the square footage.

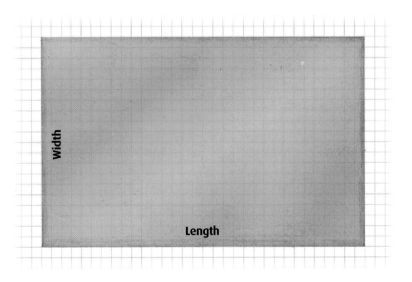

Width

Length

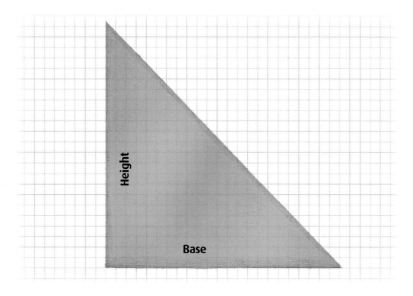

To find the area of a triangle, multiply the "base" of the triangle by the height and divide by 2. Although the base can be any one of the triangle's sides, most people let the bottom one be the base. Finding the triangle's height can be a little more tricky. On a right triangle, as here, the height is simply the upright side. On other types, draw a straight line from the top point of the triangle to the base, then count the number of squares along the line to find the height.

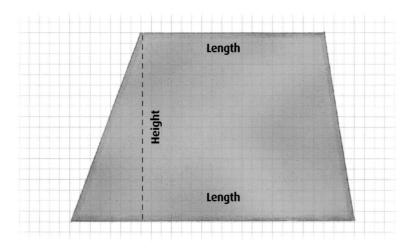

To find the area of a trapezoid, measure the length of each of the parallel sides, as well as the distance between the two lines, called the height. The area is the combined length of the sides times the height divided by 2.

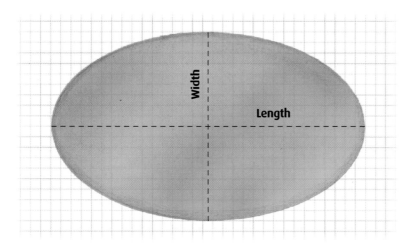

To find the area of an oval, multiply length by width, then multiply the result by 0.8. To find the area of a circle, multiply the radius times itself, and then multiply the answer by 3.14 (pi). Divide the answer by 2 if the shape is a half circle.

SOIL BASICS

Planting a lawn

You may have a brand new home. Or perhaps you've just bought an older home accompanied by a lawn that's just as old but not quite so appealing. Maybe a disease or insect has left your lawn in shambles. *You* need to plant some grass. Whether you're planting the entire lawn or just repairing a few spots, the steps are the same.

You'll find that few things give as much satisfaction as a new lawn, except perhaps knowing that you are the one who planted it. Starting a lawn involves working the soil, grading it, fixing any drainage problems, eliminating weeds, adding nutrients, and otherwise making it the best it can be. It's hard work but certainly not beyond the abilities of most people.

Once the soil is in shape, simply lay the sod, sow the seed, or plant some sprigs or plugs. Whichever you use, water well until the lawn takes root, mow before the leaves get too tall (mowing helps the lawn fill in), and start to enjoy your brand-new carpet of green.

Chapter 8 highlights

Don't want to start from scratch but do need to fill some holes?

If your lawn is in fairly decent shape but has a few thin spots or damaged areas, you don't need to plant a new lawn. Instead you can repair it. Jump to pages 179–180 for information on patching problem spots.

Recurring problems in your lawn can also be solved without starting from scratch. Overseeding with new improved varieties that resist pests is a simpler solution. To learn how to overseed, go to pages 181–183.

For information on selecting a grass and buying seed, pages 17–35 can give you a hand.

Preparing the yard for sod or seed

8

PLANTING A LAWN

Whether you're planning on laying sod or seeding, the process of getting the yard ready is the same. Most of your efforts will be directed at improving the soil—problems with the soil can lead to problems with the grass. The very least you'll want to do is work organic matter into the soil. But as long as you are at it, take the time to fix problems such as thin topsoil and uneven terrain.

Let a soil test be your guide to how much work you need to do. It will tell you whether the soil is acidic or alkaline and whether you need to make changes to the pH. It will also tell you how much organic matter to add and what blend of fertilizer to use, as well as how much. Without a soil test, you have only a general idea of what to provide for your lawn. Starting a new lawn involves a major investment of time, effort, and money. There's no need to work blindly for the want of a soil test.

Basic steps

The primary goal when preparing soil for a new lawn is to create a bed of topsoil rich in the nutrients that the grass will need. In the process, you'll be adding raw materials like organic matter and topsoil that will help you fill in low spots and correct any problems with the grade of your lot.

Where topsoil is thin, you can thicken the layer as well as smooth out any irregularities.

A healthy lawn needs a minimum of 4 inches of topsoil. Any new topsoil should have qualities similar to those of the soil that's in the yard now. Although putting rich topsoil on top of sand or clay sounds like a good way to improve the soil, what it actually does is create layers within the soil. Grass roots are reluctant to cross such layers, and water won't travel from one layer to the next until the top layer is saturated. Unless the soils are similar and mixed together well, new topsoil can create more problems than it solves.

Once the soil is spread across the yard, much of the job is like making a cake: You mix ingredients together, add a few more, and mix again. The new topsoil is rototilled in with the old, and then you spread organic matter across the surface and rototill again. (The organic matter can be peat moss, compost, rotted manure, mushroom soil, or about any other well-rotted organic matter.)

Organic matter helps provide nutrients and builds up the soil structure, but turf professionals also work some fertilizer into the soil as they're preparing it for planting. If there's a need for lime to correct acidity or sulfur to correct alkalinity, that goes on top of the soil at this point. And then it's time to mix again, not with a rototiller but with a rake.

Dealing with any existing lawn

Before you can start a new lawn, you need to get rid of any existing vegetation in the lawn area. Even if you're bringing in new topsoil and adding organic matter, the weeds, existing turf, or other vegetation would interfere with mixing these materials into the soil. In addition, established weeds might continue to prosper.

There are four ways to kill the existing lawn: spraying a nonselective herbicide, solarizing, stripping with a sod cutter, and smothering. All take at least a few weeks to a few months to eliminate the old turf and weeds. Be sure you add this time into your scheduling.

Begin soil work several weeks before sowing seed or laying sod, depending on the method you use to remove existing vegetation. The soil should be ready to go by the time you're ready to plant. For warm-season grasses that time is late spring or early summer. Cool-season grasses are best started in late summer or early fall.

▲ Herbicides containing glyphosate will kill all vegetation that is green and actively growing, usually in one to two weeks. Once the grass is dead, scuffle the soil to bring up weed seeds, water, and wait for the seeds to sprout. Spray the new weeds. Repeat three to four times, until no weeds sprout after spraying, scuffling, and watering.

▲ Solarizing involves heating an area to kill weed seeds and pathogens in the soil as well as vegetation. The process works best in sunny areas when temperatures are above 70°F (21°C). Water, then cover the area with clear—not black—plastic. Bury the edges in a shallow trench to keep the plastic in place. The site will be clear in one to two months.

▲ A sod stripper, available at rental centers, cuts existing grass in 12- to 18-inch-wide strips. Roll up the sod and compost it or, if it is very weedy, throw it in the trash. Scuffle the soil, water, then wait for weeds to emerge. Spray them with glyphosate or hoe them down. Repeat until no more weeds appear.

▲ Smothering involves blocking light to the grass and weeds. Spread several layers of newspaper across the lawn, wet them, and cover with 4 to 6 inches of compost or other organic matter. This should kill the lawn in two to four months, after which you can work the compost and paper into the soil. Instead of newspaper you can use black plastic, weighing it in place. This method takes longer to work, the plastic doesn't biodegrade like the paper does, and you'll eventually need to dispose of it.

Grading the slope of a yard

PROJECT DETAILS

SKILLS: Measuring, excavating
PROJECT: Correcting the slope of a yard

TIME TO COMPLETE

Time depends on the size of the yard and the amount of correction required.

STUFF YOU'LL NEED

TOOLS: Mason's line, 3-foot stakes, line level, tape measure, lime, or landscapers paint, rototiller, landscape rake, lawn roller
MATERIALS: Topsoil, soil amendments

▲ Grading involves everything from scraping off the topsoil to digging and rototilling. This is not a job you want to do by hand. Consider hiring a contractor for this part of the job and doing the rest of the work yourself.

The perfect slope

A slope with a drop of 1 foot in 50 will keep water moving through the grass instead of puddling. A drop greater than 1 foot in 3, however, will result in erosion. Anything in between 1 in 50 and 1 in 3 is an acceptable grade for a yard. A slope outside that range needs to be regraded.

The slope of your yard is important for two entirely different reasons. First, you don't want water building up in low spots and turning part of the yard into a swamp, and second, you don't want water running into your house and flooding the basement.

Most yards start out with the correct slope—a drop of 1 foot in every 50—but over time, settling, usage, construction, road work, utility work, or careless landscaping may have changed the grade. When correcting the slope of a yard, the first step is to measure the current slope. The second step is to fix it as necessary.

Measuring requires the simplest of equipment. With a line, a level, a tape measure, two measurements, and a little arithmetic, you can determine the slope of your yard.

Correcting the slope, however, requires some complicated equipment, at least at the outset. The process usually involves scraping off the topsoil, correcting the grade of the subsoil, and then putting the topsoil back into place. It's a job that requires skill and equipment that the average homeowner doesn't have.

Because the problem begins with the subsoil, that's where it needs to be fixed. It won't do to just truck in some soil and rake it out into a new slope. Not only will this result in an uneven layer of topsoil, but there are practical considerations. Solving the problem by adding topsoil at the house, for example, could raise the soil level above the foundation or over the siding. Solving the problem by removing soil at the sidewalk could remove all the topsoil there and leave the surface well below the level of the sidewalk, which is a safety hazard.

You might want to consider hiring a contractor to do much of the work with the subsoil. Once the excavation is complete and the topsoil (plus any extra) is back in place, the remaining work is something you can do on your own. This includes rototilling organic matter into the topsoil, smoothing out the grade with a final raking, and rolling to compress the soil somewhat.

All in all, it's a big job, but it is the foundation of your new lawn. If you're going to the trouble of starting a new lawn, you should give it a good foundation.

1 MARK UTILITY LINES

Have all your local utility companies mark the location of the lines that run through your yard so that you don't cut through them by accident.

2 SET UP A LINE

Drive a 3-foot stake into the ground beside your house. Drive a second stake 50 feet away toward the edge of the property. (If your property line is less than 50 feet away, see "Smaller Yards," below right.)

3 CHECK LEVEL

Tie a line to both stakes, then hang a line level on it. Slide the line up or down on one of the stakes until the bubble centers between the marks in the vial.

4 MEASURE THE SLOPE

Measure the distance between the ground and the line at the house and between the ground and the line at the second stake. Subtract the measurement at the house from the one at the edge of the property. This will tell you how much the yard slopes over the distance of the line.

5 CHECK IN SEVERAL PLACES

Measure at several points along the line to see whether there are any low spots. If so, place a 2×4 at the spot and check between it and the ground to see how far and wide the low spot extends. Mark the entire depression with lime or landscapers paint. Reposition the line at each corner of the house. Check the slope and look for low spots at each location.

 WORK SMARTER

MASON'S LINE

Even when you stretch it as tight as you can, string will sag once you put on the line level. Use mason's line instead. It's available at home centers and masonry supply stores and is meant to help masons lay out a flat, level surface over long distances. It won't sag when you're trying to figure out the slope of your yard.

 CLOSER LOOK

SMALLER YARDS

If your property line is less than 50 feet away, put the stake at a distance that divides into 50 evenly; for example, 12½ or 25 feet. If the stake is 12½ feet away from the house, multiply the slope of the line by 4 to find the slope over 50 feet. Multiply by 2 if the stake is 25 feet away.

6

GRADE THE SUBSOIL

If the slope is consistently less than 1 in 50 or your yard has major depressions, you should fix the problem by removing the topsoil and scraping the subgrade to the proper slope and flatness. This is lot of heavy work and is best done by a contractor who will put the topsoil back in place once he has corrected the subgrade.

7

ADD DRAIN LINES, IF NECESSARY

Regrading and correcting the slope of the yard should solve most drainage problems. If your soil is heavy clay, however, or if you have problems with a wet basement, you may need to put in drain lines to direct water away from the house. Dig a trench 1 foot wide and 1 foot deep. Slope the trench so that it drops 1 inch every 8 feet, then place black drain line in the bottom of the trench. For complete details, see page 170.

8

ADD MORE TOPSOIL

Once the grade is correct and any drain lines have been installed, spread topsoil across the yard. (You might want to let the contractor do this work.) The topsoil layer should be a minimum of 4 inches deep to accommodate the roots of the grass. If bringing in new topsoil, be sure to till it into the old soil, as explained in the next step.

 WORK SMARTER

DON'T TILL WET SOIL
Rototilling wet soil will compact it. Test first to make sure the soil is dry. Pull up a fistful of soil from about 4 inches down and squeeze it tightly in your hand. It if breaks and crumbles when you open your hand, it's dry enough to till.

9

WORK TOPSOIL INTO EXISTING SOIL

Rake out part of the topsoil, making sure it is roughly the same depth across the yard. Rototill to work the new soil into the existing soil. This creates a transition layer between the two soils. If the new and old soil aren't well mixed, the grass roots will reach down only to the line between the two. Add the remaining topsoil and spread it evenly across the yard.

10

SPREAD ORGANIC MATTER ACROSS THE SOIL

The soil test will have told you how much organic matter your soil needs. Generally speaking you'll want to spread about a 2-inch layer of organic matter, such as compost, across the lawn. Talk with your garden center staff about what's most appropriate to use in your area.

8

PLANTING A LAWN

11 **APPLY FERTILIZER**

Add fertilizer as recommended by a soil test. If the test recommended incorporating any other amendments such as lime or sulfur into the soil, apply them now too. Rake the fertilizer and amendments into the organic matter, then till them into the top 4 to 6 inches of soil.

12 **CREATE A ROUGH GRADE AND FILL IN MINOR IRREGULARITIES**

After tilling, rake the yard to smooth out the soil surface and to remove plant debris. Check the slope in several places with the line and line level. Level the soil with your rake if necessary. Turn your rake upside down and scrape out high spots, using the soil to fill in low spots. If you're going to put in a sprinkler system, do so after raking the rough grade.

 **WORK SMARTER**

CONTROLLING CRABGRASS
Bare soil is the perfect host for crabgrass and other weeds. When you apply fertilizer after working the organic matter into the soil, use one with a preemergence herbicide to control crabgrass and weeds.

13 **RAKE THE SURFACE SMOOTH**

Rake the surface of the soil to smooth it out and to break up clods. The final texture should be fairly rough, with pieces of dirt that fall between the size of a golf ball and that of a pea. Keep the grade 1 inch below sidewalks, driveways, and patios if you will be planting sod. If you will be seeding, the grade should be about ¼ to ½ inch lower than the pavement.

14 **ROLL THE SURFACE**

Roll the soil with a 200- to 300-pound roller until it is firm enough to support your weight without leaving a footprint more than ½ inch deep. If rolling results in low spots, fill them with topsoil and roll again. Water the soil and let it settle for about a week. If weeds pop up, spray them with glyphosate. Rake out any rough spots that develop, then get ready for planting.

 **CLOSER LOOK**

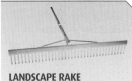

LANDSCAPE RAKE
A landscape rake is made for smoothing out soil when grading. The wide head easily evens out surfaces, the rounded tines move soil without digging in, and the top edge is perfect for scraping down high spots.

8

PLANTING A LAWN

Laying drainpipe

WORK SMARTER

GAUGING THE SLOPE

It's important that the trench you dig drop at least 1 inch for every 8 feet so that the water moves through it quickly. This gadget will help you gauge the slope:

Start with a 4-foot 2×4—sight along the edge to make sure it's straight. Tape a ½-inch spacer to the edge of the 2×4 at one end, then tape a 4-foot level to the 2×4 with one of its ends resting on the spacer.

Set the 2×4 in the bottom of your trench to test the slope. The slope will be correct when the bubble centers between the lines in the vial.

I f part of your yard turns to mud after a rain and stays that way for days, or if part of the yard is constantly soggy, the yard will benefit from having a drain line installed. If you're thinking about putting in drain lines and installing a new lawn, grade your yard first then install the drain lines following the steps on pages 166–169.

If you have a single problem spot, you may be able to drain it with a single line. If the yard is generally soggy all over, however, you'll need to run lines every 10 or 15 feet.

The drain line should start a few feet uphill from the problem spot and continue downhill, dropping at a rate of 1 inch for every 8 feet. Part of the trick in laying a successful drain line is knowing where it should end. At some point, the line has to emerge from underground.

Because the pipe has to maintain its slope of 1 inch every 8 feet even when it meets the surface, you may have to dig a swale into which the pipe can emerge and the water can drain.

Once the water leaves the pipe, it has to go somewhere. In the easiest case it goes into a pond, the street, or a drainage ditch along the edge of your property. In the more difficult case, you'll have to dig a dry well—a large hole filled with gravel into which the water drains. Sizing and digging the hole are clearly work for a contractor.

Wherever you send the water, do not drain it into your neighbor's yard, or close enough to it that the water ends up there. It not only makes for poor relations, but it's illegal. Also check your community's codes to learn exactly what you are allowed to do.

Avoid clogged lines

Drainage pipe can become clogged with dirt washed down in rain and irrigation water. You can protect the pipe and keep it open by slipping a pipe sleeve or sock over it. Or you can cover the pipe with landscape fabric. Landscape fabric is a plastic cloth woven fine enough to hold back dirt, but loose enough to let water pass through. It's the same material used as weed barrier or weed cloth.

1 **LAY OUT THE TRENCHES**

Drive two stakes 1 foot apart into the ground at the beginning of the trench and at the end of the trench. Connect the stakes with mason's line and mark along the lines with lime, chalk, or landscapers paint to show the position of the trench. Repeat every 10 to 15 feet.

2 **DIG THE TRENCHES**

Follow the layout lines and dig through the topsoil to make trenches 1 foot deep and 1 foot wide. Dig the trenches so that they slope away from the house at a rate of 1 inch every 8 feet.

3 **LINE THE TRENCHES WITH STONE**

Shovel a 2-inch layer of coarse washed gravel into the trench. Check with the level and 2×4 to make sure you've maintained the proper slope. Rake the gravel out to correct any problems.

4 **PUT PIPE IN THE TRENCHES**

Lay 4-inch-diameter perforated pipe in the trenches. If using PVC, the holes should face down. If using corrugated pipe, the perforations encircle the pipe; lay the pipe however it comes off the roll. The pipe needs to be covered in landscape fabric to keep it from clogging. You can do so in step 6, or you can buy a landscape fabric sock that you slip over the pipe now.

5 **JOIN PIPES TOGETHER, IF USING MORE THAN ONE**

If you need more than one section of pipe, connect them with a coupling made for the pipe. You do not need to glue the fittings to the pipe. Continue laying pipe until it can leave the ground, or you can dig an opening for it.

6 **BURY THE PIPE IN GRAVEL**

Cover the drainpipe with landscape fabric. The landscape fabric will keep soil from filtering into the drain and clogging it. Then begin shoveling gravel into the trench, filling to within 1 to 2 inches from the top. Cover the gravel with topsoil.

8

PLANTING A LAWN

Starting a lawn from sod

When most people put in a new lawn, they start with sod. Not only is it faster to place, but it's reassuring to suddenly see grass on a lot that was bare only a few hours earlier.

Sod starts life on a farm as grass seed and is raised with the kind of care and attention that golf course turf gets. Once the grass on the sod farm has green leaves and is actively growing roots, it's ready to be harvested. It's cut into strips with about ½ inch to ⅝ inch of soil attached and rolled or folded and delivered to your yard.

The only grasses that make good sod are ones with strong rhizomes and stolons—the stems that spread out underground and at ground level to start neighboring plants. These grasses can stand up to the slicing and rolling of harvest. Rhizomes and stolons knit the soil and grass together so they can be rolled up without separating.

The grasses sold as sod are far more limited in variety than the grasses sold as seed. In the North, most sod is Kentucky bluegrass, though ryegrass and creeping fescue are sometimes mixed in. In the South, bermudagrass, bahiagrass, zoysiagrass, and St. Augustinegrass are available as sod.

Because sod has so little soil, it dries quickly. Also when it is rolled up, sod produces heat, which can be damaging. So have all the prep work done and be ready to install the sod the day it arrives.

WORK SMARTER

KEEP SOD MOIST AS YOU WORK
It's vitally important that you don't let the sod dry out as you install it. Sod that dries out will die. Work with a helper so that one person can start watering the already-laid sod while the other continues to lay sod. If you have no one to help, be sure to set up sprinklers to water the sod as you continue working.

▼ Only a few hours ago, this yard was nothing but bare soil. Even though sod gives you nearly instant results, remember that it needs a few weeks to take root. Until then, avoid using your lawn too heavily.

1 **MAKE SURE THE SOIL IS MOIST**

Sod should be installed on moist soil. If the ground is dry, water until the soil is moist but not wet.

2 **DISTRIBUTE THE SOD**

Carrying sod from a central location to where it's needed is a lot of work. Sod is delivered on pallets. Have the sod company place the pallets around the yard, separated by the amount of ground each pallet will cover. Begin laying sod as soon as it arrives.

3 **PICK A STARTING POINT**

Lay sod so the rows are perpendicular to the slope of the yard. Start against a straightedge, such as a driveway or sidewalk. This keeps the first row straight and makes it easier to lay subsequent rows tightly against each other.

4 **LAY THE FIRST PIECE OF SOD**

Unroll the first piece of sod, keeping it tight against the straightedge as you go.

5 **LAY THE SECOND PIECE**

Unroll the second piece slightly and butt the end tightly against the end of the first without stretching either piece. Sod pieces will shrink as they dry out, leaving gaps between the strips of sod, which weeds will fill. Unroll the rest of the second piece of sod, keeping it tight against the driveway or sidewalk. Continue laying rolls of sod in this manner until you finish the first row.

6 **START THE SECOND ROW**

The seams between the end of one roll and the beginning of the next should be offset from row to row like brickwork. Do this by starting the second row with a partial roll—either one left over from the end of the first row or from a roll of sod you have cut in half.

7

CONTINUE LAYING SOD

Finish the second row, then lay the remaining rows offsetting the seams from row to row. Lay plywood paths across sod you've already laid so you don't displace the pieces as you work.

8

ROLL THE SOD, THEN WATER IT

Roll the sod lightly to help the roots make contact with the soil. Begin watering the sod within 30 minutes of installation to further encourage rooting and to keep the sod from drying out.

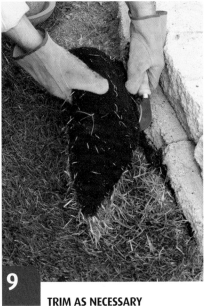

9

TRIM AS NECESSARY

Use a knife to trim sod to fit around trees, garden beds, and other interruptions. Fitting small pieces around obstacles generally doesn't work—the pieces dry out and die.

CLOSER LOOK

FROM SOD TO LAWN

Although you'll mow the lawn after its second week, the lawn still isn't ready for heavy use at this point. Keep children and pets off it until after its second mowing.

Sod is thoroughly established once the roots have reached into the soil. You'll be able to tug on the grass, and it won't lift up. Begin a regular irrigation program at this point, watering deeply and infrequently.

10

WATER SEVERAL TIMES A DAY DURING THE FIRST TWO WEEKS

Keep the sod moist during the day, watering up to three times daily, if necessary. Apply enough water to moisten the sod and soil but not soak the area. Make the last watering around 3 p.m. so that the lawn dries before nightfall. Leaving grass wet overnight encourages disease.

11

MOW WHEN THE GRASS REACHES 3 TO 4 INCHES TALL

Let the grass grow for one to two weeks without cutting to allow the roots to grow into the soil. After two weeks, stop watering for a day or two so the soil can firm up, then mow the grass to its recommended height, taking off no more than a third of the leaf blade. Begin gradually cutting back on watering to encourage deeper root growth. Fertilize after six weeks.

8

PLANTING A LAWN

Starting a lawn from seed

PROJECT DETAILS

SKILLS: Measuring, spreading seed, fertilizing, watering
PROJECT: Establishing a new lawn from seed

TIME TO COMPLETE

The actual time involved depends on the size of your yard.

STUFF YOU'LL NEED

TOOLS: Tape measure, fertilizer spreader, measuring cup, rake, lawn roller, hose, sprinkler
MATERIALS: Grass seed, lime, flour, chalk or landscapers paint, fertilizer

WORK SMARTER

SPREADING THE RIGHT AMOUNT OF SEED
Too much seed can be as much of a problem as too little. When you apply seed, put enough in the hopper to cover 1,000 square feet—the amount needed will be on the package. Measure off 1,000 square feet of your yard—an area roughly 31 feet by 31 feet. Find the spreader setting that opens the hopper about 20 percent. Put the seed in the hopper, start walking at a steady pace, open the hopper, and cover the area. Unless the hopper is empty, make multiple passes at right angles to each other to ensure even coverage.

Starting a lawn from seed requires the same soil preparation as starting one from sod, but seeding is far less expensive than sodding, and the work is much less backbreaking. Yet most people opt to use sod, perhaps because they're afraid they'll make a mistake with seed or maybe they just prefer that instant lawn they get from sod.

Seed is easy to plant and hard to fail with. Prepare the soil, spread the seed, and cover it with a bit of straw or other mulch; then water and the seed will sprout. The only worrisome part is keeping the soil moist so that the seed or the tiny seedlings don't dry out. Fertilize once the grass is established and your seeded lawn will do as well as a sodded one.

Choosing the right seed is a matter of looking at your yard and your climate. In general there are two broad types of grass: cool season and warm season, each named for the climate and temperature in which it grows best. If you are in a definite warm or cool climate, you can zero in on the grass that will work best for you. There is one exception: an area of the country known as the Transition Zone, which extends from southern Pennsylvania to mid-Mississippi and from the East Coast to just past Texas. This region is a little too hot for cool-season grasses and a little too cool for warm-season grasses. Nevertheless, cool-season grasses are preferred here, tall fescue being a favorite. Zoysiagrass, the most cold tolerant of the warm-season grasses, grows well here too. For general advice on picking a grass, see the profiles starting on page 18. For specifics, including a map of the Transition Zone and cool- and warm-season areas, see page 16.

Because warm- and cool-season grasses grow differently, and because they grow in different climates, you sow them at different times of the year. Sow warm-season grass seed in spring, cool-season grasses in late summer to early fall.

No matter which grass you choose, you'll find that it comes in several cultivated varieties called cultivars, which are listed on the seed package. Each variety has been cultivated for specific purposes, and there are countless varieties. Check with your local extension office to see if they have any particular recommendations.

8

PLANTING A LAWN

Buying quality seed

Read the package label to make sure you buy high-quality seed. Check the variety. A high-quality mix will only include improved cultivars of each grass and will list them by name, such as Brightstar II perennial ryegrass or SR 8200 tall fescue, rather than simply perennial ryegrass or tall fescue. Avoid packages in which the grass is listed as VNS, which means variety not stated.

The germination percentage tells you how many of the seeds in a package are likely to sprout. Buy the seed with the highest germination percentage and go for nothing less than 70 percent germination.

Weed seed means what it says (it's hard to remove all weed seeds from grass seed). Look for a listing of 0.5 percent or less to avoid future problems. Also watch for other crop seed, which are seeds of agricultural crops. They should make up 0.5 percent or less of the package.

Some states mandate that no more than 0.5 percent other crop seed be in a bag. A top-quality seed will contain no such seed.

Inert matter is simply a filler, such as ground corncobs. In a high-quality mix, it will make up less than 5 percent of the package.

📖 WORK SMARTER

SPREADING SMALL SEEDS
Bentgrass and centipedegrass seeds are so small they can slip through a drop spreader at uneven rates. Mix the seed thoroughly with sand at a rate of ¼ pound seed to one gallon of sand for a more even application.

1

MEASURE THE YARD AND BUY SEED
Measure the size of the yard as explained in "Measuring for Sod, Grass, and Topsoil," page 160. Buy the seed you need—the exact amount will depend on the variety of grass, as well as the size of your yard. A few days before planting, water the lawn to a depth of 6 to 8 inches. Plant when the surface of the soil is dry.

2

PREPARE THE LAWN
Kill the existing grass, rake out debris, grade the yard, and enrich the soil before planting. For more on preparation, see "Preparing the Yard for Sod or Seed," page 164. Give the soil its final grading right before planting.

3

LAY OUT AN AREA OF THE LAWN
Seed is applied at a rate of so many pounds per 1,000 square feet, depending on the seed. Because drop spreaders are calibrated for fertilizer rather than seed, you'll have to lay out an area of 1,000 square feet on your own. If the area is irregular or involves several parts of the lawn, mark the boundaries with lime, flour, chalk, or landscapers paint.

4

MEASURE THE SEED
Weigh the amount of seed in the package. Divide the total weight into the amount you need to spread per 1,000 square feet. Put one-half the amount of seed needed per 1,000 square feet in a drop spreader.

8

PLANTING A LAWN

5

SPREAD THE SEED

Set the spreader on a low setting and walk back and forth in rows across the lawn. Shut off the hopper at the end of each row and begin seeding again once you've made the turn. Continue until the spreader is empty.

6

MAKE A SECOND PASS

Put half the amount needed per 1,000 square feet in the empty spreader. Make a second pass across the lawn perpendicular to the first.

7

RAKE IN THE SEED

Rake the soil lightly to cover the seeds with no more than ⅛ to ¼ inch of soil. It's hard to not cover some of the seed with too much soil. The amount is about right when only about 10 percent of the seeds are visible. It's an art, rather than a science. Trust your eyes.

8

ROLL LIGHTLY

The seeds need good contact with the soil in order to germinate. A light rolling does the job without compressing the soil too much. Roll the lawn with a roller meant to be filled with water but don't put any water in it.

 TOOL SAVVY

SETTING THE SPREADER

When spreading grass seed, set your spreader so that it is about 20 percent open. If your spreader has a scale from 1 to 10, for example, set it at 2. If the scale ranges from 1 to 15, set it at 3. If the scale goes up to 20, set the spreader to 4.

 REAL WORLD

THE LAST STRAW

After seeding you will mulch with straw or other organic material to keep seeds moist. Avoid using too much straw; it can smother the grass. If you apply straw at the proper rate—80 pounds per 1,000 square feet—you should be able to see about half the ground through the straw.

Wheat straw, the traditional mulch, sometimes contains leftover wheat or weed seeds. Avoid straw that was used as livestock bedding; it will be full of weed seeds.

Several commercially made mulches are available. Ask your garden center staff about the other mulches they sell as well as about the suitability of other straws that may be available in your area.

8

PLANTING A LAWN

8

PLANTING A LAWN

CLOSER LOOK

WATERING LAWNS GROWN FROM SEED

Water lightly until the seeds germinate. Overwatering will cause the seeds to rot. Underwatering will cause them to dry out and die. Water enough to keep the top 1 to 2 inches of soil moist but not soaked. You may have to water lightly two to four times daily. Use a screwdriver to probe the soil for an indication of moisture depth. Change gradually to a normal watering pattern. When the grass is about 2 inches tall, make a gradual transition to a normal watering pattern. As the seedlings become established, watering every other day may be enough. Once the root system has developed, water deeply once or twice a week.

9

APPLY MULCH

Mulching the seed helps keep moisture in the soil and helps prevent erosion until the grass is established. Wheat straw is the traditional lawn mulch, but it sometimes contains weed seeds. Check with your garden center for a suitable straw or other mulches.

10

WATER TWO TO FOUR TIMES DAILY

Grass needs water to grow. Let the seeds or seedlings dry out, and they will die. Water frequently at first, applying enough water to moisten the top 1 to 2 inches of soil. As the grass germinates and begins to take hold, gradually reduce watering until you are on a normal schedule.

11

BEGIN MOWING TO THICKEN THE LAWN

Mowing encourages grass plants to spread out and fill in the lawn. Begin mowing when the plants have reached their typical mowing height, and never take off more than one-third of the leaf blade at a time. For example, cut cool-season grasses back to 2 inches once they reach a height of 3 inches. Cut warm-season grasses back to 1 to 2 inches when they are 1½ to 3 inches tall.

12

FERTILIZE

Once the grass is four to six weeks old, fertilize it, using a slow-release fertilizer at the rate of 1 pound of nitrogen per 1,000 square feet. After eight to ten weeks, give the grass a second application of fertilizer at the same rate.

Patching problem spots

PROJECT DETAILS

SKILLS: Applying herbicide, rototilling, fertilizing, watering, applying seed
PROJECT: Patching to repair a dead spot in the lawn

TIME TO COMPLETE

Time varies with the extent of damage.

STUFF YOU'LL NEED

TOOLS: Rototiller, rake, sprayer, fertilizer spreader
MATERIALS: Compost, straw, and seed, sod or sprigs

When small areas in your lawn die, you can repair them by preparing the soil and planting new grass. But the first step in patching has nothing to do with starting new grass. The first step in repairing it is to figure out what went wrong and fix it. Grass can die for any number of reasons, and unless you solve the problem, sooner or later it will reappear, wiping out the repair.

Start by taking a good look at the dead spot. Inspect it for compaction, for shade problems, disease and insect damage. The chapter "Solving Problems," page 86 to 117 walks you through inspecting your yard and finding out what went wrong. It also helps you find a solution for each problem. Follow the steps and fix the problem before you start replanting. Once you've solved the problem, try to find a grass that matches the existing lawn or that at least has a similar texture and color to the existing grass.

Depending on which kind of grass makes up your yard, you can patch with seed or sod. Most grasses can be started from seeds. Some warm-season grasses, including hybrid bermudagrasses and St. Augustinegrass, can only be planted as sod or plugs, which are round or square pieces cut from a strip of sod. Whichever method you use, preparation of the soil is the same.

Preparing the soil

1

REMOVE ALL GRASS IN THE TROUBLED AREA
Dig up and remove the grass in the problem area. Enlarge the patch to a square or rectangle to make working on it easier.

2

LOOSEN THE SOIL
Turn over the soil to break up any compaction. Remove stones, roots, and other plant matter that might interfere with your new grass as you work.

3

ADD ORGANIC MATTER
Enrich the soil with organic matter, such as compost or a commercially available product. Spade the organic matter into the soil.

8

PLANTING A LAWN

4

RAKE THE SURFACE LEVEL

Rake the soil to create a smooth surface. If using seed, the soil surface should be at the same level as the surrounding soil. If using sod, the level should be about 1 inch lower to account for the depth of the sod's soil and roots. Take care that the soil surface is even, without low or high spots.

5

WATER THE AREA

New grass will die if the soil beneath it dries out. Give it a head start by watering to a depth of about 8 inches before planting.

 WORK SMARTER

REPLANT WITH GRASS THAT MATCHES THE ORIGINAL

Each grass has a unique texture and is its own distinct shade of green. A bare spot planted with a grass that doesn't match the surrounding grass will call attention to itself. Make sure you plant a grass that matches your lawn's color and texture. Check the grass profiles starting on pages 18 to 35 for help in learning the kind of grass growing in your yard.

Buying quality seed

If you're patching with sod, cut pieces to fit, and put them in place so that they are tight against each other and the surrounding grass. Apply a starter fertilizer, and water to keep the soil underneath moist for at least two weeks. Begin mowing when you are no longer able to peel back the sod. If using plugs, plant them 2 to 4 inches apart—a bit closer than normal, so that the area will fill in faster. Keep the area around the plugs weed free.

Patching with seed

1

SPREAD SEED

If you're repairing the damage with seed, spread it at the rate described on the package. Rake a thin layer of soil over the seeds, apply a starter fertilizer, then cover with straw or other mulch.

2

KEEP THE SOIL MOIST UNTIL THE SEEDS SPROUT

Seeds that dry out will die, and you'll have to replant. Depending on the soil, you may need to water the seeds several times a day. Keep the soil moist, but not so wet that it's soggy or that water collects on the surface.

3

MOW AS USUAL

Set the mower to the proper height for your lawn and ensure that it cuts off no more than one-third of the grass blade. While the seedlings are small, they will be below the mower blade; as they grow, it's especially important to follow the one-third rule. Take care that your mower wheels straddle the patch. Scalping the seedlings—as well as the surrounding lawn—will set them back and lengthen the time it takes for the patch to fill in.

8

PLANTING A LAWN

Overseeding to improve a lawn

 PROJECT DETAILS

SKILLS: Measuring, seeding, and raking or core aerating
PROJECT: Improve a struggling lawn with a new grass variety

 TIME TO COMPLETE

Time varies depending on the size of the yard.

 STUFF YOU'LL NEED

TOOLS: Lawn mower, tape measure, rake, core aerator, fertilizer spreader, lightweight roller, sprinkler and hose
MATERIALS: Grass seed, mulch or topdressing, fertilizer

 CLOSER LOOK

GETTING READY TO OVERSEED
The new overseeded grass will grow better if you can get the old grass to take a break. This reduces competition between the two and gives the new grass a chance to get growing. If you follow a regular feeding program, stop fertilizing four to five weeks before overseeding. Vigorous growth of the existing lawn will make it more difficult for the new seeds to establish themselves. Also, about two weeks before overseeding, cut back on watering by 50 to 60 percent. The grass will respond by storing food and growing less rapidly, further reducing competition with the new seed.

You can repair a lawn that is in moderately bad shape by overseeding it. How do you know if your lawn is moderately bad? No more than 20 to 25 percent of it is dead or bare, or weeds make up no more than 40 percent of the lawn. If your lawn exceeds these amounts, you'll do better by starting over.

Overseeding is exactly what it sounds like—sowing seeds over the top of the existing lawn. This technique not only fills in the bare spots, but also gives you a better lawn with less effort.

The object of overseeding isn't merely to get grass to grow where none exists; it's also to improve the entire stand of grass by sowing better varieties. Seed companies are constantly breeding new varieties of grass (called cultivars). These new varieties are more resistant to insects and diseases and are more drought tolerant. If your lawn is more than seven years old—which is likely, since at least half the lawns in North America are—it would probably benefit from overseeding with one of the new turfgrass varieties even if it isn't in bad shape.

Part of the success of overseeding depends on eliminating competition from the existing lawn. Stop fertilizing and cut back on watering to slow growth of the existing lawn and lessen its competition with the new seed.

If you are overseeding a cool-season lawn, do so in the late summer or early fall. Overseed warm-season grasses from April through July. Cut the grass shorter than usual, plant the seeds, and then cover with compost so the new grass will have plenty of nutrients.

8

PLANTING A LAWN

1

CUT THE LAWN
Mow the grass, cutting off a third of its height. Wait a day or two and mow again, taking off another one-third. Continue until you've removed 60 to 70 percent of the grass height. Remove the clippings so the seed can work its way to the soil.

2

MEASURE THE YARD AND BUY THE SEED
Measure your yard, choose the seed you'll use, and double or triple the amount called for on the package. Because of competition and because the seed won't be falling on bare soil, not all of it will germinate.

3

PREPARE THE SEEDBED
If you're overseeding only a small area, you can rake the soil thoroughly to rough it up and create a good seedbed. On larger areas, use a core aerator to prepare the seedbed. A core aerator pulls cylindrical chunks of soil out of the ground and leaves them on the surface where they break apart. Cut a minimum of 20 to 40 holes per square foot with an aerator—the more holes you cut the better.

4

APPLY HALF THE SEED
Divide the total amount of seed you need to sow in half. Set one-half aside. Put the other half in a drop spreader set at about 20 percent of its full opening (inset). In other words, if your spreader has a maximum setting of 10, set it at 2; if it has a maximum setting of 15, set it on 3, and so on. Apply the seed, walking back and forth across the lawn.

5

APPLY THE REST OF THE SEED
Refill the spreader and apply the remaining seed traveling perpendicular to the direction you traveled when applying the first half.

6

WORK THE SEED INTO THE SOIL
Drag a rake upside down across the lawn to work the seed into the soil. On a large lawn, you can do this by dragging a weighted carpet across the lawn with a garden tractor.

7 **COVER THE SEED AND SOIL**

Enrich the soil and fertilize the seed by spreading a ¼-inch layer of mulch or topdressing over the ground. See "The Last Straw," page 177, for more on mulch. See "Choosing Topdressing," page 155, for more on topdressing.

8 **ROLL THE LAWN**

Push a lightweight roller across the seeded area. This presses the seed into the soil and ensures contact between the seeds and soil.

9 **WATER THE LAWN THREE TIMES A DAY**

Keep the soil and seeds moist by watering lightly three times a day. Watering at around 10 a.m., 12 noon, and 2 p.m. will keep the lawn moist during maximum exposure to the sun. Once the grass is 1 inch tall, cut back watering to ¼ inch once a day.

10 **MOW THE GRASS**

Let the grass grow to its normal mowing height, then cut it back by one-third. Be sure to mow when the grass is dry. Mowing new grass when it's wet will pull it out of the ground.

11 **FERTILIZE THE LAWN**

Roughly six weeks after sowing seed, fertilize the lawn with 1 pound of a fertilizer containing quick-release nitrogen per 1,000 square feet. Choose a fertilizer that provides the other nutrients recommended by a soil test.

Winter overseeding

Two of the most popular warm-season grasses—bermudagrass and zoysiagrass—lose their green color when cool weather arrives. To keep the lawn green year-round in southern areas, overseed it with ryegrass, which does well over winter in the South. You can use either perennial ryegrass, annual ryegrass, or a mixture of the two, sowing it in late October or early November.

Winter overseeding is much like regular overseeding. Start by cutting the existing lawn back to about 1 inch, either bagging the clippings as you go or raking them up after you're done. Rent a slit-seeder and use it to sow the ryegrass seed at the rate recommended on the package. Drag a rake upside down across the lawn to work the seed into the grass, or drag a weighted carpet across it with a tractor. Keep the soil and seeds moist by watering lightly three times a day. Let the grass grow to about 2½ inches, then mow regularly.

8

PLANTING A LAWN

The Home Depot

Home Depot garden associates are an excellent source of information on lawn care. They have extensive training in the field, and many associates have worked as lawn care professionals. You can also visit the Home Depot website at www.homedepot.com. Type in "lawn" in the search window, and then click on HELPFUL INFO, for buying advice and lawn care pointers.

Look for the Eco Options$_{sm}$ logo in stores to find products that let you improve your home and the environment. For additional information visit homedepot.com/ecooptions.

The Scotts Miracle-Gro Company

Scotts offers a complete line of lawn fertilizers, weed and disease controls, and seed. You'll find a guide to their products and articles about lawn care at www.scotts.com. You can also talk to lawn care specialists by calling 800/543-Turf (8873) or clicking on the "contact us" link on the website.

Vigoro

Vigoro manufactures a full line of lawn products, including fertilizers, weed and disease controls, and seed. You can get product information and advice on lawn care at www.vigoro.com. Email the company by clicking on the "contact us" link on the website or call 800/874-8892 with fertilizer questions or 800/332-5553 with questions about insecticides and herbicides.

Bayer Advanced

Bayer Advanced manufactures weed, insect, and disease controls for lawns. Check their website www.bayeradvanced.com for information on their products, lawn and garden pests, and on lawn care. You can email questions to the company through the website or reach it by calling 877/229-3724.

Local Sources

Cooperative Extension Services

The Cooperative Extension Service is an outreach of your state land grant university and is funded through the United States Department of Agriculture. Officially known as the Cooperative State Research Education and Extension Service, its mission is to provide the public with the latest information in agriculture, which includes turf management. Extension offices are set up in counties across the United States. Contact your extension agent to get advice on lawn care and lawn problems, varieties of grass that work well locally, and about having a soil test done. You'll find the office listed in the phone book. Check the blue pages under "county" or in the white pages under the name of your state university, followed by "cooperative extension service."

National and Regional Sources

Better Lawn and Turf Institute

http://www.turfgrasssod.org/lawninstitute/index.html
Advice on watering, fertilizing, and mowing for homeowners

Midwest Sod Council

http://www.midwestsodcouncil.com/homeowners/home_index.htm
Information on buying and installing sod

National Turfgrass Evaluation Program

http://www.ntep.org/
Provides results of national tests of all major turfgrass species. This program is partially funded by the U.S. Department of Agriculture.

University and Extension Programs

Many universities have turfgrass management programs to train lawn care professionals. Many of the programs have websites (sometimes connected with the extension service) that provide information for homeowners. Here is a survey of sites. You can find others by typing "lawn" and your state into an Internet search engine.

Mississippi State University Extension Service

http://msucares.com/lawn/lawn/

Ohio State University

http://ohioline.osu.edu/lines/lawns.html

Penn State University Turfgrass Management Extension and Outreach

http://turfgrassmanagement.psu.edu/homelawns.cfm

Purdue Turfgrass Program

http://www.agry.purdue.edu/turf/

Texas A&M University Turfgrass Program

http://aggieturf.tamu.edu/

University of Arizona Cooperative Extension Master Gardener's Manual

http://cals.arizona.edu/pubs/garden/mg/lawns/

University of California

http://www.ipm.ucdavis.edu/TOOLS/TURF/

University of Nebraska at Lincoln

http://entomology.unl.edu/turfent/

Clemson University

http://virtual.clemson.edu/groups/turfornamental/

GLOSSARY

Aeration. The process of removing small plugs of soil from the lawn to spread microbes that help break up compacted soil or reduce thatch.

Annual. A plant that germinates from seed, grows, flowers, produces seed, then dies in one year. Annual plants must be replanted every year.

Broad-spectrum pesticide. A postemergent pesticide that kills everything it is applied to.

Bunchgrass. A grass that grows in clumps. It spreads from the crown via tillers, rather than by rhizomes and stolons. Because growth radiates outward in a tight circle from the original plant, the grass appears to be bunched together.

Chlorophyll. The substance in plants that gives them their green color. Chlorophyll and sunlight work together to convert air and water into carbohydrates that the plant uses as food.

Clay. A type of soil; one of the three components of loam, the other two being sand and organic matter. Clay is very dense, and while it absorbs water readily, it also holds it. Plants are able to get water from clay only at a very slow rate.

Compost. Decomposed organic matter, such as leaves or lawn clippings, which is added to the soil to improve its organic content and structure.

Cool-season grass. Grasses that grow best in cooler climates. Cool-season grasses have growth spurts in the spring and fall.

Crown. The part of the grass at ground level from which all growth—roots and shoots—originates.

Cultural controls. Methods of controlling weeds, diseases, and insects by improving the condition of the soil or plant. For example, watering and mowing are two types of cultural controls. When done correctly, watering and mowing results in healthy grass that can resist pests.

Daughter plant. A plant formed by a tiller, rhizome, or stolon; a young shoot of grass propagated by an older existing plant.

Dormant. A state in which a plant stops growing and turns brown or off-color, usually in reaction to an environmental stress, such as cold weather or drought. A dormant plant is not dead. Once good growing weather resumes, it will green up and begin growing again.

Fertilizer. A product that delivers nutrients to the lawn to help it grow. The key nutrients in lawn fertilizers are nitrogen, potassium, and phosphorus.

Loam. A type of soil composed of sand, clay, and organic matter in roughly equal proportions. Loam is the ideal soil for growing grass.

Mulch. A material placed over bare soil to hold in moisture and prevent weed growth and erosion. In the case of lawns, mulch is used when starting seeds. The mulch is usually some type of organic matter, such as straw, peat moss, newspaper, or burlap, that breaks down over time.

Overseeding. Spreading grass seed over an existing lawn. The main reason for overseeding is to reinvigorate the lawn with improved or pest-resistant grass varieties. In the South, warm-season lawns are often overseeded with a cool-season grass to provide green color all winter.

Perennial. A grass or other plant that grows year after year without replanting.

Plugging. A method of starting a lawn in which sod is cut into small pieces, called plugs, and planted in holes in the soil. It is a less expensive method than sodding.

pH. A measure of alkalinity and acidity. pH is measured on a scale of 1 to 14. A pH of 7 is neutral; a pH less than 7 is acidic; a pH of more than 7 is alkaline.

Postemergent herbicide. An herbicide that kills weeds after they begin growing. The weed may be anywhere from a seedling to a mature plant, although younger weeds are easier to kill than mature weeds.

Power rake. A machine with flexible tines that combs through the grass to remove thatch.

Preemergent herbicide. An herbicide that prevents weed seeds from germinating or that kills weeds as they attempt to emerge from the soil. Most have no effect on existing plants.

Rhizome. An underground stem from which new plants may form.

Rhizomatous. A plant that spreads largely or entirely via rhizomes.

Selective herbicide. A postemergent herbicide that kills only certain types of plants, such as grassy plants or broadleaf plants.

Sprigging. A method of planting grass in which individual stolons or rhizomes are placed in furrows in the soil.

Stolons. Aboveground stems that spread from the crown of an existing grass plant and from which new plants can grow.

Stoloniferous. A plant that spreads largely or entirely via stolons.

Thatch. A layer of organic matter, usually grass rhizomes and stolons, which builds up between the soil and the grass plants. Layers more than ½ inch thick can keep water and air from filtering into the soil and reaching roots, and should be removed.

Tiller. Grass shoots that form around the base of a bunchgrass, enabling it to spread into new areas.

Topdressing. Spreading compost or other organic matter across the lawn to add organic matter.

Warm-season grasses. Grasses that grow mainly during warm weather. Most are hardy only in warm climates. Warm-season grasses grow all summer and go dormant in winter.

INDEX

Metric conversions

U.S. Units to Metric Equivalents

To convert from	Multiply by	To Get
Inches	25.4	Millimeters
Inches	2.54	Centimeters
Feet	30.48	Centimeters
Feet	.03048	Meters
Yards	0.9144	Meters
Miles	1.6093	Kilometers
Square inches	6.4516	Square centimeters
Square feet	0.0929	Square meters
Square yards	0.8361	Square meters
Acres	0.4047	Hectares
Square miles	2.5899	Square kilometers
Cubic inches	16.387	Cubic centimeters
Cubic feet	0.0283	Cubic meters
Cubic feet	28.316	Liters
Cubic yards	0.7646	Cubic meters
Cubic yards	764.55	Liters

To convert from degrees Fahrenheit (F) to degrees Celsius (C), first subtract 32, then multiply by 5/9.

Metric Units to U.S. Equivalents

To convert from	Multiply by	To Get
Millimeters	0.0394	Inches
Centimeters	0.3937	Inches
Centimeters	0.0328	Feet
Meters	3.2808	Feet
Meters	1.0936	Yards
Kilometers	0.6214	Miles
Square centimeters	0.1550	Square inches
Square meters	10.764	Square feet
Square meters	1.1960	Square yards
Hectares	2.4711	Acres
Square kilometers	0.3861	Square miles
Cubic centimeters	0.0610	Cubic inches
Cubic meters	35.315	Cubic feet
Liters	0.0353	Cubic feet
Cubic meters	1.308	Cubic yards
Liters	0.0013	Cubic yards

To convert from degrees Celsius to degrees Fahrenheit, multiply by 9/5, then add 32.

Carolyn Evans
Escondido, CA

Larry Baumgartner
Lake Forest, CA

Georgia Lee Thieben
Garden Grove, CA

Tom Del Hotal
Lemon Grove, CA

Scott R. Tubbs
Acworth, GA

Many thanks to
the employees of
The Home Depot® whose
"wisdom of the aisles"
has made
Lawns 1-2-3™
the most useful
book of its kind.

Lucy Kutil
Hamilton Mills, GA

Craig Allen
Athens, GA

Russell Hattaway
Buford, GA

Lorn Patterson
Vista, CA

Tom Sattler
Atlanta, GA

Toolbox essentials: nuts-and-bolts books for do-it-yourself success.

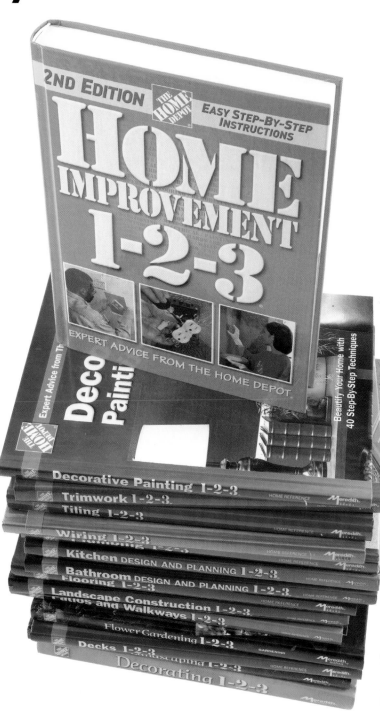

Save money, get great results, and take the guesswork out of home improvement projects with a growing library of step-by-step books from the experts at The Home Depot®.

Packed with lots of projects and practical tips, these books help you design, remodel, decorate, and repair your home or garden. Easy-to-follow, step-by-step instructions and colorful photographs ensure success. Projects even estimate time, skills, materials needed, and tools required.

**You can do it.
We can help.**℠

**Look for the books that help you say "I can do that!"
at The Home Depot® www.meredithbooks.com,
or wherever quality books are sold.**